THE
WOMAN
ALONE

THE WOMAN ALONE

Patricia O'Brien

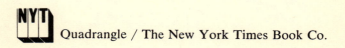
Quadrangle / The New York Times Book Co.

Library of Congress Catalog Card Number: 72-94650

International Standard Book Number: 0-8129-6240-0

Third paperback printing, 1975

To my mother and father,
ANNA AND MARTIN O'BRIEN

Contents

Acknowledgments

My thanks to Margaret Mead, Ashley Montagu, Lionel Tiger, and Ann Landers, among others, for their conversation and insights. To my editor, James F. Hoge Jr. of the Chicago *Sun-Times*, for his interest and support. To my city editor, Jim Peneff, who understood and looked the other way when I needed to work.

To my husband, John Koval, a rare and enduring person who also knows what it means to be alone. To my children, for their forbearance (with an extra bow to eight-year-old Monica who has generously suggested I entitle this, "My Mommy's Book, and I Am Sick of It"). And to my housekeeper, Blanche Krempec, who has held everything together so efficiently, I have no adequate way to say "thank you."

To the people at the University of Chicago who provided me with a "room of my own" and much more. Most importantly, Laurence Hall, a special friend and honest critic, and Harold Richman, dean of the School of Social Service Administration. To

Margaret Rosenheim and Donna Levine of the university's Center for the Study of Welfare Policy, both for their critiques and for the fellowship, that gave financial support. To Judy Nicol, a *Sun-Times* reporter and friend for sharing her perceptions and knowledge of women alone. And to Betsy Fimoff, Gwen Wilson and Mary Lou Papandria, who typed the manuscript and offered their valuable reactions as women.

Finally, to a friend who told me when it mattered the most, "Fight for the life of your mind."

Thank you, and I will, all my life.

Preface

Is this a "Women's Lib" book? Yes, in the sense that it is about both women and liberty. Women have been discriminated against in a variety of ways, but I did not set out to write a book that would document and assail. There are already on the market fine, angry polemics that document the injustices against women, and they need not be duplicated here.

This is a personal book; a question book, not an answer book; a search, not a discovery. I cannot offer a neat package of conclusions because I have not found all the answers for my own life, nor do I think what might be right for me would be right for all women.

I have tried to write about the experience of being female from the perspective of women alone—drawing first on my own experience and then moving the focus to the lives of the women I searched out, the single, widowed, and divorced women of this country, women without men, who want and need as much as anyone else to be part of a whole, not just fragments isolated from society and from one another. I would like to think that what I learned about them, and about myself, can mean something important to women, married and single, and also to men, who are and always will be part of any whole world we might hope to have.

*THE
WOMAN
ALONE*

1.

The Cardboard City

I once had a dream that deeply disturbed me. I was sitting on a grass-covered hill looking down at a red building. Somehow I knew my husband was inside the building, but although I called and called, he did not appear. I began to cry, caught by some unexplainable anxiety; only then did he come out and beckon me down from the hill. We began walking silently together on a hot, dusty road toward a bridge. A door suddenly opened in one of the concrete supports of the bridge and my husband stepped through without a word, just a farewell wave of his hand. The door shut behind him and its outline vanished into the concrete.

Desolate, yet somehow compelled to keep walking, I continued past the bridge and into a dark tunnel. Dozens of people, men and women, were walking silently, each unaware of the other, scattered as far as I could see. Then in the distance I thought I saw a circle of light. Soon I could see what appeared to be a city, a place of sunlit, white-washed buildings, color and motion. Although my strange companions remained silent, I felt easier and more hopeful. The details of the city became increasingly clear. An elevated train . . . a Ferris wheel with colored streamers . . . flags . . .

Finally I came to the end of the tunnel. The city spread out before me, but not as a place warmed by sunlight—instead, as something oddly one-dimensional, lit with a strange flat glitter. I realized it was nothing more than a vast expanse of painted cardboard. I looked into the still faces of the people walking with me, expecting some reaction of horror or anger. Nothing. No concern, no comprehension, just blankness. I could bear this alien dream no longer. "You idiots! Fools!" I screamed, desperately certain there would be no calm voice of reason and authority to speak up and prove me wrong: "Don't you realize we must all be dead?"

I awoke to the sound of my own highpitched cry. And although I never dreamed this dream again, it became part of my life because I began to live it: in the process, I met and grew to know some of the people with me in the tunnel. I sought them out, at first looking only to the men (surely they could provide the comfort, the authority to change the direction of my dream), and then, with increasing awareness and a sense of care and belonging, to the women. I learned something about who we were, why we were in the tunnel, and why we had been unable to speak. I like to think I have reached the cardboard city and can now walk on. There is something better ahead.

Most women marry. They do so because the pressures that propel them into a world where everyone counts by twos are almost irresistible. As a child of the fifties, these pressures for me meant early marriage, many babies, and tears if my husband forgot a bouquet of roses to commemorate our anniversary. Earlier, in high school, they had meant wistful envy of the first girl to show up with a tiny but awesome diamond on her left hand. Each day after school I would memorize the array of diamonds in white velvet boxes in the jewelry-store window at the corner, choosing my favorites, wanting my own. I memorized the silver flatware patterns and couldn't make up my mind whether I wanted "Silver Sculpture" or "Autumn Leaves." I dreamed of elegantly simple wedding gowns and explosions of sexual realization, which usually took the form of being gloriously (but hazily) raped in a hayloft. Good convent product that I was, I also dreamed of a stalwart husband, motherhood, and God.

I did not question the order of things. My friends, my teachers, my parents did not question the order of things. Those few strange misfits in my conservative world who argued against Senator Joseph McCarthy or the Catholic Leap to Faith (which precluded all questions) were equally disliked and avoided. Similarity was valued, difference was suspect. It strikes me as odd now, how quickly we ourselves forgot the pain of being different. My father had walked the streets of Boston during the Depression looking for work, and he still remembers vividly the signs posted in shop windows: NO IRISH NEED APPLY. Even my name was chosen for its ethnic neutrality—my mother had wished to name me Bridget, after my grandmother in Northern Ireland, but she and my father were afraid this strong and honest name would conjure up images of comic slatterns and housemaids. When we moved to Los Angeles, being Irish was not a stigma; in fact, it almost became an advantage—an identification tag in a city of rootless, questing people.

For myself and my friends, expectations were mapped out in advance and we docilely accepted them as our own: high school, a little college, marriage. Partly, I realize now, this total unquestioning was the soporific mood of the fifties and partly it was Catholicism, but living in Los Angeles contributed the right shade of Technicolor that fused it all together. We were products of the Baltimore Catechism and Hollywood movies, a heady mixture of dogma and romanticism that kept us happy, convinced, and relatively untouched by reality. I read *The Robe* for spiri-

tual uplifting during senior retreat at my convent school, thinking as I read each page, I swear, of what a great movie it would
make. Marriage was a mixture of Mary on her way to
Bethlehem with Joseph and Elizabeth Taylor in her MGM wedding gown vowing to cherish Nicky Hilton. Indeed, in my world,
marriage was made both in heaven and on celluloid, and one
image was remarkably like the other.

We did so value conviction—certainly not the conviction of a
rebel or heretic, but the unworrying conviction of consensus, the
kind most comfortable to traditional Catholics. As Mary
McCarthy has said, there was a sense of privilege fostered in us
because we were repeatedly told how lucky we were to be born
into the one true religion. We grew up feeling sorry for Protestants. Sorry for people with only one arm or one leg. Sorry for
dead cats in the road. Magnanimity came easy, but not authentic
compassion and understanding; these virtues were reserved to
God, who had need of them in dealing with all the sinful people
in the world. We grew to adulthood, untouched and untouching.
I wonder, is this why I was so shaken upon discovering loving,
needful people beyond my own tight and ordered world?

"You can do anything, be anything you want to be," my
father told me as we walked together on a frosty Christmas Eve.
I remember feeling thrilled and important, but that was the fun
of dreaming. I ran for class president, won gold cups at speech
contests, and poured over college catalogues, but I made no
true plans for myself, and felt no loss for not having done so.
My father made me think big, but for me, at that time, what
was there to "think big" about?

Our magnanimity was extended politely to those who were
only slightly offbeat or not worth bothering about: the fat girls
with gaping skirt seams who gobbled Look candy bars in the
lunchroom, the "oddballs" who joined the band and tooted
brassy, unfeminine horns, the girls who wanted to become doctors
and not nurses, the bookworms who never set their hair in wet lit-

tle pincurls, and above all, those few classmates who were not concentrating on getting married as soon as possible. What happened to them, I wonder? What did they do?

Margaret Mead has said unmarried women were virtually nonexistent in the fifties, which was true. We couldn't afford to tolerate them. By the end of my senior year, unengaged, I could barely tolerate myself. Years of slathering Noxema over pimples, rolling on the living room floor to batter down my hips, and obeying the advice in *Seventeen* magazine ("Be a good listener and above all, don't let that special person know you are smarter than he is") finally earned me the next best thing to an engagement ring—a fraternity pin. And just in time: on graduation day. I was well primed: misty-eyed at the prospect of entering something called Maturity and loving the prospect of marching toward it under hoops of roses in the convent garden.

My steady boyfriend was an earnest college junior from a nearby Jesuit university, and he was available to act out the drama. "I want to be pinned," I told him. I remember us standing on the stone porch overlooking the lawn filled with dressed-up parents, arms entwined, listening to the band tune up for "Pomp and Circumstance," feeling terribly important and grave. Then he jumped into his car and drove twenty miles to Pasadena for his fraternity pin, I waiting anxiously, fearing he wouldn't make it back in time. He did, and I had the longed-for romantic conclusion to graduation. My classmates gathered around enviously, my mother looked nervous, and we announced proudly to everyone that we were now "engaged to be engaged."

I knitted argyle socks for him, sitting for hours with my dangling spools of purple and gray angora (his school colors), feeling very domestic. They fell apart in the wash, but it didn't matter by then because summer was over and we had broken up. Recently I came across piles of old letters in a rotting box while cleaning out the garage. Among them was a large picture of this handsome, grinning boy-man, inscribed "To Pat, My Sweet Little

Teddy Bear.'' How unreal and humorous that time seems now. When I look at my graduation pictures I see a triumphantly self-satisfied young woman sticking out her chest so the fraternity pin will show up well in the photos, and hanging on to a tall, equally self-satisfied youth. I guess it seems more sad than humorous.

He went to law school in California and I went off to college in Washington, where shortly afterward I met the man I did marry. We were young and happy and vowed to be true forever. My father made little jokes: ''Here she is, I fixed her teeth, kept her from falling apart. Now it's your turn.'' We all laughed. We played out our parts in the fairy tale. I finished my sophomore year with poor grades, spending most of my time reading *Modern Bride* and maintaining my virginity with as finely drawn a line as possible. (Catholic girls were very good at that.)

Then he went back to college, and I stayed home to work as a switchboard operator until our December marriage. I used to sit during idle moments at that switchboard, staring at the diamond on my left hand as it caught the light, watching it sparkle, dreaming of neat little apartments and neat little babies born of erotic mating. (Even with all the teen-age fumbling and exploring in cars at drive-in theaters, I had no true idea of what sex was all about.)

At only one point do I recall a sense of loss: when my younger sister, off on her first year of college in Washington, called home excitedly to tell about her new experiences. I sat at one extension, my parents at the other, the three of us telling Mary how great it all sounded and how much fun she would have, and I couldn't forget that only the year before, the excited calls had been from me. I lectured myself: You've met the right man, and now it's time to settle down. But the doubts did not wholly go away; they in fact became so disturbing at one point that I almost faced them.

It was just before the wedding invitations were ordered. My mother was at the kitchen table, talking about the wedding, and I stood in the doorway listening. Suddenly, surprising myself, I began to cry.

"What is the matter, Pat?" Mother asked.

"I don't know," I said. "I feel strange. I'm not sure."

Always practical, Mother folded her hands on the table and said, "Pat, take the money you've saved and go see him. Make sure—once you're married, there is no turning back. And honey, please do it before I order the invitations."

I agreed, and flew to Seattle on a dawn plane, uncertain, wondering all the way. But when I arrived, he met me and within a few hours I felt my world was tipped straight again. We talked about the importance of what we were doing, reassured each other, and spoke knowingly and—we thought—wisely of how a good marriage meant sharing fifty-fifty on all the problems and we could certainly do that. ("Sharing fifty-fifty" was the closest most of us ever came in the fifties to talking about the emotional complexities of marriage.)

I flew home the next day, and the invitations were ordered and mailed. From then on, I thought mostly about flowers and white runners and wedding cakes.

Once during that waiting time I went with some friends to visit a former high school classmate, who had married first, been envied the most, and had just given birth to a child. We cooed and giggled over the baby, and secretly I thought how mature my friend looked, moving around busily, heating bottles in her new blue satin duster. Her parents had filled the room with plush pandas, flowers, and chocolates; a maternal Disneyland in one small apartment. "Soon I'll have all this too," I thought.

Two years later, already a mother and expecting my second child, I visited again. My friend had just had her second baby, and was tired and cross. As she walked into the kitchen to fix coffee, she picked up a bottle of syrup. It slipped from her hands, and thick goo and bits of glass covered the floor, seeping into the cracks of the linoleum. We both stood and stared at it, thinking of the mess it would be to clean up. Disneyland was gone. The box of Spic and Span under the sink was more important now.

My wedding day came. I awoke to the sight of my bridal gown hanging on the door and my father standing by my bed smiling and mussing my hair. "I won't be waking my little girl up ever again," he said. It was a storybook day. All the details went smoothly, and when it was over, when the streamers were on the car and horns were honking and people laughing, I threw my bouquet—carefully aiming for a girlfriend who was a year older than I and as yet unmarried. She missed and was downcast. But she married within a year anyway. I wonder, where was the mandate written? We all knew what it was: each princess must find her prince. If she failed—or lost him—she lived the reverse side of the fairy tale with all the other widows, divorcees, and spinsters in America. It is still so.

I knew nothing of this world during the long years spent bearing and rearing children, working as an Avon lady, and typing term papers to help put my husband through graduate school at the University of Oregon, years of isolation from all but my family and neighboring wives, whom I would repeatedly invite over for coffee and companionship, and after they left, I would wonder at my depression.

I could not understand what was happening. I had everything I was ever supposed to have wanted, yet I would find myself crying while I folded diapers. Was it loneliness I felt? But how could I be lonely? People were around constantly. My life had shape and direction and substance—what was wrong with me? In fact, I had been alone only one time in my life, a night shortly after my fourth daughter was born. I remember twice turning off the lights and trying to go to sleep, each time getting up and turning them on again, irritated with my cowardice but too filled with nameless fears to resist. Finally I settled down in the living room to wait out the night, sleepless, a butcher knife beside me. I was then twenty-seven years old.

Slowly but steadily the romantic expectations on which I had built my life began inevitably to give way to the reality. Something harder, more honest but infinitely more frightening was taking shape. I began to question everything: my church, my marriage, my rights and responsibilities. But I did so with incredible timidity: afraid, afraid, always afraid. To question the precepts of Catholicism was to invite the damnation of hell. To question the truth of my marriage was to question authority and to shake the roots of life for six people. But once the questions began I could not stop them, and they led me out to sea as inexorably as the evening tide.

Between my third and fourth pregnancies, the questions became unendurable. I decided to go on a retreat to a monastery in Portland, Oregon. I knew how peaceful a retreat could be. For three days I would talk to no one, communicating only with God and a temporarily silent world. Before my marriage I had gone to a cloistered convent, sleeping in a little room with bars across the window, and had found it one of the most deeply peaceful experiences of solitude in my life. But the experience at the Portland monastery was not the same. Doubts of the truth, of the efficacy of my religion, had become tormenting. I sought out the retreat master for counsel, taking to him the now jumbled package of literalism that had been my mainstay for so long and, in effect, asking him to patch it up again. He could not. He was at first the kindly patriarchal figure I knew and valued: "If you have doubts, my dear, you must put it in the hands of God," he said. "You must make the leap to faith."

I finally dared to push against this comfortable assurance. "I can't, Father," I said. "I've got to know some reasons." We talked. He was gentle, understanding, then firm; finally cold. I knew what was happening, and it was so frightening that I felt dizzy. He raised his voice. I raised mine.

"Father, if I don't confess to you my doubts, I can't receive the sacraments, can I? And if I confess them to you, and can't tell you I am sorry for having them, you can't absolve me, can you?"

"Just say you are sorry," he shouted.

"But I'm *not* sorry," I shouted back, hoping somehow for a miracle to change the course I was taking. I didn't want him to pat my hand and look the other way in the confessional after this talk. He *knew* I wasn't sorry; he knew being sorry had nothing to do with my problem. I wanted him to be consistent with the religion that I counted on to be consistent; but within that consistency I now knew there was nothing but a dead core and, oh God, what did one *do* when the core was gone?

We finished, both baffled, both tormented. He couldn't believe my stubbornness. I couldn't believe he had no answers. I walked out into the hall, down the silent corridor filled with other women on retreat nurtured by their missals and beads, and I knew I had nothing left. They stared. Our voices, the priest's and my own, had cut into the quiet air, destroying the fiction of unassailable holiness we all took for granted.

I attended Mass once more. There were about fifty of us in the small chapel for the morning service. Everyone went to the altar rail for Holy Communion except me. I was dismissed from my church; or, I had dismissed myself. Whatever had happened, I couldn't believe it was done.

Many evenings my husband and I sat down together at the kitchen table after dinner was over, the babies in bed, and tried to wrestle with all that was happening to me, to us.

We were in no way prepared, both of us feeling totally vulnerable and helpless. I have since read again the letters I wrote to my husband shortly before we were married, and the abject tone, the teasing, happy servility ("Be sure you learn lots of things so someday you can teach them to me"), even now makes me feel sad and tired; sad for that girl who put all her energies into shaping herself as an appendage and for the young man she married; tired with the realization that it probably could not have been any other way, given who we were and how we had been formed.

In an effort to firm the boundaries of our lives, I decided to pick up the fragments of my abandoned education and begin again. He encouraged me, and the university accepted not only my transcript, but me—with interest and genuine help. We bought an old Plymouth for $100 and I drove to school each morning, singing with the radio, thinking new ideas and feeling new emotions. I loved that car. It gave me wings.

New expectations were growing too, built on an education and a beginner's confidence that I could be competent in work I loved: journalism. For me, that meant serious, full-time commitment. Already I knew too many housewives back at the kitchen sink with their degrees and Phi Beta Kappa keys, still frustrated, still unhappy. It was going to be different for me. I had discovered Betty Friedan under the hairdryer and held fast to new goals.

After graduation we moved to Indiana, where my husband began teaching at the University of Notre Dame. I took a job as a reporter for the local newspaper, enjoying the experience of knowing I had chosen work I was both suited for and loved. It didn't take long to realize the extent of my good fortune—only long enough to meet and talk with some of the men locked in with early career decisions and growing families, who would never have a chance to reach out for anything other than a steady paycheck. Are they not as trapped as many women? At the same time, I realized I was considered odd by the wives of other professors at the university. That knowledge preyed on all that was conformist in me, all that feared being "different." The university wives did not work. Those few who broke this rule were teachers or nurses, good nurturing professions, and so escaped disapproval. I could not escape it so I avoided its source, confining my interests to my family and to the daily deadlines that mark the life of a reporter.

Work and home mixed uneasily. I belonged to no one world, existing marginally at the edges of two, but without the power to accept the rewards or responsibility for either. Wanting to please had been a large part of my morality. When I ceased trying, I lost the feeling of being good. I could never have it again because the question that would not leave me, that demanded an answer was, What had I ever done or desired wholly on my own?

My husband and I began going to a psychologist for marriage counseling. The result was a year of expensive, nondirective therapy ("Now what do *you* think is wrong?"), of floundering, false insights, long, painful attempts to understand each other as we drove the twenty miles to and from the clinic each week. One time it all connected, frightening both of us. An old wound was poked during a bitter session, then ripped open. I screamed and cried and he screamed back; he pounded his fists and I ripped at my hair and we ended up limp, enjoying that strange peace for a short while that only two people in constant, painful conflict find through periodic, violent catharsis. "The two of you have got to get off the fence," the therapist finally advised. "You've got to either decide to make your marriage work or get divorced."

How, we asked, do you push a button or turn a lever and make a marriage "work"? How can you ignore the unhappiness and confusion that doom each solitary, genuine effort? On the other hand, how do you sever what has become all of life for a man and a woman? How do you cut through the tangle of emotion and come out as two whole people? And how do you resolve a conflict that is rooted not only in the relationship of two people, but in the society within which they live?

Yet out of that session came a decision. I was to go away.

On January 12, 1970, a bitter, icy morning, I settled myself on the cold wooden seat of the aging South Shore commuter train that connected South Bend, Indiana, with Chicago and looked out the window at my children waving good-bye. Their smiles were bright and uncertain. Monica, who at five was the baby of the family, stopped pretending and began to cry angrily, frantically. Seven-year-old Maureen put her arm around Monica in an attempt at comfort, but Monica only cried harder with the realization that her mother was really leaving. ("I will be home every Friday night," I had told the children the night before, adding promises of frequent phone calls and special weekend bedtime stories to ease their pain and my own. "And you'll go back to Chicago every Monday morning," said Maureen with understanding finality.)

Through the train window and my own tears, dimly, I saw my husband, his hand in Monica's hair, smiling tensely, waving. I had thrown the anchor for this family to him. All because I had reached a time in my life where I was compelled to take a journey away from—outside of—my marriage, a journey away from isolation in search of a personal wholeness I had never known.

Where and how had not been problems. I had taken a job as a reporter with the Chicago *Sun-Times*, a job I wanted and needed to grow professionally. I was to live in Chicago during the week and commute home eighty miles each Friday. In this way we thought perhaps we could find a new direction for ourselves and our children. Under this arrangement, I lived alone away from my family for two years.

"Good-bye! Good-bye!" The train pulled slowly from the station. Stumbling in their floppy galoshes, the children ran the length of the platform, waving, and I strained to catch a last glimpse of them all. My husband had turned his back and was already walking toward the car. I knew then I was forever caught, even though perhaps forever free. The tearing of flesh was complete.

If this book was intended to be a defense of my own experience, I would go back over the past few pages and expand them to a hundred. But long ago I decided never to defend this decision that was almost inevitable when it finally came. The temptation to do so has sometimes been overwhelming. "How the hell could you go away and leave your children? How could you stand it?" a fellow reporter asked abruptly one morning at work. I couldn't answer. How do you articulate a void filled only with guilt and private pain?

There is a passage in Thornton Wilder's *The Eighth Day* that surely must touch other people as it has me: "Family life is like that of nations: each member battles for his measure of air and light, of nourishment and territory, and particularly for that measure of admiration and attention which is called 'glory.' It is like a forest; each tree must fight for its sunlight; under the ground the roots engage in a death struggle for moisture . . ."

My journey to Chicago was a search for air and light.

2.

Into the Tunnel

A new job and an alien life. Nervousness and uncertainty. I made many simple mistakes at first, pretending to know and understand when I didn't.

I have since watched with sympathy other women, waitresses, for example, in their shiny black dresses, older women unused to working, hurriedly trying to figure a bill correctly when customers are signaling impatiently from all over the room. I have watched clerks under the watchful eye of a store manager helping women choose a dress or a blouse, confused over what is or isn't in fashion, and afraid of admitting it. They work at grocery check-out counters, drugstores, movie theaters, laundries, offices and factories, these women with their tired feet and anxious expressions. There are no husbands to bring home paychecks or to give emotional support. Usually they don't want to work, but they must. In one sense, I have nothing in common with them. I chose to work, but for most women alone the world of work doesn't offer substantial rewards. In another sense, I

feel a kinship because they so obviously want their dignity as I
wanted mine when I first came to Chicago—and I was as uncertain as they of hanging on to it.

Everything overwhelmed me that first month—the weather,
the fast-paced atmosphere of a large newspaper, but particularly
the mechanics of everyday living. Initially I lived in a North Side
high-rise apartment some distance from the newspaper, which
meant learning bus schedules and routes. I kept getting on the
wrong bus. Dependency on others to see to details was so deeply
rooted—men had always opened the car door, they knew how to
get from here to there, and they didn't bother much with buses.

Part of the problem was my intense self-absorption in attempting to change direction without self-confidence. I was expending vast amounts of energy trying to succeed, all the while
expecting to fail. I had walked out onto a diving board and now
stood at the end with nothing to do but jump, and suddenly I
wondered if I could swim. I wanted everything. I wanted to be a
star reporter; I wanted to love and to be loved; I wanted to meet
not only the needs but the desires of my children; I wanted to
stand on a hilltop in Greece and fly on skis down the mountains
of Switzerland; I wanted to be rich and famous and happy. Even
wanting all that took energy. Mine flew off in many directions
without focus, because of an inner environment shaped long ago
to a socially acceptable form inimical to embracing the world. I
was diffused. I didn't want to be forced to choose. Sylvia Plath
has described this diffusion with her analogy of the fig tree, full
with the fruit of all the good things of life. To choose one means
to lose all the rest. Those who cannot decide must watch as each
fig turns dry and black and falls dead from the tree. I couldn't let
that happen. So I had to reach, reach constantly for them all.
And that meant never resting, always thinking, always hoping,
always planning. It meant I was an ambitious woman, not a socially attractive thing to be.

There were small good moments: among them, a box of fresh

blue checks with my name on them. Though most of my income was used for family expenses in South Bend, I felt inordinately pleased that those checks were all my own, that what happened to the small amount of money I used for living in Chicago was up to me, no one else. This knowledge gave not only a sense of my new independence but something more. Privacy. I had never known it and did not yet value it. But I recognized it.

I also loved the little family grocery store at the corner near my apartment building. Each evening I would wheel a wire cart around, indulging myself in things like cans of lima beans (my husband had never liked them), Pepperidge Farm chocolate cake, English chocolate bars, or a steak for one dollar. I felt strange buying quarts of milk instead of gallons, and stranger still when I had to throw half of it out when it went sour or the small loaves of bread when they got moldy. Milk and bread never had a chance to go sour or get moldy in a home with four children. I wondered more than once, how did single people manage to use up food? It seemed to me bread should be packaged in half-dozen slices and milk dispensed by the glass for solitary apartment dwellers. I had entered a Lilliputian consumer world and it was intriguing.

After shopping I would carry the bag to the building, go up in the elevator (silently, although it was often crowded with other singles carrying brown paper bags; we stared at the flashing floor lights and did not talk to each other), down the corridor, turn the key in the lock and enter the apartment. At first this was a difficult moment—I had never, as far as I could remember, entered an empty house or apartment alone at night. I used to leave the door slightly ajar and then go from room to room checking to make sure no burglar or rapist was waiting to pounce when I closed and locked the door. I was forever coming across brisk two-paragraph stories in the newspaper about hideous incidents befalling women alone: the nurse strangled with her stocking; a secretary who came home from work, surprised a burglar, and was hanged from the living-room light fixture.

But when the door was finally shut and I was alone, I didn't worry. It was peaceful. I loved those quiet evenings. I would fry the dollar steak and slice a tomato, then sit down with dinner and the paper to read, no voices, no chaos, no anger or strain, no responsibilities intruding. Afterward I would wash my one plate (without filling a sink with soapy water—it seemed like such a waste), fix a cup of coffee, and settle in for an evening of reading, listening to the wind shriek around the side of the building. For weeks, this was all I needed. Just to be alone.

My children were voices on the telephone, interrupting each other to report on their activities, and the eagerness of their voices followed me into sleep. I needed them, I realized, as they needed me—and the mysteries of how a family works did not need to be totally unraveled to understand that. But for that time, in that way, I needed also to be apart from them.

Conversations with my husband were usually brief and carefully cheerful; infrequently long and unguarded. We honored the cold distance between us as we would honor a pledge, each unable to ask anything of the other.

I had no friends in Chicago, which didn't matter at first. I was too preoccupied in adjusting to a strange environment to miss them. But after the first couple of months it wasn't enough to spend evenings with a book, a candy bar, and a cup of coffee. I began dialing friends far away, friends who knew me, friends who would sit patiently at the phone and listen and respond for an hour or more. What would lonely people do without a telephone? But I wasn't surprised at my own loneliness; I had expected it and wasn't going to make the same mistake I had made at different times in the past: running back from the unknown to what is understood and familiar.

A friend suggested I join a church social group, but as a renegade Catholic I would have felt like a trespasser in any church. I could never belong to any other and was forever alienated from my own. Often at five o'clock at night I was reluctant to leave the bright and busy city room. I liked being part of it. I would work on notes, make phone calls, or read the first edition of the next day's paper all the way to the want ads, just to stay around a little longer. Sometimes I would be invited to join a group for a drink after work; sometimes I would be invited to dinner.

Most people thought, understandably, that I lived a strange life. Sometimes I would try to explain, most often not, because they were absorbed in their own lives, and I had to figure out my own. The multitude of small fears, grown large for want of confrontation, were still to be conquered. And yet already I was being confronted with something that looked and felt like a new form of isolation. I was "different," that odious label I had spent so many years slapping on other people, never myself. Had I simply traded one kind of isolation for another?

I knew very little about the Women's Liberation movement, but my own experience was teaching me the difficulties of being accepted without a clear-cut marital status. Mine was uncomfortably hazy at that point. I couldn't be easily catalogued and filed.

The underlying assumption seems to be a woman "should" belong to a man, and if she doesn't for too long a time, something is amiss. People disapprove of women without men, not in an overt way, but by exhibiting a vague, general cautiousness toward what is not known or understood (for example, neighbors speculating about the friendship between two female schoolteachers who buy a home together). The stereotypes about women alone haven't changed much in the past twenty-five years. I began to realize I would have to be dealing with them myself, and it was a jolting recognition of the extent of my isolation.

Married women are too often dependent cripples, but I could see that living alone in a society built on marriage meant other curious dependencies to be avoided, such as fashioning oneself into a stereotype in order to avoid social disapproval. For instance, I saw around me examples of the businesswoman who announces her unattractiveness with as much meticulous attention to detail as a model making up for an assignment, asking to be allowed to withdraw from the race. If she persists, the pressures decrease. She will no longer be looked upon with disapproval because she hasn't married. She has successfully proven what is "wrong" with her and now will be left alone, reclassified as an aging spinster who couldn't find a man. Or, the woman so eager to marry that she retools for every man she meets. Her ideas, her likes and dislikes, undergo chameleon-like changes until she marries or the time comes when she wonders just who she is. That kind of identity crisis must be no less painful than the one I endured as a housewife who did the same thing years before. I wondered, which stereotypes would apply to me? Runaway wife? Dilettante? I knew one thing: none would provide protection from social disapproval.

I knew also I could sidestep some of the problems by continuing my routine of coming home each night with a comforting bag of groceries, locking the door, and watching the rest of the world on television. Except I wouldn't. The cost for this self-exploration was too dear. It was time to reach out and touch other people to see what we shared, even at the risk of being lonelier than ever.

I wanted friends, realizing that my appreciation of solitude was shallowly rooted. And yet I also sensed that such an appreciation meant strength—if I could pursue it not by locking doors but by opening them.

These lines from a song explain a little of what happened, and although I have them jumbled, they do say what I would like to say: "I have tried in my own way to be free; I have tried to reach those who reached out for me." Sometimes I made mistakes. But I am grateful for the warm experiences and I don't regret them.

Spring came, then early summer. A pattern of life was by now well established: each Monday morning I took the six o'clock train from South Bend, and each Friday night I returned at eight in the evening. My children accepted the routine, even though Saturdays were often lost days spent in exhaustion doing nothing. Sundays were lonely, particularly at night when I was preparing to go back to Chicago. The two little ones would sit and watch me wash my hair and put it up in rollers and we would talk, bright and fast. (Maureen has since told me she still hates to see me washing my hair because it always signaled the end of the weekend.)

Once I was hospitalized in Chicago for a week with eye trouble and couldn't make it home. The day I was released, the family came up to visit for the afternoon and we went to a park. It was a beautiful, clear day, cyclists pedaling everywhere, sailboats bouncing white and free on Lake Michigan, parents playing catch with their children. I was grateful they had come. I wanted to spin out a long lovely day, but I had forgotten the length of the drive back to South Bend. My husband was packing things up and preparing to leave within a few hours. He and the children piled into the car, all except Maureen, who was playing at the sandbox. I went to get her and we sat together at the sandbox without speaking. Maureen took a stick and drew in the sand the words "I love you." I took the stick and wrote, "I love you, too." The car horn honked impatiently. It was time to go.

I have never felt so lonely in my life as I did that day in the bright sun, listening to the voices of summer and pleasure that were not for us.

Maureen wanted to take some sand with her in a bottle, so I filled it for her, keeping my face down to hide the tears. But she knew. (Later, much later, I learned of a ritual Maureen followed with her "Chicago sand" at home. She would sit on the

brick steps and carefully pour the white grains out on the cement, write "I love Mama" in them with her finger, and then
carefully pour them all back in the bottle.)

It was at times like this when I would have given anything to
belong wholly to my children's world, but I had stepped away
carrying fragments of myself and had not yet put them together
in a new and honest form. That had to be accomplished first.
But I think I knew that summer day something of the pain of a
divorced father, of what it must be like to love your children by
the calendar, infrequently, without the relaxation of having time
to waste lavishly, always knowing you must give them up to their
"ordinary" lives in which you play no part.

August 1970. For months there had been talk about the
display of strength planned by the Women's Liberation
movement—Women's Strike Day, a day when all women in the
country would be exhorted to drop their menial chores and
gather to protest their second-class status. I had only a
peripheral interest; the liberation movement had not yet drawn
me in any clear, positive way. I was one of the women trying to
redirect the course of their lives who didn't want anything to do
with other women in the process, which is a common reaction:
middle-class blacks don't want to remember the ghetto. I felt,
simply, that I was more intelligent than most women, and so I
dismissed them as boring. There had been too many years of
Tupperware parties, neighborhood barbecues, and Saturday
mornings at the beauty shop. In those days, for all our coffee-
klatsching, for all our exchange of information on baby care and
diets and detergents, we were women sharing only the
miscellany of our lives, and rarely, so rarely, did we open our
hearts. We were housewives, and our friendships were based on
an exchange of complaints. When we were depressed, unaware
that we shared a common emptiness, we went to our family doctors and they gave us something to calm our nerves. We talked

endlessly about so little, and I wish I could go back and change some of that. We should have known each other.

Originally another reporter was scheduled to cover the Strike Day activities in Chicago, but she was on leave at the time and the assignment was passed on to me. I hadn't wanted it. I felt I was the wrong person to cover Strike Day. Carrie Nation and her hatchet were still mixed up in my mind with the early suffragettes, those strong, fierce women I knew nothing about except through the comic strips, and they all seemed strange and absurd. The women I saw in news photos dumping bras and girdles in trash cans and waving their fists at men embarrassed me. Surely there were better ways, more feminine, more polite ways to object to the way men treated women. I would laugh when men pointed their fingers at newspaper pictures of women picketing and made some witty comment about "what these broads need." But even then I secretly admired the courage of those women. Some of the things they were saying sounded remarkably like what was going on in my own brain.

As a joke, one morning at work I pinned on my dress the official brown and white button that said "Women" and "Strike—August 26." People in the office commented and laughed, but they soon forgot it and so did I until later in the day, in the Loop, I walked into a church that interested me because of its distinctive architecture. A pleasant, round-faced woman greeted me and offered a tour of the church. But then she spotted the button and was immediately disconcerted. "What's that?" she said, poking her finger as if she were testing a rotten tomato. "A Women's Strike Day button," I replied. She looked flustered and upset. "I'm afraid you had better come another time; we're not showing any more people around today," she said, taking a step back from me. I left the church, feeling bemused and strange. It was a totally new experience to be suddenly unwelcome because I apparently espoused unpopular ideas. Later, I wrote a light feature story about what happened the day I wore a Women's Lib button, trying with humor, to get across something of what was troubling about a society that reacted with distrust and anger to anything different.

On August 26, crowds of women and curious men began assembling in Civic Center Plaza shortly before noon. Placards were hoisted and microphones connected, and an atmosphere of excited expectation hung over the crowd. No one knew quite what to expect because there had not been a similar gathering of women—all ages, all backgrounds—for many years, certainly not in my lifetime.

I've covered quite a few meetings, rallies, and demonstrations, even a riot or two. At some I have felt a special trembling in the air, like a chord of music cutting through all other sounds, commanding, demanding attention. I felt it that day at Civic Center. I felt it shiver down my back, through my whole body and out to other women—who sent it back to me. I shoved back and forth through the crowd, talking to women, scribbling notes, listening to speakers, watching the hostility of the lunchtime girl-watchers as they lounged by the fountain hooting and laughing. Their day was spoiled, and I suddenly realized how much I disliked them. They did not seem to be the same good-natured observers who whistled their appreciation when you walked past on a sunny day in a new dress, making you feel good, attractive, feminine, the way a woman is supposed to want to feel. Their prerogative to inspect and mentally undress had been challenged, and they didn't like it at all.

Was this my radicalization? I really don't know. Are we able to freeze-frame the exact moments when we change, or do we only focus in retrospect on the most obvious pivotal points to impose an order on events? My commitment to the women's movement came cautiously, then in a rush, but it was never total. At times some women's groups have sounded as disturbingly didactic as the Catholic Church, and I hadn't escaped one absolutist portrayal of what I was and could be only to replace it with another. What I sensed that day was primarily a unity, a precarious unity to be sure, but something authentic enough to include us all: the secretaries, the schoolteachers, the tense young women backpacking babies, the angry women, black and white, the curious housewives in for a day of shopping from the suburbs. It was a shock to look at all these women, not as competitors or aliens, but as people like me. (Months later, talking with Lionel Tiger on his theory of male bonding, I tried to explain this first experience of connection with women. It was very hard. I had no language—a lifetime of being a woman, and I had no language to explain the realization of belonging to my own kind.)

I looked around the crowded plaza that afternoon and for the first time, precisely because I felt unity with them, I wondered about the isolation of women—not just the physical isolation of wives from a working world or wives from single women or even the additional emotional isolation of women from men, but the psychic isolation that keeps so many women, married or single, but particularly women without men, lonely yet with no capacity for aloneness. *Why do women find it so hard to be alone*? Why, I wondered, are we so afraid of loneliness that we flee from solitude, fearing emptiness? And why does this fear so often mean unhappy marriages or bitter and lonely lives?

Women looked at each other that day, half-embarrassed, self-conscious, unsure. They were not used to seeing themselves as individuals making contact as individuals. Being part of that mixing, milling crowd mattered deeply to me because I was trying hard to find out how to be alone without being lonely, how to train myself to self-sufficiency when I had never expected to value or need it. I felt deprived of fundamental strengths. Before I could reach out to other people, I would have to get myself all together. And I thought that perhaps, by opening myself to the experience of other women, I might succeed;

that learning more of the experience of being female from the perspective of women alone would illuminate dimensions of life hitherto obscured.

A popular image of the woman alone is the aging spinster with her bottle and telephone. She has become a cliché for melodrama and novels. Like all clichés, it is based on truth. These women abound. I have met them, drunk with them, and listened to them. Their loneliness comes from unfulfillment, an unsatisfied psychic hunger, from fear fed by self-pity or simply a dread that no one will come to the party. Sometimes it can be a desolation so profound it is indescribable. But loneliness is no kin to solitude: there was no need for community campfires at Walden Pond.

Alexis de Tocqueville, Margaret Mead, and others have written of the insistently gregarious personalities of Americans, the flocking together that produces in our time, for example, unbelievable crowding even in the places to which we retreat for respite from the world. Observe a park campsite: tents pitched stake to stake, cars honking, babies crying, dogs barking, people standing in long lines to chop wood and use bathrooms, their lives and diapers and card games all mixed together in what has come to be called a "vacation." Why?

Margaret Mead said over twenty years ago that the reason we cluster together with such determination is because "nowhere in childhood or youth is there any training or any practice in self-sufficient isolation." Certainly this is true of the life experience of most American women. Yet isolation is a harsh companion to self-sufficiency. Must we be isolated? Philip Slater argues that Americans have such a developed ethos of individuality, such a relentless admiration for self-reliance, that we have within us self-sufficient isolation in the form of a virus rather than a virtue, an essentially masculine view which misses the fact that self-reliance is not the hallmark of the American woman, although it is part of the mystique.

John Locke has told us we all, men and women, exist as individual atoms with no organic connection. Americans have traditionally been a lonely crowd, creating communities for protection, yet philosophically and metaphysically alone. "I have found no exertion of the legs can bring two minds much nearer to one another," said Henry Thoreau. Probably a stout-hearted individualism was required by the struggle of the Pilgrims in a new and hostile world and the push later to settle the West. Social Darwinism, capitalistic expansion, all such factors contributed to the atomistic nature of Americans.

But there is another dimension. What I want to talk about are the specific problems of women: the lonely woman in the lonely crowd. De Tocqueville admired female independence born of a new and mobile society, a society freed of European restrictions, but not independence rooted in the self-confidence and social freedom to do as one pleases with one's life. Women are reared now as they have always been in this country, with the spoken and unspoken assumption from the cradle that they will marry. The persistent and sometimes enervating "search for identity" that women seem endlessly embarked upon is inevitable in view of their early training for a role that has little to do with the uniqueness of the individual. In contrast, a man is raised with a sense of what he is to be, not whom he is to marry, and he is therefore identified by what he does. He is a plumber, or president of the bank. A woman is identified by whom she marries— she is the plumber's wife. A woman from Alabama, ill, two divorces behind her, put it to me starkly: "From the time I was a little girl, I knew I was nothing unless I got myself a man."

Once married, a woman shapes herself to her husband, the "Pygmalion effect," as sociologist Jesse Bernard calls it. The conditions of marriage, built on the role of the man as prime mover and provider, produce this result. It goes beyond the image of a hapless, helpless dependent female and deep into married life as it is lived by even exceptional women. In a comment on the role required of the wife of a politician, Marvella Bayh, wife of Senator Birch Bayh of Indiana, has said: "I've always longed for a career of my own because I never really did have one . . . I live completely through him . . . But I suppose it would be a rude awakening if something happened to him. Not only would I lose a husband, a best friend and a breadwinner, but my own career." (And why is it that lists of "most admired women" usually include so many wives of famous men?)

Some of the troubled self-questioning among wives today stems from the fact they are realizing now the extent to which they live their lives through their husbands—instead of all at once in the rude shock that awaits them after divorce or widowhood. But most wouldn't have it any other way. A man is security. He means groceries in the cupboard and shoes in the closet. He means friends and status. He means, ultimately, all those things that a widow or divorced woman left without money or emotional support no longer has.

If there is a trap that women can set to perpetuate female helplessness and dependency, it is to raise their daughters as marriage material and not as individuals with other life options. It is so easy. Read them only fairy tales about princesses (who marry handsome princes) and witches (*they* are usually alone), buy them only dolls and toy stoves and brooms and cooking sets, and if they seem more interested in math than boys, discourage them. But to do these things is to set the scene for marital turmoil in the next generation, to move our children even further away than we are from loving relationships between men and women that not only work but grow.

Even those who would change the order of things for themselves accept the concept of marriage as security. A young writer hunting for a better-paying job explained to me with dignity as well as disturbing self-knowledge that she was doing so because ''I don't want to have to marry for money.'' Although women are approaching marriage more carefully, with less romanticism, they are still convinced that true security means marriage, rarely realizing the burden this puts on men to deliver an impossible package. Indeed, the nuclear family—one man, one woman, and their children, isolated from broader family bonds—has not compensated either man or woman for their own inadequacies or the deficiencies of life, but has instead created intolerable demands for intimacy and meaning.

Most women still don't realize they have a potential for separate psychic existence, which involves taking primary responsibility for one's own emotions and adjustments to life. Within this separateness is true security, the best kind of all because it allows for freedom. But freedom, as Sartre reminds us, is terrifying, so most married women spend their lives avoiding any serious confrontation with themselves. Women alone must either face such a confrontation or retreat to the bitterness and isolation supposedly the lot of all women without men. Most give up. This became particularly clear to me after writing a series of articles on divorce, which resulted in a steady flow of mail that lasted for over a year. I began dreading the ordeal of opening thick letters filled with court records and intimate personal details of lives of divorced women who were clutching in any direction for help. Those women were so utterly incapable it was frightening. I remember one, a middle-aged woman trying to support two children on $65 a week, who was unable to go to work because there was nothing she could do: ''Where did my life go?'' she wrote at the end of her long letter. ''I just never *was* and I'm so afraid.''

Are women, then, lonelier than men? Of course not. To claim this would be to ignore the evidence of human experience all around us. What I am discussing here is ontology, which is perhaps the ultimate metaphysical puzzle, the whole concept of

Being and the relationship of the I to the Other. But I intend to
bite off only a small piece of that to chew. I do think women
are lonely in a different way from men. In part their loneliness
comes from their dependency, while a man's comes from the absolute requirement that he be not only independent but able
to support a woman's dependency. Sometimes, unable to take
this pressure, he dies early—a form of suicide. His identity
comes through work. During the Depression men went off to
jobs each day that no longer existed, pretending there was still
work because without work they were nothing. Engineers laid
off when the government cancelled aircraft contracts in Seattle
also continued the fiction of driving to town each morning so the
neighbors would not know and would not pity. Others retreated,
closeted themselves in their home, unable to face the fact that
they no longer had jobs. Willy Loman, the tragic figure in *Death
of a Salesman*, without work or dignity, is legion.

A particular incident on Women's Strike Day illuminated for
me the deep gaps in understanding between women of different
classes and life styles. "Why don't all these women go out and
get a job?" one woman cried angrily. "What are they doing
here? Trying to be like men, that's what they're doing! Why
don't they go out and scrub floors like I had to do? They want to
sit in the boss's chair, and they'll never do that while there's a
man with pants on!" She saw the demonstrators as middle-class
women with time to kill, women who didn't have the faintest
idea of what it was like to go to work at six in the evening to
clean an office building and ride a lonely bus home at two in the
morning. None of those middle-class women knew whether or
not her kids turned out all right, whether she managed to pay her
bills, or whether her rheumatism was painful at night. What did
they have to say to her? What indeed?

Women need to establish communication with each other. We
understand so little of each other's lives, yet we are so quick to
pronounce judgment on one another. We need the parallel

strengths of solitude and community to deal with discriminatory practices perpetuated by a male-dominated society, to change attitudes, to do away with stereotypes and face ourselves honestly. At the same time, women need men and men need women. Without each other, without some form of mutual reliance, we lose our humanity. If we could only rid ourselves of the myths and false expectations—even the comfortable ones. If we could know ourselves better, know other women, then perhaps we might establish deeper and more honest relationships with men. Is it possible? "I don't know, but it would be fun," one woman told me wistfully.

Many women still cling to the myth of female weakness not only because it is part of their conditioning but because, as author Mary Ellmann has pointed out, they know how to exploit it so well. But that power boomerangs when women are no longer young and pretty and find themselves alone. It also boomerangs when women decide to deliberately put it aside and show their personalities honestly—and find they have lost the capacity to do so. "Love doesn't work here in America," said a disconsolate college senior. "You start living with someone and you have been so busy learning to know him you don't know anything about yourself, and neither does he. You find out, by God, that love doesn't make a damn bit of difference."

A question being asked so often now is whether what is genuine and natural for women is something different than for men. But how can we know, when what we accept as natural is usually only normative?

3.

Women Alone

"Are you planning to be here more than a week?" the YWCA director asked with a smile, her pen poised over paper.

"Yes," I said. "But I don't know for how much longer after that."

"Two weeks?"

"Maybe. Maybe longer."

"Are you single, widowed, or divorced?"

"Married."

She nodded briefly and asked no more questions. "You'll enjoy the fourth floor best," she said. "It's quieter."

I paid my money and she gave me my room and mailbox keys. "Please be very careful of your keys," she told me. "The women here get nervous over the idea of people losing them. We have to change the locks then." I followed her down the cavernous first-floor corridor to the elevator; the operator, an old man, was asleep on a stool. She woke him, and the ancient lift creaked slowly up to the fourth floor.

The halls in the vast stone structure of the Chicago McCormick YWCA twisted off in every direction. It was a little dreary, a little cold. But it was very quiet, and I liked that. The director showed me my room, a tiny narrow cubicle at the end of the hall. It was large enough to hold only a single bed with a pink chenille bedspread, a chair, a desk and a lamp. Just the basics. I wanted nothing more at that point, physically, mentally, or emotionally.

"It's perfect," I said.

It was January 1971. I had left the high-rise apartment and was to live at the Y for six months, quite comfortably.

The fourth floor was for the "regulars," the women who usually moved in and stayed for a long time, the women who didn't turn their radios up loud or shout from room to room. On the contrary, they rarely talked to one another. Each evening from behind my own locked door I would hear the quiet click of doors closing up and down the hall. But the walls were very thin.

One night as I lay in bed, a woman began to cry in the next room. Not loudly, just a tired cry, the same tired crying sound I've heard more than once late at night in a maternity ward. I lay there and listened for two hours, haunted with my own memories, knowing I could turn my head to that wall and whisper something and be heard. But what? Finally I fell asleep.

Some of the women on the fourth floor had lived at the Y for many years; they were timid people, single or sometimes widowed, who needed the protection of this comfortable fortress, a place where they could retreat, complete with guards and sign-in sheets and sirens that went off at night if anybody disturbed a barred door. For others, living at the Y meant a package of total care. Each morning you left your room and when you came back it was cleaned and dusted and your clothes were hung. The cafeteria fixed breakfast, and the kitchen help did the dishes. Most women have not lived lives where somebody else takes care of the housekeeping mechanics, and they are usually uneasy in such situations. But perhaps because somewhere in their lives they had lost the resilience to cope with daily uncertainties, or just because they wanted their minds free for other concerns, most women at the YWCA preferred what I think is best described as the tidiness of the life offered.

Men were allowed only on the first and second floors, but after ten o'clock the iron gates came down across the stairway and the building was closed for the night. Those of us not properly sealed in at that time were required to sign a roster at the front desk, a procedure which made me feel like an over-age college sophomore, somehow guilty if I had to put down my name and write one or two A.M. after it. Yet I enjoyed the anonymity and extended my stay week by week. ("You can save money paying by the month," the man at the desk said repeatedly. "But I don't know how long I'll be here," I answered each time. Finally he gave up and accepted me as just one more eccentric.)

The Y was an oddly uncommunal place. The young women changed every few days and the "regulars" met together only to watch television. Sometimes I would join them. But it seemed unnatural to be watching television, which for me was a family experience that meant hushing children and making frequent trips to the kitchen, a *community* kind of thing, not sitting silently with a roomful of strangers. You had to have a consensus vote to change the channel, but how do you get a consensus when no one speaks? I remember one evening when two women stood up simultaneously and asked if they could change the station. They both became flustered in the awkward silence that followed. It wasn't a hostile or rude silence; it was more like embarrassment. If I read the expressions on the faces correctly, it was as if a rule had been broken. Then, from the back of the room, a little Chinese woman who never spoke to anybody, who had slept from seven until midnight each evening for ten years in front of the television set, spoke up: "I like *this* station," she said. Her voice rang through the room. The two women immediately sat down. All heads swiveled back to the screen, the tension evaporated, and each woman retreated to her own private bubble once again.

Unless I was out for the evening, I usually stayed in my room. I liked it there. At that point, I needed periods of total aloneness to be forced into myself. I would fill the tub and soak for an hour, reading books on women. Some of them made me shake with anger because of the truth of what they said; others were so depressing I could not finish them. I went from one to another, piecing together something of a history of my own sex, a history that had never been offered in school or anywhere else in my life. If blacks have been robbed of their own heritage of knowledge and pride, so have women; and I think this realization was the most angering and depressing of all.

One morning as I was leaving for work, I stepped off the elevator onto the main floor into a confusion of floodlights, wires, and people. A movie company was filming a scene in the lobby with actress Candice Bergen. Curious, I stood around with the rest of the onlookers. ''We *never* have much excitement here, do we?'' remarked one eager observer. Hers was the first and only casual comment made by one of the women in my direction the entire six months I lived at the Y.

The film was about a young woman coming to the big city for the first time who checks into the YWCA. Candice Bergen walked in struggling with a suitcase, staring around at the high ceilings, a little awed; the classic scene of a young, potentially vulnerable woman coming to a haven of security. It was interesting, even though most girls I had observed checking in certainly didn't look awed. The scene symbolized a particular search for security that there is little need for now. Young women are more inclined to take an apartment with a roommate than to accept the home substitute that the Y was originally intended to provide. But the older women, the widows and spinsters on the fourth floor, for example, are women who still need havens. There are very few.

Not long after I left, the McCormick Y was closed down because there are not many young women who want the iron gates and the sign-in sheets anymore. I have wondered what happened to the women on the fourth floor. And to the little Chinese woman who slept in front of the television set?

Once while living there, I passed a man on the sidewalk next-door staring at a wrecking crew tearing down an old apartment building. He was muttering, angry, oblivious to other people on the sidewalk, just watching the huge ball crash into the beautiful old brick. I watched too for awhile, and the rapid destruction made me wince. Suddenly he leaned down, picked up a rock, yelled something unintelligible, and threw it hard at the metal ball. The rock bounced off without a discernible sound; the man stood there silently for a few more moments and then turned and walked away. I understood how he felt. Later, when I heard about the old Y closing down, I too felt like picking up a rock and throwing it. At something.

Why did I stay there? I don't know really, but I did develop a remote kind of affection for the place. I had come strictly for immediate convenience, intending to stay until I could find an apartment, and instead had lingered. People at work couldn't believe I actually *lived* at the YWCA. Puzzling over my reasons, a friend once announced he was convinced I was trying to retreat to the convent of my youth. Warming up to the idea, he declared I was a nun, "aloof, trying to slip past the Mother Superior." I certainly didn't feel like a nun (though signing in at night did make me nervous). It wasn't that. The Y was a place where I had stripped my life down to the barest essentials, to the minimum of responsibility. And I had gained the maximum of privacy. I didn't seek friendships among the women living there because I felt that I had entered into a sort of unwritten pact when I moved in—I could move about within my private little bubble if I didn't violate anyone else's. I had chosen aloneness as a route to finding my own individuality. Would it work? I didn't

know. I couldn't know, at that point. So I set out to discover
what the experience of aloneness was like for other women; in a
sense, I set out to find the woman in me I wanted to know.

In the process, I met and talked with women from as varied
backgrounds and experience as I could find: divorced and
widowed women, working women alone, single careerists, welfare mothers, students, activists, prostitutes, nuns, lesbians, ac-
tresses—women who would never dream they had anything in
common. I thought they did: the experience of being alone. I
saw this experience, then, from a variety of perspectives, and
found some women living in little boxes, their lives bleak and
isolated; others joyful and free. Most of them do not want to be
alone. But some have found the rarest security of all, the ability
to live peacefully with oneself.

I didn't realize it at that time, but I had started looking for the
substance of this experience two years before, on a hill in
Ireland. This was where it had begun for my mother. She is my
first portrait of a woman alone.

My mother's name is Anna Gilbride. She comes from a farm
family in County Fermanagh, Northern Ireland. She was the
eldest of six children, and kept herself and her brothers and
sisters enthralled with dreams of someday going to America.

I have since visited the old house at Cole Hill where my
mother's childhood ended and her work life began at the age of
fourteen. In the summer of 1968, before the bloody revival of
the war between Catholics and Protestants, I climbed the hill
back of the house with one of my mother's sisters. "This is where
Anna used to sit and tell us stories about America," she told me.
"She always said she'd get there someday and we would laugh
and say, 'Oh, Annie,' but other times we knew she meant it."

I sat down for a few moments under the same tree and looked
out across the hills to the horizon, trying to imagine what it had
been like to live with a dream like that—a dream that had no

hope of reality for a fourteen-year-old housemaid. I was beginning to understand something of the spirit of a woman who
walked away from everything she knew and took a chance on a
strange country and a strange life, alone. Would I have been
able to do that? I don't know if I would have had enough faith in
myself. I felt that day on Mother's hill, as I do now, proud to be
her daughter. (I do not intend any sentimental comparison between her journey to America and mine to Chicago, because they
were fundamentally different. However, her life has been important to me in understanding something of the endurance and accomplishment of women who do not back off from isolation, but
rather face it with all its risks in order to expand the boundaries
of their lives.)

One afternoon, over tea at the kitchen table, Mother told me
part of her story:

"When I was fourteen, we moved from Drummully Lane to
Cole Hill. It took all my parents' savings to buy a forty-acre
farm. We had to stock it, so daddy bought our first cow for forty
pounds. That was a lot of money then. We bought a second one
and it got sick and died; I remember it lying in the byre and my
daddy and mother worrying about it going to die. At night all
the neighbors would come and try to raise it up, get it on its feet,
but it was no use. The cow died and we needed money. I was
only fourteen, but I was the eldest and I had to go to work.

"I remember I was in the house and my daddy came in and
said, 'Annie, Sam McClennon—they need a girl.' Sam McClennon was standing outside at the end of the house, pretending not
to notice us talking at the door. As we walked out, Daddy said,
'They pay good wages. We'll try for eleven pounds. All right?' I
nodded my head, tickled to death to go. I wasn't happy at home,
and I wanted to be away. But then Sam McClennon said, 'Oh,
no, she's just a little girl. She isn't strong enough for the work.'
He stood there and looked me over, and shook his head. My

daddy said, 'She's fine; she's a good worker.' So I was hired for eleven pounds for six months.

"It was a nice home and I stayed there for a couple of years . . . After that, I worked for other people. My best job was with the stationmaster. His house was nicer than a farmer's home, by the railroad tracks. But I didn't want to be a maid; the mistress had me wear a uniform, and when she wasn't home, I'd take my cap and throw it down the hall. I'd go out after working and watch the people going places on the trains, and I knew that what I wanted to do more than ever was go to America, but it was growing bigger in my head and smaller in my pocket.''

"Finally when I was eighteen I went to Belfast and worked as a pantry maid in a hotel. I met an old lady and we used to talk, and one day she said, 'Go to America, Annie. Look at me—I waited, and waited, and never did what I wanted to do. Don't let that happen to you.' I started going down to the docks on my day off and I saw a sign: 'Three pounds to Canada,' it said. I signed up right away—I didn't even know where in Canada! There was a quota system, and I wouldn't be able to get from Ireland to the United States for five years, and I felt I was getting too old to wait any longer. This way, I signed up to work for a company in Canada and in return got the low passage. But I was under twenty-one, so I had to get my parents' permission and the parish priest's permission. I wrote home and my father answered with a wonderful letter, telling me it was all right to go. Then he went and talked to the priest to find out what kind of country Canada was. The priest told him it was a wild country, but a lot of young people were going there anyway . . .

"I went home for a little while and got my few things together, and then my father and I went back to Belfast. I sailed on Friday the thirteenth, in August 1926. I was so excited when the boat left the dock. Then I looked up and saw my father, his hat in his hands, waving, and I think he was crying. Suddenly I realized I might never see him or my mother again.''

   She did—but it was many years later.

   Mother found Canada a vast, empty country upon her arrival
in Ottawa. She worked for two years there, as a housemaid, a
waitress, a clerk in a company store. But they were enjoyable
years and she has memories of many friends, many dances, and
snowy sleigh rides to Quebec. It would have been easy to stay.
Comfortable. She bought a black satin dress for seven dollars
that she wore to the dances, a dress she carefully folded each
night and put back in its box.

   I have seen a picture of my mother, the flapper, in her black
satin dress with the fashionable braided sweatband, a solemn
picture that doesn't look as if it quite goes with the rhythm of the
Black Bottom. It didn't, of course. Even stepping into the era of
the twenties in the United States, a young woman from Ireland,
Mother kept her own rhythm. She knew she was different from
the time her boat docked in Canada and she said curiously to
one of her new friends, ''Where are we supposed to stand to get
off?'' And he turned and pointed to a nondescript group by the
helm: ''The immigrants are over there. That's where you go.''

   By the early thirties, she was an American citizen. An
American woman who had followed her own dreams and made
them come true.

   At any given time, one out of three adult women in this country are alone, whether they like it or not. Most don't, which is
hardly surprising. These women live in undefined worlds,
usually without reliable social status, under pressure to be self-
reliant in a society that doesn't particularly value self-reliance in
women. Perhaps none of this would be important, if women
didn't think it was—but they do. They are fully aware that marriage is the preferred state; they are fully aware they are shut out
from many of its advantages, and indeed it shouldn't surprise

anyone that there are very few merry widows or gay divorcees. Why are so many women single? And how do they adjust?

There are a variety of reasons why women are alone, but usually it is the result of a catastrophic event: a divorce or death. There are also many women who have never married, either by choice or because they did not have the opportunity. Few women actually choose permanent aloneness, and most resent the presumption of oddity. "It's a very strange thing at my age to still be single," author Jane Howard has said. "To be thirty-six years old and never to have been married is to feel in a constant state of apology." The extent to which the women I have met successfully and happily built lives for themselves seems to correlate closely with their ability to relax about marriage. "It would be nice to be married," said one divorced woman. "It would be very nice. But I'm doing all right, and I can be happy if I have to remain alone." She paused, then added, "If I choose to."

The problems for a woman living alone are severe, and it seems to me that most women either face them with a great deal of strength or with none at all. The presence or absence of strength doesn't seem necessarily dependent on money or security. I have met some desperate, unhappy women buttressed on one side by alimony payments and on the other by a supportive family. And I have also met a woman recuperating from a painful back operation, forced to go on welfare, who was an exceptional battler, a person who made *me* feel secure because of her equanimity toward life.

It seems reasonably certain that the number of single women in this country will increase in years to come, again for a number of reasons. For example, the rising divorce rate. Why is it rising? I believe one reason is that the critical age for women contemplating change in their lives is going down. Married women are responding to social change by putting themselves through a sometimes painful self-affirmation process, a process already so publicized that the questions are familiar to everyone: "Who am

I? Where am I going?'' ''Self-fulfillment'' and ''search for identity'' have become such stock phrases in Sunday supplements
that what they describe is too easily dismissable. But this soul
searching implies major change for both men and women—which
means we all should be aware of what is happening in the minds
and hearts of women.

There are other routes to singleness: younger women are not
in as much of a hurry to marry as they have been in the past. In
1970, 36 percent of all women between the ages of twenty and
twenty-four were single, compared with only 28 percent in
1960. The reasons for this are complex, and no one knows exactly what it may mean for the future. Some go so far as to pre-
dict the death of marriage, but there is a powerful magnetic pull
for most of us toward an institution that promises love, stability,
and loyalty—regardless of the divorce rate. ''I can't run down
marriage. My weakness was in staying with mine as long as I
did,'' feminist Betty Friedan told me. ''But what people are seeking in marriage are among the best things we need and want.''

Yet marriage has left a hunger. For all our efforts, the family
as we know it seems unable to satisfy the hungers of the many
lonely people within it. But we have no reliable substitutes, although many people are searching, experimenting with different
life styles. Usually the alternatives for a woman involve some
form of sharing a semipermanent relationship with a
man—either in a commune, sharing an apartment, or as a man's
mistress (I wish there was a better word, but there isn't). None of
these alternatives gives the woman any assurance of continuity,
the kind of assurance she has been taught from the cradle to expect. Without it, her relationships are precarious; she doesn't
know any other way to structure security. An ironic aspect of
relationships outside of marriage is that, sooner or later, if they
end, it is often because a woman has begun to push for a marriage contract—hating herself for doing it, but unable to stop.
''He loves me because I am free and live my own life, the very

reasons I want to be loved for," said a secretary in Washington, D.C. "But the longer I love him, the less free I feel, the more I want to make our relationship permanent. And that's driving him away."

I doubt if this classic dilemma for women is any closer to resolution than it has ever been, and unfortunately it contributes significantly to the dissembling which so many women exhibit in their relationships with men. (Many women remember their mothers cautioning, "Don't let a boy know how much you care." "Be sure to play hard to get, or you might scare him away.") Women have been so afraid of "scaring him away" that once they "catch" him, they need a contract to close all doors, forgetting that locks make prisoners unless the two people want nothing more than simply to clutch at one another. Sometimes this happens within marriage. Other times it happens within an arrangement, but the results are often the same. The point is, women are not necessarily finding psychic freedom simply by avoiding marriage.

I think there is one particular phenomenon that is changing married and single women alike, that is contributing to the growing number of women in their twenties and thirties who have been divorced within the last five years—and that is the availability of reliable contraception. The Pill. The intrauterine device. Women are experiencing a whole new concept of freedom with the realization that they can decide—on their own—not to bear children. Unmarried women do not have to marry to legitimize their sexual needs anymore. Some arbiters of social morals at first predicted wholesale promiscuity. (Certainly no one knows how many marriages are no longer taking place that would once have been solemnized hastily while the bride could still fit into her wedding gown.) But among the women I have talked with, it isn't happening that way. The freedom they feel is tempered with new confusions and problems.

For although the Pill has added dimension to female sexuality, it has also exacerbated anxiety. It impels a woman to acknowledge her own sexual responsibility, and such an admission does not harmonize well with the sexually passive role considered "natural" to women. Sexual passivity is one of the comfortable myths women have helped foster about themselves, perhaps because it enabled them to blame men when things went wrong. Sex was for man's pleasure, not woman's. It was all right for a man to "sow his wild oats," but not for a woman; *she* was of finer stuff and did not demonstrate her feet of clay. For years we laughed at the Victorians for these ideas, but the attitudes remained oddly residual until the advent of contraception.

Along with this, the Pill has forced reappraisal of traditional moral values; it is now no longer possible to ignore the fact that sex is often a continuing, normal part of life for unmarried as well as married women. Yet it wasn't until March 1972, for example, that the United States Supreme Court declared a Massachusetts law unconstitutional that made it a crime for single persons to buy birth control devices. Some form of guilt is still imbedded in the attitudes of young single women whom I have met. They continue to feel vulnerable to the judgments of their parents, their church, and all those vague "other people" who disapprove of sexual activity outside of marriage. "It's ridiculous, I know," said one young woman, her voice exasperated. "I have been living with a man for three years and we go through elaborate precautions when our parents come to visit—I put all his clothes in a special closet and lock it all up, and it makes me mad every time I do it."

Social planners were surprised when they found that the Pill was not lowering the illegitimacy rate among teen-agers as much as expected. Unwed mothers explained that it somehow didn't seem "right" to plan for sexual encounters; that meant deliberate promiscuity. Most women, whatever their ages, do not want to be branded promiscuous. It is a label reserved solely for their sex that makes rigid presumptions about a woman's life and personality. It is still true—at younger age levels—that if sexual intercourse just "happens" with someone you care about, the unease is not as great. Even among women in college, anxiety is still present although reliable contraception has contributed to freer sex lives. Reflecting on the life styles of herself and her friends, an Oberlin College sophomore observed with discontent, "Everybody's doing a head count of people they have slept with around here. They're still upset somewhere in their minds. I think the 'freedom' part of sexual freedom is more myth than reality."

For married men and women the Pill often has meant a jarring transition from traditional roles: the woman is no longer sexually submissive but indeed may consider "sowing wild oats" herself. I am thinking particularly of my own generation, where the Pill changed so many unshakable convictions of what was possible and what was not. Ultimately, it has added deeply to the questioning about marriage. I recall—as other women have told me they do also—the mixed feelings of relief and uncertainty I felt when my obstetrician handed me my first prescription for the oral contraceptive, giving me so matter of factly a slip of paper that I knew (however obscurely at that point) would change my life.

Part of the new ability to make independent plans and decisions for many women, again among my generation, was an eagerness to explore their own sexuality. First, the Masters and Johnson studies came along and legitimized the fact they had any. Second, it was obvious that traditional values and attitudes toward sex were changing, and it was more than X-rated movies popping up at the neighborhood theater. It was an unexpected fluidity in mores, which promised both dimension and danger. Both men and women had rising expectations for their interpersonal relationships, including freer sexual expression. The human-potential movement gained momentum, and married couples huddled in encounter groups from the Esalen Institute in Big Sur, California, to churches in New York City. It was remarkably easy for novice leaders to take people apart emotionally, but not so simple to put them back together again. Men and women began searching out "meaningful relationships" with other persons, which meant sexual encounters and confessions later at the kitchen table to spouses, all in the spirit of new and more open marriages.

There are no reliable statistics that would tell us if the number or rate of such liaisons has increased, but I am very much aware of the remarkable number of women who, in other days and calmer times, would never have dreamed of breaking with traditional mores so drastically but who have now done so. However, I don't think women are able to handle the standard pattern of male infidelity that allows the home to stay secure, with extramarital relationships kept strictly on the sidelines. The compulsion to confess weighs heavily in a culture that demands monogamous wives. I would guess the increase of divorce among middle-class couples has in part stemmed from women experimenting with freer sexual expression outside their marriages and having the Brave New World blow up in their faces.

I do not believe that anyone yet has fully comprehended what the introduction of reliable contraception has meant to many women, both married and single. Perhaps the story of just one woman—a woman I will call Nina Janeway—will provide an illustration.

It was a bright, snowy day. I walked with her from the courthouse where she had just received her divorce decree out onto the street. We were both a little confused over what to do next. Do you celebrate a divorce? Or cry? The conflict pulls both ways. "Let's go get a drink," she suggested, and I agreed.

Nina Janeway is a tall and beautiful woman of thirty-five who, until a short year before, had led a comfortable and predictable life as the wife of a doctor. We walked together to a nearby bar, which seemed especially dark because of the brightness outside; we sat down and she began nervously drumming her finger on the table. "I expected to feel very different," she said with a smile. "But instead I just feel empty." She began to tell me a little of what had happened.

"I have two children, and we both decided we didn't want any more, at least not right away, so I began taking the Pill about two years ago," she said. Because she was finally able to make some reliable plans after the years of bottles and formulas, she decided to go back to college.

"Some of my new friends had more in common with me than with my husband, which bothered him, but we continued our regular social patterns, often having friends over in the evening, going out—that sort of thing. One evening we were both planning on going to a psychology seminar, which interested me more than him, but he had agreed to go. The baby came down with a fever. He urged me to go alone, so I did. It was an exciting evening, and I didn't get home until almost midnight." She paused. "I'll never forget that scene. He was sitting up in bed, his arms folded, glaring, when I walked into the bedroom. He demanded to know where I had been. I was so surprised—and then I began protesting, telling him what he already knew, but I felt sick. He hadn't trusted me. He knew I was excited about new things, and new people. And I realized that night, he didn't like it. He didn't like it at all."

From then on, Nina Janeway found herself in a continuing conflict between her husband's expectations and the things she wanted to do, a conflict that made her resentful and eventually led to the end of her marriage. There was no relief, no joy. Not even enough anger to make the day seem inevitable. She saw clearly that no one had won anything. We talked for a long while, until the shadows outdoors dulled the snow.

As we left, she said, "You know, some of the women in the

neighborhood have hinted that they envy me. How can they possibly feel that way? They think I'm free. That is really funny. Who wants to be free when it means being alone?''

I think there is a restlessness among many married women. Even though studies show that most wives profess total commitment and happiness, the national divorce rate has almost reached the point of wiping out half the marriages begun each year. More liberal divorce laws that allow a union to be split solely on grounds of ''irreconcilable differences'' have certainly contributed to the rising rate, but some experts believe these new laws simply allow people to end marriages already dead. The answers for the rising divorce rate have to go beyond the standard ones. Men have joked for years about the ''old lady'' or the ''ball and chain,'' laughing at Jiggs running from Maggie's rolling pin, but the truth is they are happier and emotionally healthier within marriage than their wives. As Jesse Bernard reports, married men show fewer symptoms of mental illness than never-married men, they live longer, and, if widowed or divorced, half of them are so anxious to remarry that they do so within three years.

Marriage is good for men, but the case is not so convincing for wives. They are indeed restless—some are writing up marriage contracts that split the work at home equally, others are hiring baby sitters and going to work, others are opting for such ordinary tension relievers as shopping sprees. (I met a Boulder, Colorado, housewife on an airport bus who leaves a note on the dining-room table for her husband telling him she is going away for a few days, not saying where. ''I never know until I get to the airport,'' she told me. She flies to a city she has never seen, checks into a hotel, goes sightseeing or shopping, and flies home as promised.)

But for those who finally decide marriage means too much misery, the answer is divorce or separation. Once divorced, most women face overwhelming problems and anxieties, compounded by guilt over a broken marriage. Many I have talked with would remarry just as fast as possible if they had the opportunity. But it isn't easy. Often left with the responsibility of raising all the children, untrained to move into well-paying jobs, and living in a culture that provides little support or approval for divorced women, they feel cut off from the world once shared, however vicariously, with a husband. It is no illusion. They *are* cut off, although it is arguable who among all women alone are left most bereft of support. Widows have their memories, divorced women their anger, and single women their cats. Probably the only single people with easily available support systems are the swinging singles who group together in apartment buildings on the West Coast.

The point is, most women alone think they would be happier—or at least better off—married, even if they have had a bad experience ending in divorce. Why? The easy answer is security. But when I've asked that question of women, I've received many answers, some sure, some uncertain, most thoughtful. I remember particularly a young social worker curled up in a chair, talking at length of how she wants to avoid the traps she has seen her friends fall into in unhappy marriages. "When you get right down to it," she said finally, "a man alone is cool. A woman is not." I liked that. I thought of it another night when I met a woman who tried to be very cool.

It was in a North Side apartment where a group of women had met for a discussion. She was our hostess, very thin and tanned, wearing Indian prayer beads over her Saks linen dress. Around midnight she poured a new round of drinks, then sat glaring at me. We had been talking about women, and she had become increasingly annoyed over the direction of the conversation.

"Look, baby," she said in a soft, throaty voice, "I've worked damn hard to get where I am. I have eight hundred people who listen to me. Now you listen. At work, I'm a bitch. Sometimes I can't turn it off, but my work is IMPORTANT.'' She made the word sound like a plea. ''But I'm a real woman, a feminine woman. So don't you talk to me about Women's Lib. I love being a woman. I love sleeping with a' man. I love love. And don't you talk to me of housewives and stupid salesclerks.'' Her voice rose. ''You goddamn stupid woman! Why can't you understand?''

I understood it was about time for me to get out of there, but the woman next to me on the sofa patted my hand and smiled encouragingly. ''Don't mind Sharon,'' she whispered. ''It's her age.''

I stayed. Sharon suddenly seemed more of a vulnerable person than a threat. I had met many like her, women who fit certain middle-aged stereotypes—single, successful, a heavy drinker; a kind of woman a certain type of man boasts about ''servicing'' to his friends. The loneliness for women like her can be unbearable. Their jobs (she was a director in a medium-sized corporation) are indeed important, but not enough to provide a comfortable sense of identity. They are proud of their accomplishments, and on the job make a point of not yielding to a man in any way. Sharon looked every inch the successful businesswoman, but she carried on her shoulders an enormous fear that someone, somehow, somewhere, would find out how old she actually was. She told me later how she carefully falsified her birth records so that they tell the world she is forty instead of forty-nine. The deception was possible because she does indeed look much younger than she is.

''It's important that I maintain my image,'' Sharon said. ''I didn't plan to fake my age, but when I got this job, the personnel director was explaining about the retirement benefits, pensions, and so on. Then he asked, 'How old are you?' And I knew he expected me to say I was in my thirties; I could tell the way he

looked at me. So I thought quick. I was forty-five at the time.
'I'm thirty-six,' I told him. There was this dead silence. 'Oh,' he
said. He thought I was even younger. I couldn't take a chance
then. So I altered my birth certificate by putting it through a
series of reproductions and then sent them a Xerox copy. It can
be done.''

It's hard to understand the burden of fearing age that single,
successful career women often have. I walked out of Sharon's
apartment much later that night, depressed, because I suspected
her secret was no secret.

Recently a friend asked curiously, ''Have you found any truly
independent women alone?'' The difficulty in answering that
question is that we, as a society, cannot define what is true independence for anyone. We understand financial autonomy.
But can any of us ever be totally emotionally independent? I
doubt it.

So it is not a question of whether I have met a truly independent woman. There are many financially independent
women who are able to make their lives more comfortable, more
mobile, and more varied than is possible for most women without husbands. What my friend really wants to know is, have I
met many women alone who are happy in their aloneness? The
answer is, not many. Not in the sense of being sufficiently independent of the fear of loneliness that they are able to see themselves as whole beings and not just as floating parts. Not in the
sense of being able to accept aloneness as a possibly permanent
condition of their lives. I have met numerous women who pretend they need no one, but in their pretense is such obvious
emptiness.

The women who live alone most happily (as far as that
description applies to any of us) are those whose independence
is involved more with a sense of purpose than with simple self-

affirmation. For example, Jane Kennedy, a woman of exceptional courage and resilience; or, to describe her in another way, an ex-con from the Detroit House of Corrections.

I met Jane Kennedy a few months after her release from prison for damaging Dow Chemical records in Midland, Michigan. Her case had attracted considerable attention. She had twice sacrificed parole by refusing to promise never again to engage in "active nonviolent" antiwar activities. This embarrassed and angered prison authorities: they were caught in the position of offering her a way out and instead having it become an effective dramatization of the ridiculousness of keeping her in jail. "She's the most troublesome prisoner I've come in contact with in more than forty years," the prison warden complained to a reporter. "Every time she's told to do something, she always asks why."

Jane Kennedy is no fiery young activist. She is forty-five, divorced, and was formerly the assistant director of nursing at Billings Hospital in Chicago. Her involvement in the antiwar movement was the result of trying to live the principles she espoused—not by comfortably sitting back and complaining but by risking her own safety.

After a year in prison Jane Kennedy's health is fragile. I realized this the moment she opened the door of her small apartment in the Hyde Park section of Chicago's South Side. Blue jersey pajamas covered her thin figure, and she held a small kitten in her arms. She greeted me with a smiling apology: "Sorry for the pajamas, but I spend a lot of time resting these days." The toll of the year in prison—much of it spent in solitary confinement—shows on her face and in her nervous, quick gestures. While we talked she sat cross-legged on a sofa bed, her long gray-brown hair constantly tumbling over her face. I asked her what she enjoys doing now. "I'm trying to read a lot," she said. "But I have a hard time finishing a book because my own thoughts keep intruding.'' These thoughts revolve around what she saw happening in prison—not just to herself but to all the women referred to by the matrons, not as persons, but as the ''count.''

''I feel now this absolute inability to communicate about the prison scene,'' she said. ''I didn't understand anything about the kind of hypocrisy that goes on here, in the free world, until I was there. For the first time in my life I lived in poverty with other poor people, and I'm convinced now we live a lie in this comfortable world with warm places to live and ice boxes filled with food.'' Her hair tumbled; agitated, she pushed it back. ''I'm not sure all of what I mean by that, but it has to do with such things as tolerating eight million unemployed persons and then arresting some woman because she steals to buy food for her kids, putting her in prison, calling her a criminal, and then taking her children away from her family—because they aren't providing an adequate home.''

As I listened to this woman, I realized it wasn't middle-class liberal concern she expressed; it was the angry conviction of someone who has walked on the dark side of life in this country and wants urgently to convey to the rest of us what exists there.

Because she was a questioner, because she challenged prison routine, she spent a good amount of time in a place called ''the Hole'':

''It's a five by eight room with a door and a sink with running water, a bed and a mattress. There's a tiny window with wire meshing—all you can see out that window is either darkness or light. The door also had a tiny window: I used to press my nose up against it and try to look out. We were fed once a day. There is nothing to do. No one to talk to. You cannot even turn out the light—it is controlled by a switch outside the cell and covered with wire mesh. My clothes were taken away and I was given some kind of granny gown—you are supposed to get a fresh one every day, but they didn't bother. So I washed it every day in the sink and covered myself with a towel while I dried it on the radiator. It was December and very cold.''

The worst part about solitary confinement was the sensory deprivation, she said. ''After five days, I knew it was possible I would begin hearing voices. I knew it would be all right—that I would eventually get out and I wasn't going insane. But look, all the other women prisoners were poor, without education, and most of them were black. What do you think it meant to them when they began to hear voices? Some women I knew there became terribly frightened. After getting out of the Hole, they would do anything they were asked to do, because they were afraid they were going insane. And that is the whole point of that kind of treatment. This is humane?''

Jane Kennedy's life at this point is an odd combination of peace and imminent peril. She may have to go back to prison on a second charge, this time for burning draft records in Indianapolis. ''I don't want to go back. Oh God, no, I dread it,'' she said.

If she escapes another bout in prison, Jane Kennedy intends to live alone the rest of her life; she is in fact one of the few women I met who has expressed no interest whatsoever in marriage. Once, years ago, she did marry and was divorced, a fact few people realize about her—probably because she does not fit any particular stereotype of a divorced woman. Her dedication to changing an inhumane system gives her a special status as a woman alone—a special sense of purpose, a unique social identity. She is in many ways a lucky woman: she is part of a movement that provides structure and support. Perhaps this has been responsible for her calm acceptance of celibacy.

''It has been years and years since I've had sex, and I don't miss it, although I think it's a lovely thing and I wouldn't mind it at all. But it's nothing I can't live without,'' she said. ''I didn't purposely choose a celibate life, but it has made what I have done much easier to do." She stopped and thought a moment, then said, "It has freed me, actually. I have not had to be responsible to another person, and because of that, I was free to act out my convictions. And now I am free to live them in another way."

Before I left, I placed a phone call from her apartment. On the dial was a red and white sticker: WARNING: THIS PHONE MAY BE TAPPED No, I thought, Jane Kennedy was not an ordinary woman alone.

Few women would choose a sexually celibate life. Few women would choose a life of risking public criticism if they could avoid it. But the point is, few women alone have a strong sense of purpose in their lives, nor do they perceive a wide range of choices open to them. If they are single, they want to be married. If they are divorced, they are trying to plan new lives but are hampered by guilt and uncertainty. If they are widowed, they often have experienced a drop in status as well as a drop in financial security.

Widows are, in fact, probably the most physically restricted, most helpless women alone. "The rights a woman receives in marriage and most of her duties in this role in our society cease upon the death of the husband," sociologist Helena Z. Lopata has said. In other words, widows suffer total role loss, an overwhelming event. Moreover, widows over the age of sixty-five have been discriminated against financially. Until recently, they received much less on the average than men in Social Security payments. In a sense, they have been caught coming and going: encouraged to stay home and raise their children and later penalized for not having worked. Loneliness becomes a major problem for them, particularly for those whose children are often thousands of miles away and who are without the friendships that once were shared with their husbands. The jolt that awaits many women who have built their lives around the working friendships of a mate is that, once he is gone, there is no place for them at the company picnic anymore.

Yet widows are not expected to admit to loneliness because if they do, in our culture, that means something is "wrong" with them. They haven't "adjusted" as fast as all their busy friends and relatives think they should have. When you think about it, though, the prevailing assumption is that there is "something wrong" with any woman alone. This last is important. It is the feeling that many women who are alone have about themselves. The more I realized this, the more I felt they were missing something that was within reach, something difficult to describe but possible to achieve—something married women want but which eludes them within the restrictions of marriage.

All women need to be stronger and more individualistic than they have hitherto wanted, tried, or dared to be. Perhaps women alone have a unique chance to gain this personal strength if they redefine who they are in relation to a society that undervalues them. But that means understanding more of what life has been like for women alone of other years, other centuries; it means putting oneself into a larger perspective. And then moving on to the future.

4.

From Witches to the Cosmo Girl: The Woman Alone Through History

When I was a little girl, it seemed every neighborhood had a witch. Ours was an old, bent woman who appeared outside her dark and (we thought) cobwebby house once a day to water plants and tidy her porch. I had to walk by on my way to school, excited and fearful. Would she be outside? Usually when I reached the hedge that divided her property from the house next door, I would run as fast as I could, quickly glancing over to see if she was there. If she wasn't, I would be both relieved and disappointed.

Why are old women alone cast so often as witches? When I think back to the images of my childhood it seems old men were always kindly creatures who pulled children into their laps, told Br'er Rabbit stories, and fixed bicycles. They grew bright rose gardens, and when I walked past to go to school, they waved to me and I would wave back. I knew, absolutely, their houses had no cobwebs.

The witch figure as a woman alone appeared frequently in ancient myths and legends: the evil woman who fled from her husband's side on a broomstick, leaving her skin next to him to deceive him into thinking she was still there. Margaret Mead described the recurring symbol of the witch in *Male and Female* as a statement of human fear of what can be done to mankind by women who do not bear children. Only strange and unnatural beings would flee from their destiny. The witch was a danger to mankind, to be stalked and destroyed, and the myth often became a reality. No one knows how many women have been burned at the stake or hanged as witches, but in the eighteenth century alone, thousands lost their lives because of primitive fears. The witch is also, I think, a symbol of our fear of aging women. If a human being is valued basically for her reproductive function and attractiveness, what is there left when these qualities are gone? An old crone, with certain capacities left, probably enough to make trouble.

The image of the witch as an old woman alone did not even occur to me until one night when I was reading my children a bedtime story from a beautifully gruesome book. They loved it. Their eyes were shining, and they were wiggling in anticipation of the climax when the witch would die a terrible death. She always does. The princess is always united with the prince, who is usually responsible for killing the witch, and they get married. The fairy tale supplies the proper finale, pairing the man and the woman and getting rid of the ugly crone.

In *Walden*, Thoreau tells how visitors to his pond would retreat before night, leaving him alone in single communion with the water, the land, and the sky. "I believe," he said, "that men are generally still a little afraid of the dark, though the witches are all hung, and Christianity and candles have been introduced." I like that quiet observation enormously because we are indeed still "a little afraid of the dark," the darkness in our own minds.

Women alone have been part of that darkness, simply because

they haven't fit properly into the image men have had of women since they reworked the story of creation. If woman is not the rib from man's side, the helpmate subject to his greater wisdom and power, what is she? These apprehensions, translated into reality, have historically meant severely restricted lives for single women. In our time, the restrictions are still present. A woman has three basic choices: she can marry, go on welfare, or become financially independent.

Before the advent of the nuclear family, single women were able to remain protected within the large, extended family that both welcomed and had room for maiden aunts and spinster daughters. Today most homes are small, three-bedroom affairs that barely provide enough living space for a mother, a father, and growing children. And yet, in that odd, balancing way history has of providing alternatives, the middle-class woman of the twentieth century doesn't face the same social stigma for working that her nineteenth-century counterpart did. In the past, to become independent was to become inferior. (Unless of course, a woman was lucky enough to inherit money. Jane Austen once observed: "A single woman with a narrow income must be a ridiculous, disagreeable old maid, the proper sport of boys and girls, but a single woman of fortune is always respectable, and may be as sensible and pleasant as anybody else." But the state might scheme to take away her wealth, which it managed at times to do. In nineteenth-century England, a serious proposal was made that went a step beyond: single women should be sequestered in institutions as surplus commodities, their property confiscated by the state.)

Female independence no longer means inferiority, but independence, as Simone de Beauvoir has said, is not enough. Certainly education and industrialization did away with the absolute helplessness so often the fate of women who never married or who had lost their husbands. But independence has meant living in a society that requires self-assertion and yet condemns it as unfeminine if the woman should break one of the un-written rules of conduct that man has set for her.

Underlying all the criticisms and attacks on women alone through history has been the uneasy fear that women who seek alternatives to marriage and motherhood might very well find them satisfying. The images of themselves that women have been presented with (and helped perpetuate) are intended to discourage or intimidate. And even though as a nation we are committing ourselves to cutting back the birth rate, women who do not marry pose questions about the structure of society. Those questions are difficult to articulate, because they are so deeply rooted in our anxieties about what we are. If women are allowed to flee on their broomsticks, couldn't they possibly destroy all that has been so carefully put together by men?

In America the woman without a man has usually been pitied or disliked and ascribed low status except when she has been needed—perhaps to nurse the wounded or run the farms and factories in time of war. Generally, of course, the single woman has historically been both intriguing and a challenge to men when she is young. But prolonged singleness—even prolonged virginity—is still suspect. A widow is a nuisance or a financial burden. And you never take a divorced woman home to meet your wife.

There were few single women in colonial America. Indeed, there were few women at all, and most of them married quickly. It was common for a girl to marry at thirteen or fourteen, and a young woman still unmarried at the age of twenty was branded a "stale maid." But women were expected to carry equal respon-sibilities with the men. The hard-working colonial women died young, weakened by frequent pregnancies, with no medicines or proper care, and no rest from their work in the home and in the fields. It wasn't unusual for men to outlive two, three, or even four wives. The high death rate reinforced the belief that women were inferior to men. Even though they worked as hard as their husbands, women believed they were inferior—when they took time to think about it. Those who didn't conform were poor marriage material, and were left to spinsterhood. Yet, spared the drain of frequent childbirth on their health and energies, some of these women made remarkable contributions with their labor, eventually managing large estates and plantations. Others, widowed, did the same.

Until the American Revolution, women were not strictly confined to the home. They could be outside in the light and air, their bodies unconstricted by tight-fitting clothes. But as the cities grew and the machines came in, so did a new middle class; and middle-class women retreated into the home and civilized femininity. Their supposed delicacy became evidence of their superior sensibility. They were, of course, still expected to marry. But now they cooked and drank tea and sat in their parlors doing needlepoint, their hair frazzled with curling irons and their bodies laced in with whalebone corsets and heavy skirts. They earnestly cultivated all the feminine traits valued highly by men, including the frequent fainting spells (faithfully recorded by novelists of the time) that dramatized their dependency. Women developed what historian William O'Neill has called a "cult of delicacy" and made a fetish of beauty and clothes. (One nineteenth-century actress actually had a rib removed to make her waist the tiniest on stage. She later died of predictable complications. The reverse side of self-mutilation by women would be the Amazons who cut off their right breasts—not for beauty but so they could better hold their bows.)

History was affecting lower-class women quite differently during the early years of the nineteenth century. They and their children began moving out of the home to work in the New England mills. By the early nineteenth century, thousands of

women had left their spinning wheels at home for the machines
in the factories. The difficult and tedious work of spinning cloth
had traditionally been the responsibility of unmarried women
required to earn their keep in the home (thus the origin of the
word "spinster"); now these women had the chance to earn
something for their labor. It wasn't much.

The feminist Harriet Hanson Robinson began working in
the textile mills when she was ten. She told of how the mill girls
at Lowell, Massachusetts, were greatly pleased with their average
wages of two dollars a week in the early years, but later, in 1834,
mustered the courage to strike for higher wages (one girl throwing her bonnet into the air as a signal to stop work), with some
recognition and success. In general, the early years in the mills
meant finally some status and freedom for women without husbands. Women had no property rights; a widow could be left
penniless at her husband's or the court's whim; a father would
often leave nothing to an unmarried daughter. A woman was
not supposed to be intelligent enough to handle money. But now
she could have two dollars a week.

Harriet Robinson wrote:

> If a woman did not choose to marry, or, when left a
> widow, to re-marry, she had no choice but to enter one
> of the few employments open to her or to become a burden
> on the charity of some relative. In almost every New En-
> gland home could be found one or more of these women
> sitting "solitary" in the family; sometimes welcome, more
> often unwelcome; leading joyless, and in many instances,
> unsatisfactory lives. The cotton factory was a great open-
> ing to these lonely and dependent women. From a condi-
> tion of almost pauperism they were placed at once above
> want. They could earn money and spend it as they
> pleased. . . .

no longer obliged to finish out their faded lives a burden
to their male relatives. . . . They went forth from their
Alma Mater, the Lowell Factory, carrying with them the
independence, the self-reliance taught in that hard school,
and they have done their little part. . . . Their early experience developed their characters . . . and helped them to
fight well the battle of life.

Harriet Robinson overestimated the degree of freedom won
by these early working women, but it was true they now had money, new concepts of themselves, and a little leisure time to read
and think about their lives.

Mary Wollstonecraft was one of the earliest and most articulate defenders of the right of women to equal dignity with
men. In the fall of 1792 she wrote *A Vindication of the Rights of
Woman* in six weeks, decrying the servility and vanity of
women, saying in her Introduction, "My own sex, I hope, will
excuse me, if I treat them like rational creatures, instead of flattering their fascinating graces, and viewing them as if they were
in a state of perpetual childhood, unable to stand alone." She
hammered away at a society that saw no need to educate
women, fully aware that without education, women could not
possibly be independent. A proper education, "or, to speak with
more precision, a well stored mind, would enable a woman to
support a single life with dignity," she wrote. Mary
Wollstonecraft did not hold back her assessment of her own sex:
"I have throughout supposed myself talking to ignorant women,
for ignorant ye are in the most emphatical sense of the word."
And again: "How many generations may be necessary to give
vigor to the virtue and talents of the freed posterity of abject
slaves?"
This brilliant woman's plea came only a few years before the
first barriers to education for women began to break down. In

1821 the Troy Female Seminary in New York became the first institution to offer a high school education to women. No longer were women totally confined to music and dancing lessons with a smattering of writing and arithmetic. They could go to school, and soon the nation's commitment to public education for all brought them into the classroom as teachers—an opportunity for single women to leave the home. Women teachers were not valued as highly as men, therefore they were paid much less. And the more women who entered teaching, the lower the status of the profession (a not uncommon pattern in this country). At the same time, society expected a high standard of respectability. "Women teachers were expected to behave like members of a strict religious order . . . as though they had taken vows of chastity, obedience and poverty," writes author Trevor Lloyd.

It is hardly surprising that an undercurrent of frustration existed parallel with these first opportunities for women. But opprobrium of a more virulent sort was reserved for women who took up writing as a means of expressing their ideas: "the damned mob of scribbling women," as Nathaniel Hawthorne scornfully called them. Writing novels was not only one of their first major independent means of support, but it enabled women to enter into the business in equal competition with men—a significant innovation. Before 1820 one-third of all American novels were written by women. As author and critic Leslie Fiedler points out, the birth of the novel was truly "a critical moment in the emancipation of women." However, much of what women produced was maudlin and sentimental trash, which drew strong criticism from exceptionally talented women such as George Eliot. (It isn't difficult to understand why women with major creative gifts tend to be impatient with the less competent; they know society is far readier to generalize about their capabilities from the evidence of the majority.)

Single women were particularly criticized for writing, because they were not supposed to know about intimate relationships between men and women. Nor were they supposed to be familiar with the intellectual or political issues of the time. In Victorian England, sensibilities were shocked when Charlotte Brontë and Harriet Martineau dared write about serious topics without indulging in the romantic nonsense so popular at the time. One reviewer suggested that only married women, preferably middle-aged mothers, should be allowed to write. The ultimate criticism that kept many women writers timid and uncertain was that no "lady" could write on sensitive or controversial topics. Women therefore frequently took refuge behind pseudonyms. The effect on their creativity and their personal lives was often tragic. Single women were particularly victimized by the demand for docile, domestic qualities. They were characterized as tough, aggressive, and ugly, and according to author Elaine Sowalter, they "were made to feel that their struggles to find meaningful and profitable employment for their lives were ultimately futile. And there was a real belief single women who wrote were merely seeking an outlet for their pent-up emotions and fruitless passions."

What of the image of women given us by male writers? Probably the classic portrayal of a woman alone is the adulteress Hester Prynne in *The Scarlet Letter*. Hester is presented as something of a seventeenth-century feminist, a fallen woman forced to wear on her bodice the great A "that glows like a red flame in the dark," but she is a flesh-and-blood woman, not a typical wispy character of the type popular when Hawthorne wrote in the mid-1850s. Her fate, however, is predetermined by her passion. Hawthorne and other writers of that time, particularly James Fenimore Cooper, were the first to present the theme of what Fiedler has called the Fair Maiden and the Dark Lady—innocence and experience, etherealness and passion. The heroine who eventually marries the hero is blond and feminine, the epitome of what a woman should be. The lesson is clear. Those who would be Fair Maidens must embody the traits of feminine virtue that preclude awareness of the darkness, of the evils of life; they shall be granted husbands. The Dark Lady is left alone.

Before the opening of the West, the stereotypic spinster was a horsy type, a woman with a loud voice or a gruff manner, usually suffering from unexplainable robust health. She was an unfortunate who sometimes found tolerance for her eccentricities if she lived in a family that endured her presence with reasonable good grace. She existed on their charity. But when the Western migration began, there was a reversal. Men at first continued to marry the Eastern beauties with pale skin, fair hair and tight corsets, trundling them across the prairies in covered wagons. But the journey was too arduous for many of these women, and their graves dot the landscape from Illinois to the Oregon Trail. A process of natural selection began. The men wooed the stronger women, the sisters of the beauties, the women who would have ordinarily been restricted to a life of spinsterhood.

These stronger, hardier women made it West, and contributed to one of the freest eras for women in our history. No one could afford fainting spells when the Indians circled an isolated homestead. Pioneer women ran the farms, drove the wagons, and shot game, same as the men. Many of them became widows in that lonely, dangerous land. A traveler, describing a huddled group of women and children he happened upon while crossing the Great Plains in 1852, is quoted by author Gerda Lerner:

> An open, bleak prairie, the cold wind howling overhead, bearing with it the mournful tones of that deserted woman; a new made grave, a woman and three children sitting near by; a girl of fourteen summers walking round and round in a circle, wringing her hands and calling upon her dead

parent; a boy of twelve sitting upon the wagon tongue, sobbing aloud; a strange man placing a rude headboard at the head of the grave.

And yet many of these widows continued westward, ran their own farms, reared the children, and endured the hardships of a new and raw life. They were respected women, and the esteem in which they were held was reflected in the pioneering laws in the Western states giving women legal rights. In 1850 Oregon decreed single women could be granted ownership of land. In 1869 Wyoming became the first state to grant women the vote.

But the era of the independent woman didn't last long. As the West settled down, women reverted to the traditional images. The daughters of the pioneers shed their mothers' independence and self-reliance, tightened and lengthened their skirts, and presented themselves as proper, civilized women waiting for the right man. The forthright women were once again the spinsters.

The Civil War had a significant effect on both the image and reality of women alone. The mystique of the tragic love took root, allowing many women who had lost a husband or lover in the war to live out their lives in dignity. They were recluses from society, and attitudes toward them were generous—for years the mystique was extended to encompass all the frail mysterious maiden aunts who had presumably suffered the loss of their One True Love. (Suffering, of course, was required. Such women were not supposed to be happy.) People generally have remained sympathetic to the idea that a woman alone might not have been able to marry a particular person; it fits in well with the romantic concept of one love, and one love only, for a woman.

But the Civil War was also a time when women alone proved themselves invaluable on the battlefield; this was the time of Clara Barton, Dorothea Dix, and Mary Bickerdyke, women who nursed the wounded, initiated sanitary procedures that cut down infection, set up kitchens for the fighting men, and in general provided incalculable aid to two governments totally unprepared to give medical service to their soldiers. Gerda Lerner writes: "In all, at least 3,200 women on both sides made a career of nursing in the Civil War. Hardships and male prejudice dogged their steps and pursued them even after the war. They had great difficulty in winning recognition for their services and many of them were left in want and ill health. . . . Yet the entry of women into nursing during the war was a turning point in making nursing a new profession for women."

It seems strange in retrospect that women had to endure severe hardships to gain a foothold in the nursing and teaching professions, which are now considered such "natural," nurturing occupations—and into which many young women are channeled who could better use their talents elsewhere. But there was one profession always open to women alone. Prostitution. The oldest of them all.

In the 1890s playwright George Bernard Shaw had the audacity to suggest in his play *Mrs. Warren's Profession* that working-class girls were much better off as prostitutes than they were in the factories. Although his point of view horrified the middle class, many single young women found it was true. A man's reverence for womanhood did not extend to the poor who did housework for his wife or ran the machines in his mill. In America, the influx of immigrants in the late nineteenth century brought desperate competition for factory jobs. Women had to accept low pay and long working hours, or lose their jobs to even more needy immigrants. Working women were sometimes expected to get down on their knees to scrub the factory floors after a ten- or twelve-hour work day, and those who dared complain were fired, left without funds to support their families. The prevalent attitude of the time was no lady would work, therefore no working woman was a lady. Given such an attitude, if a young woman lost her job, where else could she turn except to prostitution?

Considering the working conditions in the factories, Shaw's point of view was exceedingly humanitarian. The development of technology had not reached the point where the heat, noise, and dangers of the complex machines were totally controllable, and arsenic, lead, mercury, and phosphorus were used in many industrial processes with little or no effort to prevent poisoning. Industry exploited working women for years with inferior or dangerous working conditions. It was not until the Triangle Shirtwaist Factory fire in 1911 in New York City, in which 145 girls and women were killed, that the state legislature moved to pass legislation requiring safety procedures and regulations. The public had begun to pay attention to the problems of working women.

Another significant fact of life for women by the end of the nineteenth century was widowhood. The death rate of men of working age in 1890 was twice as high as it is today. The lack of safeguards caused numerous fatal industrial accidents. Pneumonia, tuberculosis, and smallpox added their toll to a death rate that killed one out of every five husbands by the age of forty-five. This left half a million widows under the age of forty-five, many with young children, facing the prospect of no livelihood and no social position in the community.

Robert W. Smuts, author of *Women and Work in America*, quotes a bitter account written by the daughter of one of these women:

> At that time . . . the status of Wife and Mother, always spoken of in capitals, was sentimentally precious. . . . No matter how poorly, through incompetence, neglect, or misfortune, her husband "protected" her, she was allowed the airs and graces of a woman apart. . . . Then the blow fell and the treasured Wife became the poor Widow, the

object of family bounty, not infrequently grudged, the grateful recipient of left-overs, the half-menial helper in the households of women whose husbands had simply not died. The more precious and delicate her wifehood had been, the less chance there was of her being equipped for earning a livelihood.

For all the dangers and unhappiness, the post-Civil War era was a time of opportunity for hitherto "useless" old maids and young women. By 1890 they constituted three-fourths of the entire working force of women outside the home, mostly working in the factories and as housemaids. Teaching was still the only profession open to them, but it could hardly yet be called a profession. Most schoolteachers had only six or eight years of elementary education, and it was not until 1907 that Indiana became the first state to require that all licensed teachers be high school graduates. Nursing was still a low-status profession, with formal training denied to most of the forty thousand nurses in the United States in 1890.

By the turn of the century, significant changes were taking place: among them, a rising demand for women in office jobs and a trend toward more flexible divorce laws. A crucial event had occurred: the invention of the typewriter. Office jobs meant easier working conditions for women. Many of the young girls who flocked to these jobs were not desperate or poverty-stricken and had higher status in society than their chambermaid and factory counterparts. Work could finally be pleasure. Women had enough money earned by themselves to spend as they pleased. They were realizing basic survival did not depend on finding a husband. Trevor Lloyd has called this fundamental realization one of the foundations of the Women's Liberation movement.

At the same time states were changing their divorce laws, so it was a little easier for women to end their marriages. The stigma of being a divorced woman was as strong as ever, but at least a woman who left her husband was no longer necessarily reduced to dependency on charity or relatives. She could find work as a clerk in a department store, as a telephone operator or as a typist. The inadequacies of marriage were already under attack, and the divorce rate doubled between 1880 and 1900. It was in 1879 that Ibsen's Nora announced proudly to her husband, "I believe that before all else I am a reasonable human being just as you are," not just a "little skylark, your doll," and proceeded to carry out the most famous scene in literature of a woman turning her back on marriage. Radicals came forward with ideas for shaking up the structure of marriage; Isadora Duncan, for example, proposed a system of divorce on demand by either husband or wife. Few women supported radical ideas, but many were undergoing major changes in how they viewed themselves, their marriages, and their world. They were more aware than ever before of their helplessness within marriage and their vulnerability outside it. And the search for a resolution contributed to the growth of feminism.

To understand the emergence of feminism, one must first understand the pressures on women that accompanied the emergence of the nuclear family. Contrary to what historians believed for many years, the modern nuclear family of a man, a woman, and their children is of only recent origin. Philippe Aries in *Centuries of Childhood*, a study of family life in France from the late Middle Ages through the eighteenth century, concluded that domestic privacy as a family ideal hardly existed at all before 1700. People lived crowded together in community settings, eating, sleeping, living in groups; even queens birthed their children in crowded rooms. Yet we have nurtured the vague idea of the modern family as having existed through the ages, even to the point of believing it went into a period of decline in the nineteenth and twentieth centuries. "On the contrary, it had perhaps never before exercised so much influence over the human condition," said Aries.

Once the family was removed from the community, the pressures, emotional and practical, on the individual accelerated. At the heart of the family was the woman—she was the wife of virtue and strength, the manager of the home, the one responsible for rearing the children. "In completing the transformation of the family from a loosely organized, if indispensable, adjunct of Western society into a strictly defined nuclear unit at the very center of social life, the Victorians laid a burden on women which many of them could or would not bear," William L. O'Neill has said in his history of nineteenth-century feminism, *Everyone Was Brave*.

Woman was expected to be pure, domestic, loving, and always, always submissive to man. She was elevated and degraded at the same time. Her mind was believed to be inferior, but her sensibilities were proclaimed as superior. Her job was to darn the socks and save the soul of her husband. Perhaps inevitably, this little pink cloud of veneration and domesticity became an impossible place for flesh-and-blood women.

At first the early feminists linked their efforts with those of the blacks struggling for enfranchisement, but after the shock of being excluded from the suffrage victory for blacks granted in the Fourteenth Amendment (1868), they realized the fight for the vote would take many more years. The struggle ate up the energies and efforts of hundreds of dedicated women, finally culminating in victory in 1922. But it was a hard-won victory, and the price was dear—getting the vote had exhausted the women's rights movement. Other goals, just as worthy, were lost as women retreated from their years of militant feminism. Women were still shut out from many jobs, and those they had were low-paying. Education was still a distant privilege, not a right.

Just recounting the efforts of the feminists would take at least a chapter. But I cannot pass by without paying homage to those remarkable women whom I knew absolutely nothing about two years ago, a fact I find deeply depressing. How could women have been so totally robbed of their own history? How could we have known little or nothing about Susan Anthony, Carrie Chapman Catt, Elizabeth Cady Stanton, Margaret Sanger, Victoria Woodhull? How could it be that Dorothea Dix, who was the first to investigate the wretched conditions in American jails and fight for reform, was turned into a pseudonym for an ''advice to the lovelorn'' column? And farther into nineteenth-century history, how could we know nothing about the black slaves Harriet Tubman and Sojourner Truth, two women who were among those fighting the hardest against oppression of both their race and their sex? In 1817 Sojourner Truth actually dared sue in a New York State court to have one of her children released from slavery—and won her case. Wasn't this a significant enough event in American history to have qualified for our history books?

One morning I joined a friend for coffee at work, bringing with me Mary Wollstonecraft's *A Vindication of the Rights of Woman*, which I had only just discovered. I told him how deeply moved I had been by this imperfect but passionate little book. He asked to see it. I gave it to him, and he read a few pages in silence. His jaw dropped. ''My God,'' he said. ''1792?''

The beginning years of the twentieth century marked a new era of educational opportunities for women; for the first time, they stood in their caps and gowns with the men and were handed a rolled-up scrap of paper, the college degree, which would guarantee them a place in the world of work. For some of these women, the degree was both a guarantee of a niche in that world and a guarantee of spinsterhood. Men did not flock to marry women who preferred a career to keeping house. Even now, the degree is often a source of frustration for women who continue to receive educations which, most of them discover, they have few opportunities to use after they are married.

But for some early-twentieth-century women, there was something peculiarly new in their lives: a sense of mission that produced forthright individualists with a clear idea of the value of independence and a willingness to accept the limitations. This fervor carried many women into settlement-house work, but it also produced its own isolation. The life of Jane Addams, for example, is a study in how far the human spirit can remove itself from others. "Although in her day cool distant women were common," writes William O'Neill, "Miss Addams was notably detached." A major intellect, Jane Addams became a legend for her innovative concepts of social work practiced at Chicago's Hull House. But she related to the group, not to the individual, and lived her life emotionally removed from other people, even her closest co-workers.

In a warm and thoughtful essay on what life was like for an educated woman at the turn of the century, sociologist David Riesman tells of how his mother was handed her degree in 1903 from Bryn Mawr College, along with honors and a fellowship to study in Europe. "My mother's family was too traditional, fearing the fellowship would lead to spinsterhood, and she herself was too timid to embark on such an independent course," Riesman writes. And so instead she was wooed by a young doctor. But she did not succumb immediately: "She postponed marriage . . . for five years, while she read novels," writes her son. The life of Riesman's mother followed a typical pattern for women in those days—a fostering of their own sense of cultural superiority which required disdaining the pedestrian achievements of men; a nurtured snobbery to replace what was not allowable to them—yet it was not enough and they knew it. Riesman says his mother spent much of her life "waiting vicariously on the men's table, feeling frustrated because of inability to deploy talents she was not actually sure she possessed."

The pace of life quickened between 1910 and 1920. The world went to war and a way of life vanished, its successor emerging at the end of the decade as something strange and untested. The roots of mid-twentieth-century feminism were already down: the emergence of the nuclear family had put intolerable pressures on women, although they were among the last to know. How could one complain as washboards and maids gave way to washing machines and no maids? College-educated women who went to work were no longer in a minority; however, attitudes toward them were mixed. Most of them went into teaching.

One of these women, now retired from a long and successful career as a college professor and administrator, described for me the strong public dislike that she and her colleagues had to endure:

"I started teaching at a time when the question of teaching and marriage could not be resolved," she said. "A teacher did not marry, and married teachers could not work. It's very hard for people to understand that today. We were keenly aware of what people thought, and it was an emotionally damaging thing for many women. But I think most of us who started teaching in the twenties did so with the idea that we were only going to do it *until* we married." She did not marry and does not now regret it, although there were times in her life when she thought she did. "In a way, I was afraid of marriage," she said. "I had seen my mother and my aunts, all women with tremendous abilities. All of them married. They chose very nice men, but men who were not their equals. I watched them crack up, one by one, including my mother. I didn't want that to happen to me. I guess at that time I recognized that a high-powered motor has to have something to operate on, otherwise it ends up just spinning its wheels.

"I never came to some great decision that I would give up marriage for teaching," she went on. "When you ask me these questions, it makes me think back to the man I almost married—I've been asking myself, why did I really break up with him? Because of my family responsibilities? Because of my career? I think not. I think the true answer is, he was such a damn bore. A perfectly fine young engineer, but a fatuous one hundred percent American red-blooded jerk." So much for male superiority.

The most popular image of women in the twenties was, of course, the flapper. Here was the epitome of the freed woman—no stays, no corsets; bobbed hair and wild parties. Girls flung off the restrictions that had impeded their mothers' lives, ignored their admonitions, and savored what they felt was "real" freedom in the relaxed sexual atmosphere. The flapper was eager for self-fulfillment and impatient with the old and traditional, but she still emphasized her feminine dependency. Her way of asserting what she felt was individuality was to be daring—to shorten her skirts, experiment with sex, and in general live up to the label of "blazing youth." Freedom meant Zelda frolicking in a fountain with Scott Fitzgerald, not getting a college degree. So it goes. Enter the Jazz Age. But enter the Depression too.

During the Depression, men selling apples on a street corner was not just a cartoonist's cliché. It really happened. And "Apple Mary" was also out on the street selling, because many working women had lost their jobs to male breadwinners. When men were out of work, women who worked were resented. On the other hand, there were beneficial aspects: in many families women took on odd jobs to help out when a father or husband was unable to bring in enough money; by the end of the thirties most middle- and upper-class single women worked. Society had come to accept this phenomenon, and most important, women accepted it. Women's aspirations were very high—they were going to college, had won the vote, and had expectations of entering professions.

The thirties were years when the independent, resourceful woman was popularized both in books and on film—and everyone went to the movies. Rosalind Russell bustled around in her business suit giving orders to the men, and Katharine Hepburn, in the 1936 production of *A Woman Rebels*, said curiously to a friend, "Don't you think that myth about the dependency of women was created by men?" Well. This was innovation. And yet by the final reel, Rosalind Russell has melted into the arms of Cary Grant and become a real woman. And, after years of being a crusading journalist and weathering a terrible scandal, Katharine Hepburn hides her face in the comforting arms of Herbert Marshall, who delivers the closing line before fadeout: "These modern women are so weak."

The independent woman was fine, admirable—just so long as the man took over by the end of the film. It was an image of female independence that people could live with more or less comfortably. And because the media both reflect and transmit values, the Hollywood woman on her own became a prototype personality for real women who wanted to have their cake and eat it too: a career and the stamp of approval of men. The game rules became: Play it strong if you wish, but defer in the crunch. (The women who played this game most successfully are often among those who today cannot understand why women complain about being shut out of professions and jobs: "What's the matter with them?" they ask. "*I* never had any trouble.")

There were other interesting heroines of the thirties who proved so durable that they were still around when I was in high school. That's when I discovered those remarkable sleuths, Nancy Drew and Judy Bolton. They became my heroines. Daring, independent women who solved murders and mysteries, the Hardy Boys of the female sex. In retrospect, it seems surprising they were still popular in the fifties (and are yet today) when those of us who devoured *The Password to Larkspur Lane* were taking sewing and geometry in school, with the tacit understanding between ourselves and the nuns that only the former would do us any good. ("Nancy," says Dr. Spires, "you have a wonderful mind, and a talent which I respect very highly. Above all, you have common sense—which is far from being a common thing at all . . . I need some help in solving a strange mystery, Nancy Drew. . . Will you help me?") And off we went, Nancy and I.

The celluloid heroines of the thirties gave way to the realities of the forties, when women were once again needed without comedy or patronization. I had an aunt who came to California from the East to work in the aircraft factories, our own Rosie the Riveter. I remember as a child the excitement of having a relative doing something important for the war effort, something more than just bringing rubber bands and paper to the school Liberty Drive. We didn't laugh at Rosie; we fought for places in the car to ride with her to the factory with our mother, awed by her lunchpail and tales of wearing a face shield against the sparks while she built airplanes. But after the war she went back East, and I don't know what happened to her. I do know what happened to other women like her. They went home and got married.

America came through the forties and into the fifties heartily sick of war. The world needed more love, people felt, and who of course were the naturally gentle, naturally loving and mothering human beings? Women, of course. As the age of romantic love was reinstated, the pressures to marry became stronger than they had been in at least twenty years. It was not considered strange for single women to work any more, but there was no sympathy for them if they did not ultimately marry. It wasn't popular to want to be alone. (Greta Garbo has repeatedly insisted her famous quote wasn't "I want to be alone." It was, she says, "I want to be *let* alone.") For widows, long periods of grieving were no longer considered appropriate, and the practice ended of a woman shutting herself off from society, wearing black and somber clothes after her husband's death. No matter that a bereaved woman might be at a loss in preparing an independent life; she could not retreat to the bosom of her family or hold back in dignified grief as did the Civil War spinsters and widows. She lived alone or with another woman, either for companionship or out of financial necessity. Sometimes this shut her out even more, because it was no longer considered perfectly normal for two women to live in the same household or for an unmarried brother and sister to share a residence, as it once had been. The tyranny of the *de rigueur* nuclear family was at full strength, and everything outside that structure was viewed as being somewhat unnatural.

Exceptional women forced some changes in these attitudes, women like Eleanor Roosevelt, who almost single-handedly gave new depth and dignity to the popular image of the widow. With her drive and discipline, Mrs. Roosevelt also made accomplishment appear to be a more realistic goal for women alone than ever before. Still, many women whose expectations for better jobs and fuller lives had been high saw hoped-for opportunities fading. They were no longer content to remain in the undervalued professions of teaching, nursing, and social work. They had gone to college, won the vote, and wanted to be lawyers, doctors, college professors. Sometimes they made it. But, as Margaret Mead observed, this was a time when "the more successful a man in his job, the more certain everyone is that he will make a desirable husband; the more successful a woman is, the more most people are afraid she may not be a successful wife."

Education for women was then, and is still now, considered more of an insurance policy against failure—something to help pay the rent if a girl doesn't get married. Career achievement has remained related to singleness, and yet the conflict is that the achievement most valued is still marriage.

The dilemmas and frustrations of new possibilities thwarted by traditional restrictions brought an eruption of resentment from women in the late sixties. But that resentment was not apparent in the early years of the decade. The calm of the fifties still prevailed—and millions of people were more interested in the fascinating discovery that single women had sex lives.

In 1962, I remember standing (pregnant) at the grocery check-out counter one evening reading an unusual little book that was generating all the interest. This was Helen Gurley Brown's *Sex and the Single Girl*, the ultimate ''how to get a man'' book of its time; totally, cheerfully sex-oriented. Recently I bought a copy of an updated version and read it through once again, realizing as I did so that its initial popularity was at least partly because it spoke directly for the first time to some of the private problems of women alone. It took for granted that these women had sex lives. No one had admitted that publicly before. The book gave single women an image of themselves that, though hardly liberated, was a welcome substitute for the fractionalized images most of them were used to. Miss Brown's magazine has since evolved into the supposed liberated answer to *Playboy's* Playmate: the *Cosmopolitan* Girl. The illusion of potency presented by *Playboy* becomes the illusion of freedom presented in *Cosmopolitan*: it is all right for the Cosmo Girl to be aggressive, for example, so long as her aggression is sexual. It is all right for her to be competitive—if it is with other women for the attentions of a man.

Cosmopolitan has become a monthly manual on catching a man that shows as avid a concentration on female anatomy as *Playboy*. Advertisements run to full-page spreads for douches, birth control pills, and special massage pads to fight the ''globbies'' (fat hips). A recent cover features a smiling Cosmo Girl in a red bathing suit cut to below the navel, promising on the inside, ''The True Love Story of Twiggy and Justin''; ''Advice for

Girls Planning to Marry a Divorced Man''; ''Sensational New Diet and Health Discoveries''; and a quiz: ''Are You Threatening to Men?''

Now, it seems, the most encouraged image of the liberated woman is sexual. Are we going to repeat the mistakes of the twenties, when single women confused sexual freedom with true independence? Women radicals have found sexual permissiveness a trap. Their equality has got them as far as the corner coffee shop, to fetch sandwiches for the male ''revolutionaries.''

The image of today's woman perpetuated through newspapers, magazines, television commercials, and the comic strips, which are fascinating sources for both shaping and transmitting social values, is consistently linked to sex. I wonder how influenced we have been by the comics? Now I can laugh at Al Capp's caricatures while seeing his deep conservatism; and I can follow Dick Tracy without becoming upset over his obvious moralizing for ''law and order.'' But recently it seems the most traditional stereotypes of women alone are being hustled out to co-opt the liberation movement: Poteet Canyon, off on a new adventure working for an underground newspaper, falls in with a group of women's libbers including a husky lesbian wearing a ''Repent'' tee shirt and a light in her eye for Poteet; Mary Worth introduces the traditional grim ''career woman'' who invites the sexy new chemist in the office over to her apartment to work on an important formula. She answers the door in hair curlers and makes it clear (Though why at her apartment? Could it be she is unfulfilled and is unconsciously looking for the right man?) that she wants no funny business. Eventually, of course, we know she will weaken, take out her hair curlers, and become a real woman.

Where is the Wonder Woman of the seventies?

For real-life women of this decade, aspirations are again high, but they are not making rapid progress in the working world. Between 1955 and 1970 the proportion of women working rose from one-third to one-half of all adult women, but their median earnings dropped from almost 64 percent of the median men's earnings to less than 60 percent. In short, women are not finding any trouble getting into the steno pool, but they are still knocking on locked doors to most of the professions. Supporting oneself in a job is no longer the degrading thing it once was for single women, but it has not increased their status appreciably. And the world of work remains an essential barometer of personal worth, because of its value to men. Perhaps this will change as we move closer to a leisure society where there will not be enough work even for the men.

Then what?

5.

Two Is Even, One Is Odd

There is a range of ways in which we treat women alone differently; some are institutionalized, some are quite personal. Organized religion, for example, has been in some ways the most demeaning, perhaps because it attempts to tell us not only what we are but what we have any chance of becoming. I am speaking here primarily of Catholicism, because it is the only religion I have intimately known.

Heaven, I was taught by the old Baltimore Catechism, is structured after an organizational chart, with all the proper bureaucratic divisions. The highest level is reserved for those who on earth were part of management, the priests and bishops and even the nuns, though this last wasn't stressed. The second level is for those who were married, for even St. Paul admitted somebody had to produce babies, and the third rung on the status ladder is for those who lived their lives in the "single state." Although I used to worry about missing out on the top rung if I married, I didn't feel concerned about those who would rank below me in heaven. The nuns explained carefully that God would not love single people any less than the rest of us, just differently. Anyone who remained single hadn't done anything *wrong* actually, but the implication was that he or she hadn't done anything *right* either. Certainly nothing useful enough to warrant a higher position in the organization.

It took a number of years before I was aware of the subtle distinctions the Catholic Church made about women, distinctions that implied a certain moral infirmity. Mary Daly, one of the few women Catholic theologians, states it quite well. There is in the Catholic Church, she has said, ''a strange polarity between the glorification of Woman as a symbol often identified with the person of Mary, and the underestimation of concrete existing women.'' Those made of flesh and not plaster stand on shaky pedestals. I believe it is particularly significant that women cannot be ordained as priests. Regardless of how this is explained or rationalized, it can mean only that women are somehow intrinsically unqualified.

It came as a shock, for example, after living all my life as a Catholic to find out the religion I valued didn't value me. In my childhood, women were not allowed on the altar except on very special occasions, such as for receiving the sacrament of Confirmation, and then only for a quick moment to receive the bishop's blessing. The members of the Ladies' Altar Society were permitted to change the flowers each week, but they were not supposed to touch certain sacred altar vessels. If they did, the vessels were to be reconsecrated. Women, but not men, were required to cover their heads in the presence of God, and it was a curious sight on a hot summer day to see women at Mass with bits of Kleenex pinned to their heads—better a foolish piece of tissue than nothing, and no one thought it strange. It is difficult not to assume from all this that God, then, has a sex bias, presuming he is a man, of course.

In combination, church prejudices against women and against singleness have sometimes produced attitudes as humorous as they are strange. I am thinking particularly of a familiar clarification once heard at the University of Notre Dame when a newcomer would ask about students attending that (then) pridefully all-male school: "We have no women here, you know," the serious response went. "Only nuns."

In the church, the sexuality of a nun is effectively neutralized. But for other women to remain virginal for too long still means some mysterious deficiency or, at the very least, an evasion of one's natural goal in life. We were taught from childhood that we came from Adam's rib ("that petty surgical operation," as Elizabeth Cady Stanton so scornfully called it), and to Adam we owed our bodies; to God, our souls. There wasn't much left over for ourselves. If a woman remained single, the charitable presumed she was either too frail for the convent or had an aged parent to support and therefore had to remove herself from the mainstream of life.

There are many ways in which society segregates women alone, ways based on other unarticulated presumptions of moral infirmity: women alone are many times not allowed to rent apartments, open charge accounts, or be comfortable at social events where everyone comes in pairs. They are viewed with suspicion if they live with other women; ignored if they are old; and if they are divorced, their morals are monitored by self-appointed watchdogs. Restaurants will refuse to seat them or do so only reluctantly; country clubs will not accept memberships from single businesswomen who are therefore closed off from an important informal setting for conducting business that many men consider essential. But the attitudes which are particularly hurtful in a practical sense are those which affect the way a woman alone is able to earn her living or spend her money.

Some companies refuse to hire women who are the sole support of their families, the corporate reasoning being they would be unreliable on the job if a family crisis came up. Yet studies have shown that women alone often have better working records with less absenteeism than men, precisely because they have a responsibility to support their families that cannot be ignored. There are many of them. Of the more than 5.5 million widowed, divorced, or separated women working in 1968, almost all held jobs because it was financially necessary. Most of them take what they can get. They are usually unable to afford school or training before they go to work and are therefore limited in the job market.

Until recently, single men and women were financially penalized for their single status by being required to pay higher taxes than married people. Now, ironically, new tax laws make it cheaper to live "in sin" and file separate returns from the same household than to get married. One couple promptly filed for divorce, declaring they would prefer living in sin to paying higher taxes. (Surely, those legislators who concern themselves with the morals of the country will find a way to prevent a mass exodus from marriage for financial purposes?)

Women alone are considered poor credit risks by a number of companies and department stores. "I tried to get an account at three department stores; one of them refused, explaining I was a bad risk, and the other two refused without explanation," complained a young divorced woman making $15,000 a year. "A man making half what I make with six kids to support can get a charge account—but not me."

If somewhere there is a first commandment for women alone that would significantly narrow the gap between their status and that of men and married women, it would be "Make thou some money." Women who bring their financial status near that of men experience less exposure to prejudice against their singleness. No one knows this more clearly than the woman with children who must support her family on inadequate welfare payments. She is acutely aware that a public-aid check in her mailbox means exclusion from the society of "normal," hard-working Americans who see her as something useless and left over, part of the trash on the beach after everyone else has gone home. The rules regulating her life are meant to keep her where she is. Our necessities are legally defined as her luxuries. For example, "You tell me to shop with food stamps and not buy soap," challenges a welfare mother. "But I'm supposed to be clean and my children are supposed to be clean. How do I handle that?" Worse than the mother who works, then, in society's eyes, is the mother who does not work, cares for her children, and accepts public aid to do so.

There is another category of attitudes toward women alone. The essential ingredient is curiosity. These attitudes are not necessarily negative, at least not outwardly so, and are therefore harder to defend against. It is difficult, for example, to express hurt or anger to a well-meaning relative or friend who asks the classic question, "How come you have never married?" which every single woman has heard in one form or another. The impetus has been sympathy for the woman who never caught a man. How does she respond? The "how come" question implies two things: one, she never will marry; and two, she must have a very strange reason for not doing so. Where is the hidden flaw in someone who looks like she would have no trouble marrying? And if there is no discernible flaw, how can she pass up marital bliss? Usually there is the additional implication that she wants to be married—one particularly resented by that minority of women who are content with their single status.

Even if such a woman manages to convince people she really doesn't want to be married, they will thereupon make an immediate presumption of dedication. "Why do people look at me earnestly and ask me searching questions about my commitment to my 'career,' when all I want is to do my job reasonably well and live alone?'' complained a woman in her mid-forties. In the questioner's mind, there has to be something that sets her firmly apart to justify not marrying, and that means plugging in a stereotype: a woman who is happy alone must be ''driven'' to success or ''dedicated'' beyond the level of most ordinary mortals.

Sometimes curiosity shows itself in a once-removed framework: for example, obsessive interest in the sex lives of unattached women is reflected more in the brisk sales of books on ''swinging'' stewardesses than in directly expressed curiosity about a newly divorced secretary in the office. This basic curiosity is also often coupled with nervousness about a woman's singleness—again, the vague presumption that something is wrong with her. A woman I know, still unmarried in her mid-thirties, has decided in frustration to pretend she has been divorced. ''Each time I go out with a new man, there is an awkward moment when he asks about my marital status and I have to tell him I have not been married,'' she says. ''If I just offhandedly say I'm divorced, he doesn't think there is anything strange about that at all.'' Failure to make a marriage work is acceptable. But failure to marry in the first place is inexcusable.

Particularly for young single women, there is the danger that this complex of presumptions and expectations will form a buffer zone which surrounds them and removes them from the realities of life taken for granted by men. A woman who recognizes she is too buffered from reality must escape—and this is enormously difficult, because she must escape from what she values and loves. Her family, for example, can be the source of deep and destructive pressures. ''Don't you think you are taking your education too seriously?'' a concerned father may say when his daughter has been studying through sleepless nights for her exams. How does she respond? To her father's solicitude for her health? Or to his kind presumption that she is expending herself needlessly on tasks that are meant only to occupy her time until she marries?

One woman I know, a first-year medical student, has attempted to deal with this problem by physically isolating herself from family and friends in an effort to assert her individuality through aloneness. She lives in a cabin some five miles from a small town. So far her experiment has produced a combination of loneliness and independence: "I go through periods of trying to decide what my mental image of myself is," she said. "Am I doing what I want to do? Am I going to be successful? Sometimes I feel very secure and happy, but if the slightest doubt comes into my mind, I get very upset and depressed and I figure, why don't I just get a job and make money and forget this career stuff?" She is often afraid of being alone at night, but has refused entreaties from her family to move into the little town near her university. Holidays at home are difficult. "People are constantly telling me how concerned they are about the way I live," she said. "Single girls bring out the mother in everyone. Even my dentist is concerned. My family is constantly inviting me to dinner, usually with the presumption that I haven't had a good meal in a month."

All the concern has had an effect. "Someone will come visit and talk about tremendous new restaurants in the city—I know nothing about them. New records. New people. I don't know. I'm leading pretty much a one-track life, and I'm happy doing it. But I get times when I feel guilty and I think, what am I trying to be different for? Why don't I have a more well-rounded life? My father tells me I'm missing out on a lot of things—interesting jobs, new cars, and all. I envy these things a little bit."

This particular woman's buffer zone had become so oppressive that she felt the only way she could commit herself to getting through medical school was by the unusual tactic of physical isolation. But she cannot escape or reject the attitudes of others that may yet convince her she is trying too hard to be "different."

Rather than cataloguing all the attitudes of prejudice and discrimination against single women, let us see how these attitudes affect particular individuals. Both the attitudes and their effects vary widely, of course, depending on who the women are, on why they are alone—and on something intangibly personal to each of them.

One evening I went to visit an old woman on welfare. I walked into the courtyard of the apartment building in which she lived and suddenly heard my name: "Patricia? Patricia?" I looked up and saw an anxious face peering down at me from a second-floor window. I realized I was fifteen minutes late. "Yes, it's Patricia," I said. I had never met this woman before. She had the door wide open when I reached it. "I'm sorry," she said. "I thought perhaps you had decided not to come." She smiled, her face tiny, still pretty under thin, carefully plaited braids wound high. Her little dog bounded madly about the room, obviously unstrung at the sight of a visitor, and she patted his head, apologizing, "We hardly ever have any visitors, I'm sorry."

Her name was Fanny Hunter, and she couldn't believe I had come to actually *talk* with her—not to explain why her grant wouldn't cover a new winter coat or to tell her the electricity bill had to be paid. Just talk with her. "How could you care? What does anyone see in the boring stories of an old woman?" she asked delightedly. She offered me coffee. I accepted, and she put the kettle on to boil. Later while we were talking she suddenly sniffed and cried, "Oh, no!" She ran out to the kitchen, coming back a few moments later with the old kettle, burned black, a hole in the bottom. "It's ruined," she said disconsolately. For one moment, her face looked very old. It was not just a simple irritating accident; it was a real loss. Fanny Hunter had no extra money to replace kettles carelessly burned. I knew it; she knew it. There was an odd moment of silence, and I felt my heart twist because this old woman was so obviously embarrassed that she had failed to provide me with a hospitable cup of coffee. "I have a pot," she said, lifting her head. "Will you take a chance on me again, and let me boil more water?" She smiled, stuffed the kettle into the trash, and put on the water once again. Both of us carefully watched this time, because it was Fanny's only pot. And so we had our coffee.

To share even for a short time the life of an old woman left alone, without money or friends, is to realize how we strip the old of not only opportunity to live with any grace but of the chance to pretend. We all pretend, presenting ourselves at times as more bright, knowledgeable, or witty than we really are. We value the luxury to be gracious, to entertain a passing visitor in style, even if we cut corners somewhere else. But for someone like Fanny, there are no corners to cut. Living on welfare has made her timid and apologetic. What worth can she possibly have when no one takes notice of her any longer? She sits at night with her dog and a tiny, 11-inch television set which a far-away daughter sent three years ago, squinting to watch, laughing at the antics of "That Girl." "I used to look like that," she told me. "Pretty and young and gay. It is so nice to be pretty and young and gay."

Fanny Hunter's routine of life is very simple, and she has accepted it—walks with her dog, television, visits to her church. But she is afraid, afraid someone is going to come along and take away what little she has now. "I don't need any more than this," she said. "But oh, I'd miss the TV if they took it. Do you think they'll let me keep it?" I told her I didn't think the welfare people would take her television, and her face became a little less anxious.

Finally, long into the evening, she told me her deepest secret: when she was "pretty, young and gay" she had become pregnant before her wedding, and her child was born only seven months later. She looked down at the floor, worried, and I realized her humiliation was something as real to her now these many years later as it had been then. "I don't want the ladies of the church to know," she said. "If they ever found out, I'd die; I'm just a penniless little rat now. But I've got my pride."

Why, I wondered, when I left late that night, do we leave old people so totally alone? Why do we so often dismiss them as barely human, unless they are people we love? Growing old in our culture is easy only for the very courageous or the unimaginative. For men, the process at least leaves them with a residue of a former identity ("Old Harry used to be a cab driver"); for women, there is only an asexual anonymity.

I thought about it again weeks later, on the bus going home. It was late and I was very tired; the people riding with me looked as cross and impatient to be home as I felt. An old woman got to her feet, pulled the cord, and moved to the bus door. The driver pulled to the curb. The door swung open. Slowly, her legs apparently crippled with arthritis and her hands awkward holding a cane, she began to descend the steps. The driver tapped the wheel impatiently. It was an agonizing descent. I suddenly had an insane desire to give that old woman a push to hurry her up. I looked around and realized other people around me were thinking the same thing, all of us impatient and frowning, watching her get off. She had barely removed her foot from the last step when the driver pulled the doors closed and drew rapidly away from the curb. But not fast enough for those of us at the front of the bus to miss hearing what she said. I looked around and saw her draw up straight as she could and lift her fist, shaking it at us. "I wasn't always this slow!" she yelled. Her defiance, her perception, hit us all, and we looked away from one another, ashamed of ourselves.

Mary Lighton is divorced, with two children. After saving money for a year, she decided to move to a better apartment in a safer neighborhood. She began answering the ads that looked good and quickly found an apartment she liked. The landlord was friendly, agreeable to a new paint job, and she was very pleased. Then he asked the whereabouts of her husband. "I'm divorced," she told him. He immediately became reserved, quite polite, letting her know he wasn't sure the apartment was going to be available after all. And painting would be difficult . . . Although she couldn't at first believe it, he would not rent her the apartment. Indignant, she tried another place; this too looked good, but she felt cautious: "Just in case you're interested, I'm divorced," she told the building manager. Again, he was perfectly polite and agreeable and refused to rent to her. "It was obvious to me they thought I was some sort of loose woman," she said. So she searched out another apartment with another landlord, and when asked about her marital status, she told him her husband was in Vietnam. She got the apartment along with a sympathetic chat.

The attitudes against divorced women are relentlessly moralistic. "The thing I've had to realize," said this mother, "is that although it will never be expressed, I'm supposed to have done something wrong." This estimation hits particularly hard because many of these women, particularly those with children, feel they have indeed done something wrong. "A widow's adversary is death," writer Marya Mannes told me. "The divorcee's is guilt." And what is the nature of that guilt?

I doubt if many people, alone, stripped of their anger and pain, can consider themselves wholly innocent when there is a breakup of a marriage. And even if the marriage is intolerable, it is a family. One woman told me that the moment the children were informed their father was moving out, the family was destroyed: "We were at the dinner table," she said. "And my little girl had just raised the spoon to her mouth, when she realized what we were saying. I'll never forget the look in her eyes.''

Once divorced, a woman is faced with trying to provide normal lives for her children and social acceptance for herself, and the odds can be unbearably high, particularly if she is untrained and unable to get a job. Even if she does find work that allows some reasonable balancing of responsibilities, she faces the uncertain, often traumatic process of finding a baby sitter for her children. Mary Lighton has been fighting this battle for years, and she is bitter.

"Let me tell you how it works for us,'' she said. ''How it has been for three years. My daughter comes home from school, finds the door locked, and goes down to the corner drugstore. When she was smaller, she would have to ask some adult to put in her dime and hand her the receiver because the phone was way out of her reach on the wall. Then she would ask somebody to dial the number, my number at the office, and pretty soon I'd hear this uncertain voice, 'Mommy, the baby sitter didn't show again.' '' This mother is fully aware that baby sitters who may or may not appear at the specified time, and who then quit because the pay isn't high enough, or because they have bad backs, have not provided her child with anything approaching a reliable, predictable world. She acts a little tough, a little fatalistic about it. But the morning President Nixon vetoed a national child-care center program, she was close to tears. "Do you know what he said? He said he was vetoing it because it could contribute to the disintegration of family life." She shook her head. "I can't believe it, I really can't believe it."

Nancy Ann Sheridan is twenty-four and works as a secretary for an engineering company in a large city. She used to live alone in a pretty apartment with french windows; now she is comfortable only in a room with iron bars across all the windows, even the tiny one in the bathroom that she knows, rationally, no one could ever squeeze through. But it would be useless to try reasoning with her, and why should anyone? It was Nancy Ann who got raped. It happened over a year ago, and she apologized for going over the details compulsively.

"I was asleep when he broke in," she said. "He bound me and gagged me, and I kept my eyes shut. I wasn't looking at his face, so that he wouldn't kill me. Afterward, he pulled the gag from my mouth, but it was soaked in sweat and tight around my neck. He started to twist it, apologizing excitedly, saying he was trying to take it off, and I knew, I was sure, I was going to die. But the knot came loose, and he left."

She grabbed the phone and crawled under the blankets to the foot of the bed, crying, and called the police. They took her to the hospital, in her dressing gown, where she was directed to get up on an examining table and put her feet in the stirrups. "They were all so businesslike," she said. "I couldn't understand it. I knew I wasn't the first woman in the world to get raped, but my God, it wasn't exactly like having a sore foot or something. I was so stunned; I wanted to tell someone how terrible it was."

She followed their directions, putting her feet in the metal hoists with which every woman is familiar. No one gave her a sheet. A woman doctor came in with a hose and began hosing Nancy Ann's body, soaking her dressing gown.

"She never looked at me. She just hosed me out and then dropped the hose and said, 'Okay, you're all right. Get up.' I sat up and tried to ask a question, but she was on her way out of the room and never stopped. What was I supposed to do? No one came, so I got off the table and walked into the corridor and back to the waiting room, just holding that dripping gown away from me. The place was full of people, strangers staring. No one gave a damn."

"Look, no woman can get raped unless she wants it," a grinning policeman assured me. "It just can't happen." He elaborated, and in the way that anyone who is absolutely positive about something sounds convincing, his position seemed to make sense. Later, something else made more sense— the realization that if you get told something often enough you begin to believe it. I think many women wonder about rape; certainly those who have experienced it feel a confusion of indignation, fear, and guilt. (I heard frequent stories from women of having experienced a rape or attempted rape when they were children or teen-agers and never telling anyone. Not friends, husband, or parents. Why? "I felt ashamed," said a middle-aged widow. "A little guilty. A little dirty.")

There appears to be a confusion of person and property in the attitudes of some men in their response to the possibility that a daughter, a wife, or a girlfriend might get raped. And nothing quite makes Americans more indignant than a violation of property. We do not treat rape victims as cruelly as other societies, say in Bangladesh, where many of the women raped by the West Pakistanis were ostracized from their homes and abandoned by husbands and families. But we do have our own "civilized" responses, such as the treatment this young woman received at the hospital. It was, in a sense, a punishment. And she, in retrospect, feels equally damaged by what happened at the hospital as by what happened in her bedroom. And why was there no sympathy at all from the woman doctor? Does this say something about the enormous gap between women in their understanding of one another?

A footnote: A few weeks after the incident described above, the wife of a prominent businessman in that same town underwent a similar experience after being raped. She, backed up by her husband, complained vigorously. An investigation was launched, and the hospital was forced to change its "treatment" methods.

And what about the authentically independent woman? The woman who isn't helpless, worried, or in need of a sense of identity from a man? What attitudes does she face? She loves her work in the way a man can love his work, as a sustaining, fulfilling part of life. Unlike her married male colleagues, she doesn't commute to a comfortable home in the suburbs with a wife and children, but instead may have to settle for a series of relationships, each of which seems almost enough—but not quite.

Carolyn Menninger is a bright and competent young woman who has established an independent consulting firm, which consumes a great deal of her time. She drank half a dozen cups of coffee one morning while we talked, her fingers nervously tapping the cup. She was like a helium-filled balloon tied to a chair, reasonably still, but you knew, once untied, she would head straight to the sky.

"Nobody has to take on the things that I take on," she said. "Sometimes I think I would give anything to have a day alone, but I wonder if I haven't forced myself not to have that day. I think I've set it up for myself. There are very few men that can accept my responsibilities, very few that can accept the fact I am totally committed to a certain type of work that sometimes means I have to break dates, or cuts into the time that I can spend with a person." She wants to marry, but she is finding that her vigor and enthusiasm for work become a threat to men, even though they initially like her independence. She has not yet totally adopted the veneer of not caring that many women in her position prefer to the vulnerability of being perceived as lonely.

"I met one man, oh, he respected and admired me, and it was just marvelous, because it made up for his deficiencies. That's another trap. Sometimes I think I'll never find the man who can accept me and enjoy the fact that I'm being my own person. There aren't many." She laughed and shrugged, and privately I thought, "How unfair. There really aren't many men like that." I do think more men are changing their attitudes toward forthright independent women, but not without uneasiness. "We

have all played games with each other for so long,'' one man
confided. ''It's hard to change.''

One group of women alone are finding attitudes changing
quite rapidly toward them. These are the numerous nuns who
are discarding their traditional black capes and veils for short
skirts and blouses and Villager print dresses. Some of them re-
joice with a new sense of freedom, and others feel bereft of
status. ''We have one nun in our order who put on the new habit,
stared at herself in the mirror, took it off, and refused to wear it
again,'' a nun said. As a child, I recall the awe I felt of nuns.
They were different, special, because of their clothes. I once
mustered enough nerve to ask my fourth-grade teacher if she
really had hair under her cap and she answered yes, indeed, but
she kept it cut short. I knew sister never lied, but how could she
possibly look like other people?

The mystique of the nun has definitely ended, and with it has
gone the aura of automatic respect which many of these women
needed more than they realized. The convent is no longer a
security blanket, a lesson a nun I shall call Sister Mary
Llewellan has learned:

''When I used to wear a habit, I got special treatment in
stores, but not now,'' she told me. ''Last week, I was robbed in a
department store. I couldn't in any way be identified as a sister.
The store detective was irritated; he got after me for having a
purse and got after me all the way around. He didn't identify me
as anybody with any kind of intelligence, just a dumb woman
who had her purse stolen. I had been bruised by the person who
grabbed it, but the detective didn't care. I told him I wanted to
call the police, and he said, 'What good is that going to do you?'
But I insisted, so we went to the store office and he dialed the
police station, irritated, and I asked for the phone. I said, 'This is
Sister Mary Llewellan,' and that man's whole face changed—his
whole response. It didn't make me feel very good. Here I was, a

human being who had got knocked down and asked for help, and hadn't got it. I was just another woman to him. But if I had been in the habit, would it have happened? I doubt it. I wasn't used to being treated like everybody else.''

This nun finds that the absence of an identifying uniform has generated a curious mixture of revelations about other people and herself. She has lost automatic identity. But at the same time, she has gained a sense of touch with other people. "I think the habit was kind of a moat between myself and others," she explained. "It just wasn't real. We lived in a framework that impeded intimacy.''

I know another woman, one who is truly alone. She works as a waitress and sometimes as a prostitute, and she lives in a tiny room with flaked yellow walls, hung with tie-dyed silk scarves she made herself. She has a quiet way of moving, graceful, though her body is soft and thick. She is twenty-three years old and a chain smoker. Her name is Deirdre. Her teeth are bad, and the day we met I wondered absurdly, "Why isn't there some father, somewhere, joking about fixing her teeth?" She is wary of police, and defensive about being a prostitute. "I'm not really one," she explained carefully. "Only when I need the money.''

Deirdre has worked out her own code to explain to herself what she is, and it makes her feel more comfortable in a world that accepts her as a business commodity and rejects her as a person. For Deirdre, the "sense of touch" is also important. That is why, she says, "I would rather go down on a man than let him have intercourse with me." How could this potentially intimate and loving act be less personal? I asked. She smiled. "Because I don't have to touch him with my arms or my body," she said. "All I have to do is use my mouth, and that's a lot less personal to me.''

If there is one thing most women alone seem to share, whatever their age or class or however much money they have, it is a sense of expendability. It ranges from the desperation of a middle-aged divorced woman whose ex-husband has just skipped town with her alimony, to a wealthy elderly woman's vague fear of being sick and alone. As far as I can judge, it is the source of a deep and desolating loneliness in some women. At a more benign level, it is often the simple knowledge that families and social circles won't collapse without one's presence, that husbands won't grieve, that dinner parties won't be ruined. A younger woman whose one source of wholeness, of continuity to her life, comes from her parents knows they spend much of their emotional energy on worrying why she hasn't married. An older woman can become obsessed with the idea that she might become ill and die on her kitchen floor before anyone would ever discover her plight. (One woman I know says she has carefully planned her own suicide if she becomes so ill she cannot care for herself.) At its worst, it is the engulfing vacuum that comes from the loss of a sense of interconnection with other people.

I don't want to overemphasize this, because it is not always as despairing a thing as it sounds. We all are alone, just some more so than others. In a sense, fear of abandonment is just a different twist on the universal fear of death, and there are women who do not wish to be needed or wanted by anyone, as there are men who do not wish to be needed or wanted—or so they say. Moreover, many women alone have close friendships that sustain them all their lives. And, of course, they are often sustained by their responsibilities.

Reinforcing this sense of expendability are the attitudes of our society that demand an accounting from a woman for not being married. They can be so vaporous, so intangible. But basically so unfightable. How, for example, does a woman respond to an evasive landlord who tells her a vacant apartment is not for rent when she knows it is her divorce decree that makes her undesirable? Whether or not one agrees with their tactics and occasional histrionics, the Women's Liberation movement must be credited with having tackled these intangibles and exposed them for what they are. But prejudicial attitudes may be so ingrained and so insidious that decrying them can appear absurd: we have to be *taught* an awareness of them.

I remember, for example, years ago at the University of Oregon when a black leader on campus protested about an ad run on national television by a gasoline company. The ad showed two cars racing on the desert sand, one black and one white. The black car ran out of gas before the white car, which was fueled with the company's product and was, therefore, superior. I thought it ridiculous when the black leader protested—for heaven's sake, the color of cars a racial issue? But I would never laugh now. It was indeed a racial issue, because it was both a response to and an affirmation of our deeply subconscious attitude that white is better. The good cowboy always rode a white horse; fair man always won fair maiden; white cars went farther than black cars.

All of us, men and women, are strongly influenced as to how we assess ourselves by how we perceive *others* assessing us. Consider what happens to a man who loses his job. He is no longer necessary or even desirable; he is neither a cog on the assembly line, a commuter on the train, nor a participant in the lunchroom poker game. But he at least is free to seek out another job—to present himself with certain qualifications, go through a process of reevaluation, and build a new sense of identity. It is more difficult for women. In our society, the basic affirmation of self for women is usually through marriage, and women who are not married are made acutely self-conscious of the fact that society must make special arrangements for them.

An anthropologist who has explored what this means to women is Ashley Montagu, who told me: "The big difference, first, is that women who are able to move around independently, on their own, are respected by virtually everyone. A divorcee, on the other hand, is considered a person who has committed a crime. She has thrown a monkey wrench into the machinery of social life, and what can you do with her? There she is. As for widows, there is a sort of dehumanized attitude towards them; a process that affirms that they really don't exist. They are there—but they are not real. In other words, people wish they would go away.''

He described the typical response of guilt that women alone so often feel: ''They think they've failed. It's like the murderee who is being murdered by the murderer. It is not the murderer who feels guilty, but the one who was murdered—for getting in the way.''

The loneliness of women who ''get in the way'' of the orderly functions of society is closely related to the degree of their dependency for self-awareness on other people; for those most deeply dependent, the ''inner space'' of womanhood described by analyst Erik H. Erikson becomes empty space. They are often defensive or very busy proving they need nothing. Or they retreat into the despair of their own helplessness.

It sounds fearful. Does it have to be that way?

6.

Living

Who wakes in a house alone
Wakes to moments of panic
(Will the roof fall in?
Shall I die today?)
Who wakes in a house alone
Wakes to inertia sometimes,
To fits of weeping for no reason.
Solitude swells the inner space
Like a balloon.
We are wafted hither and thither
On the air currents.
How to land it?

From *Gestalt at Sixty*, by May Sarton

Understanding how women live alone means first understanding the differences among them. Are they alone by choice or by
chance? Did it happen suddenly or over a period of time? With

guilt, or without? Do they wish to remain alone, are they desperate not to, or are they aware of both the benefits and drawbacks of singleness? What are their realistic options? Do they have varying chances because of age, class, wealth, or fame? Are they flexible? Are they sustained by a strong sense of purpose or strong religious beliefs? How do they value their work?

It isn't enough to draw dividing lines between widows and single women and divorced women; sometimes they share particular opportunities and characteristics and sometimes they don't. If there must be divisions drawn, I would differentiate in terms of reactions to aloneness—women either "cope" or they build. Much that divides the "copers" from the "builders," I believe, originates in childhood. Those who would build often retain an enduring image of a mother as a strong person; not necessarily a superachiever either as a housewife or a careerist, but a woman with a comfortably rooted image of herself that she was able to transmit to her daughters.

Different women I have interviewed identified their mothers as strong people in different ways. Some openly said they disliked their mothers but respected them. Others spoke of these now distant women as loving, whole human beings whose example had made their own lives not only endurable but rich with flexibility. "My mother taught us we were born to handle our own way of life," proudly remembers a widow now in her sixties. "She was the boss in the house. But more than that, she was the queen."

And their fathers? Some women say there was an unbalanced matching of personalities and strengths; others recall an egalitarian relationship between their parents, based on a realistic division of interests and abilities. As one woman put it, "My mother handled all the crises that were financial or of a practical nature. My father was the stronger one emotionally. And together they were like a solid wall."

For these women, the builders, the father's attitudes toward education played a crucial part in how they later viewed being alone. Most were encouraged by their fathers to expand their vision of themselves by expanding their minds: going to college was seen as serious business, not merely a hiatus between youth and marriage. A father's support gave them positive images of themselves which remained in force even if they married and were later widowed or divorced with no career to fall back on. College had been an undertaking to develop individual talents and capabilities—and seen as such by one or both parents. But sometimes it was not so much a parent's belief in education for its own sake; it was seen as sheer necessity. Doris Wilson, the executive director of the YWCA in Chicago, is single, black, and convinced that the fact she was brought up believing she must be prepared to support herself has given her a greater degree of freedom than is enjoyed by most women. "I believe a black single woman is much freer," she said. "I knew I had to get an education, either to help my husband or support myself. White women have been programmed that their role is to be a wife and a mother and be taken care of. I've never had that fantasy."

All of these are simply observations of patterns seen among certain women, not absolute statements. Asking why some women handle aloneness better than others is something like asking an octogenarian the secret of long life: for every one who avoided tobacco or ate raw steak every day, there is another who smoked for eighty years and never touched meat.

With recognition of their diversity, is there any one characteristic shared by most women alone? I would say there is, and I would identify that characteristic as their meticulous attention to planning. Women who are totally alone, without children, plan their lives with great attention to detail: they map out the hours of their days, setting down certain routines they do not allow themselves to break; they plan dinner parties and vacations far in advance of the event; they will almost choreograph their contacts with other people. They do all this for the very common-sense reason that they cannot take anything for granted. There is no structure that will generate things happening if they don't make them happen, unlike the household of a woman with children, where the daily routine means a variety of expected and unexpected events—PTA meetings, skinned knees, new math lessons, Girl Scouts, Boy Scouts, good or bad report cards, crayoned drawings that say "I love you," a mixture of warmth and worry.

This attention to planning is sometimes obsessive, often exhausting, but it is needed. It allows a woman to plan a European vacation over the Christmas holidays so she won't have to sit alone in her apartment and be reminded she has no one during this, the most family-oriented of all holidays; it helps her circumvent lonely weekends when sitting around on a rainy day reading the Sunday papers isn't enough. It is a way of providing norms and constraints on oneself when there are none applied by society. In the same way, so is the fact that large numbers of women alone keep dogs, cats, parakeets, potted plants; something, anything, that demands regular attention and care. I asked one divorced woman about this, a woman with a dog and a cat in her apartment, and she added another reason: "I keep pets because they are a source of giving and receiving affection I can depend on."

Planning is a crucial element of life not only to the ordinary woman managing to support herself on an ordinary salary, but also to women with special life structures, women who have achieved a certain degree of fame or fortune. Writer Marya Mannes has told me that without a carefully built discipline, a pattern to her life, she would be lost: "If I didn't have my writing, and if I didn't have an enormous sort of zest for living—alternating of course with periods of depression like everybody has and feelings of great loneliness—I don't know what I would do. It's very tough to really do everything yourself, for yourself."

Without planning, a woman alone lacks discipline over herself, and may worry about succumbing to what one widow described as "a very selfish way of life." This woman, her children grown and gone, lives now in an apartment building she describes as "dingy and deadly," with circa 1935 furniture in many of the apartments, places where little old ladies she doesn't want to be like have lived for twenty years. "When I came here," she said, "I threw myself into fixing the place up, and that helped so much. I had such fears of falling apart, of not caring about the place and not eating meals on time, not having anything to discipline me. I was scared." She realizes she can do anything she wants to, when she wants to. "I can eat when I'm hungry, not when it's time to prepare dinner; I can go on a trip when I feel like it, come home whenever I want to, save my money or spend it." She isn't as frightened now, but she has become a planner; the very freedom at her disposal is a thing to constrain.

The instinct for meticulous planning comes with time; women without it, women who while away their lives, helpless to provide themselves with any goals, are the kind of women Margaret Mead described to me as "lonely and bitter, women who could be useful to society, but instead are doing nothing but housekeeping, dusting houses three times too large for them." Often widowed, these women are the most vulnerable to loneliness. Sociologist Helena Lopata found ample evidence that widows are unable to adjust readily. In a study conducted in Chicago, she found 48 percent of the widows identified loneliness as their greatest problem; an additional 22 percent referred to loneliness in conjunction with other, more tangible problems, such as finances. Unused to being alone, widows are also unused to planning and became victims of their own dependency. They may be financially burdened, but their greatest burden is emotional.

There is a different kind of planning alien to most women, and that is long-range planning. This is not the same as carefully worked out events and programmed responsibilities as described above. It is instead a projection into the future that involves considering possible life plans and their various stages, choosing certain options, and preparing for them. It is a very common thing for ambitious men: "By the time I'm twenty-five I'll be doing this, and when I'm thirty, I'll be doing this—" Rarely do young women map out life and career plans in similar fashion. Even though their interests have expanded beyond those of young women in the fifties, who thought almost exclusively of marriage, they look ahead only to short-range goals: a college degree, a job in another city, a date for Friday night.

This failure to take the long view works against women who never chose to remain single, yet never met the right man to marry. Very few women actually choose singleness. It is more a process of rejecting alternatives. (Gloria Steinem, explaining the progress of her own single life, said to me, "It was more a matter of knowing what I didn't want than what I did want.") Some of these women move into their forties without ever considering how to enrich their lives if they remain alone. They inch along through the years in dead-end jobs. How a woman values her work is deeply important to how she values herself and her future. Widows, divorced women, and single women are much more likely to resign themselves to dull jobs than married women.

Some women actually avoid signing up for pension plans or health insurance until a point in their working lives when they must pay higher costs for lower benefits. Lacking a long-range image of themselves, they resist accepting the possibility that they may always be unmarried. They grew up believing eventually they would marry, saw most people they knew marry, and cannot now accept the fact that they have not married or have failed at marriage.

This nonacceptance takes various forms, one of which is revealed by a term frequently used by women who live alone:

"cope." They don't tackle a problem and solve it—they "cope," living from one day to the next. But coping can be an important survival technique, when it involves deliberate short-range planning. Consider the situation of the wife of a Vietnam prisoner of war: "I think the hardest thing is the uncertainty of it all; you can't live with an indefinite time period. I could live with the knowledge that he will be home in five years. Or if it was ten years, I could live with that. But you can't live with no time frame at all. So you cut time up into sections. I'm living from now to November."

Widows working their way through the initial period of loss do the same thing. Divorced women will look back a year after and wonder how they got through the difficult transition period. "I just looked ahead to the end of each week," said one. Eventually they must tackle specific long-range problems: where they will live, how they will work, future plans for themselves and their children. But the short-range successes are sweet victories. "I was driving back from Michigan on Labor Day, when the fan belt broke on the car," said one divorced mother of three children. "I looked at it and saw it was broken so I wrapped it around the fan. I actually got it on—I didn't get it on right, but I got to town. The kids were so relieved—I know they feel more secure just from seeing that I know more what to do now than I did before."

To move into a life alone that offers any real options, a woman has to move beyond the coping phase—easy to say, very difficult to do. There is almost a natural law operative: the more you want something, the less chance you have of getting it. Actress Lauren Bacall has described this "natural law" quite perceptively: "I think you can want something a lot and not get it. But if you stop thinking about it, the chances of getting it are greater. Somehow if you're unfocused on it, that's when it comes to you. When you're searching for something desperately, that's when you don't find it. Desperation does not make us attractive to other people.'' But it is so easy to lose and so hard to win in this strange game: a woman who is alone may be presumed to be desperate, and therefore pitied and passed over—even if she isn't. And for her to disclaim this stereotype is to invite accusations of defensiveness.

The element of time is very important to whether or not a woman builds on her life alone. For single women, avoiding early marriage gives precious years for the self-identity search—done leisurely at no one else's expense, with more lasting results. One successful woman, now in her early thirties, recently married for the first time. ''I went through a crisis five years ago,'' she said. ''But then I got busy in my work, things went very well, and finally I realized I didn't *care* about being married—that was a wonderful feeling. I realized I didn't *need* it. Am I happy now that I'm married? Oh yes, but I'm not happier. I was already happy.''

Adequate time to follow her own star seems to be fundamentally important if a woman is to succeed in a career. After studying 125 top women executives, Professor Margaret Hennig concluded that ambitious young women should establish themselves first and then get married. The women in Dr. Hennig's study came to terms with their feminine side at the age of thirty-five, when all of them suffered an identity crisis. They had reached middle-management level and realized that if they ever wanted marriage and a family, the turning point was right now. They had left something out of their long-range planning efforts, and so they set out to be more womanly—apparently succeeding, because all of them eventually married.

Many a young woman could appreciate the common-sense advice of Dr. Hennig, but at the same time wonder if she would have the option of marriage if she waits until she reaches her thirties. It is unfortunately true that, although a bright and attractive woman of thirty-five may still feel comfortably on the right side of the hill, for most women, it is an age that means

twilight rather than high noon. (The thirty-five-year-old spinster in "Rachel, Rachel," for example, tells a friend sadly:
"I'm in the exact middle of my life. Nothing ever comes around
again.")

But time to develop individual potential, to plan a career and
do interesting, varied things, is not available to widows and
divorced women. Divorce and widowhood come with heavy
pressures, sometimes subtle ones difficult to single out and
assess. Author Eve Jones describes one of these pressures on
widows as "a complicated self-condemnation that arises from your
inner urges to cease mourning and take up the threads of life
creatively again." Although the widow is given sympathy and
support for a limited time and is expected to be lost and unsure,
she is also expected to fold up her widow's weeds and get back
into the normal pace of life as soon as decently possible. (But
not so soon as to strike the neighbors as unseemly. I recall the
criticism occasioned by Elizabeth Taylor's retort to a questioner
shortly after the death of her husband Michael Todd in a plane
crash: "Mike's dead. I'm alive," she said.)

The women who move beyond coping usually demonstrate a
particular flexibility, and are quite capable of rejecting society's
notions of what behavior is appropriate to them. They quickly
recognize that hitherto familiar ways of relating to other people
must change, because they themselves must change. A woman
who goes from a life of dependency in marriage to fixing fan
belts will have different ideas at the end of a year. She may be
working in a bank now, while her former friends are still
housewives in the suburbs. She has different things to say, to do.
If she has begun going out with men, she may find her friends
faintly disapproving. She may risk a major move—I know one
divorced woman with two children who bought a car for $200
and drove across the country to start a new life, determined to
break with all that was old even though she had no guarantee
about the new. Not even a job.

Many divorced women are looking around them in the

suburbs and realizing there is no place for them there. If they want to build new lives with independence, they cannot continue sitting pat in communities of married couples and living off alimony. "It's something I wish I could now do without," a North Shore divorced woman said. "As long as I accept alimony, I know I'm not really self-sufficient. That's one reason I'd like to sell this house." Another woman, a mother of three living in a thirteen-room Evanston home, said: "Taking care of a big house is a constant worry. I have grown to hate this one." Other women in similar circumstances indicated that they intended moving into the city, into a milieu where it is easier to be alone, as single women have known all along. Sometimes this is a practical decision, particularly for a mother working in the city. ("How would I get home in a hurry if we lived out in the suburbs?" said one.) But it also can be a risky decision, because the move may mean leaving good suburban schools for schools with lower academic reputations, greater drug problems, and more racial tension. Though they are more willing to risk the unknown than they used to be, many women are still hesitant about experimenting when the outcome looks ambiguous for their children.

But their aspirations and expectations have sharpened in recent years, partially as a result of the women's movement, partially as a result of the tumultuous social change going on all around us. Yet self-justification and liberation rhetoric are not much help to a woman left alone to raise a family of children when she never expected such an outcome. There is conflict and dilemma as long as there are children, and often what may be good for a woman alone doesn't necessarily look so good for her family. Moving to the city is within this category. Yet if she doesn't have the courage to do what is right for her, she cannot build anything substantively new and better.

Moving to the city will solve some problems and add new ones. It will provide a woman with privacy—she will be able to come home late without the neighbors talking, but this new gift of privacy also means she doesn't know her neighbors. It means no lawn to mow, no home to keep up, no taxes to pay, but it also means busy streets too dangerous for your eight-year-old to ride his bike on. It means higher costs for food and baby sitters. But perhaps the greatest advantage for a woman alone is that the city gives her an environment where she is not considered out of step with the rest of the world. She may not know her neighbors, but they include other mothers, single women, widows, bachelors—a variety of people alone whom she can seek out if she wishes. In short, living in the city can mean a mixed bag of freedom, variety, and loneliness. Women with families to raise who are considering such a move perhaps should have a glimpse of what living in the city means to other women alone—for example, that special breed of people who live along the city boundaries of most major urban areas: the young people somewhat enviously described by marrieds as the "swinging singles."

In Chicago they live on the North Side. The high-rises and brownstones and four-plus-ones (cheap wood-framed four-story buildings built over an open basement garage that sprouted everywhere for a few years after builders found a loophole in the city code that allowed four-story non-steel-braced construction) stretch north along Lake Michigan's blue shore for about eight miles. They are filled with thousands of single men and women, some a few years out of college, others in their twenties and thirties, who have gravitated to the North Side for the particular combination of convenience and companionship the area offers. Because of their numbers, the city's entrepreneurs have responded with singles bars, buildings that have meeting rooms to encourage mixers, and a variety of shops, theaters, and events that are intended to draw their interest and their money. It all sounds gay and interesting. But is it?

"Living in a high-rise was fine for a year; now I want to get

out of there. There's something so artificial about meeting people in a programmed way,'' said a disillusioned young secretary.
And consider the singles bars. The first time I visited one the
most striking thing was the way people seemed to be having such
a great time. Everyone danced furiously, laughed, and chat-
tered; no one seemed to be just sitting calmly with a friend. All
the women smiled and all the men talked. There was such a tir-
ing artificiality to it all, programmed conviviality that meets
a need, but wears thin with too much exposure.

A study of how singles in Chicago respond to an environment
specifically catering to them was recently reported in *Society*
magazine. ''The popular image of the 'swinging singles' spawned
and nurtured by the media is clearly false. There is little in
the bars to attract these people, especially the women,'' the
researchers concluded. They said that after six months it is
rare for a woman to continue seeking social contacts at a singles bar, although a man will continue going for a longer period
of time in search of ''an environment that feeds his psycho-
sexual fantasies.'' He seeks and often finds sexual companions
among the high school graduates who frequent the singles bars,
who ironically are looking for husbands (usually unsuccessfully).

Men and women alike resent artificially arranged meeting
places, such as the party rooms and mixing lounges in the high-
rises, and are uncomfortably reminded of the self-consciousness
of standing around alone at dances in high school. Women are
particularly uncomfortable because they feel they are being ap-
praised: how they look, their figures, the size of their breasts,
the way they wear their hair. (I found the laundry rooms to be
the closest thing to a natural environment while living in a
high-rise—it was easy to talk with a neighbor as you both hunted
for a missing blue sock; the most natural thing imaginable and
yet, in the lobby or the elevator, that same neighbor would be
a diffident stranger.)

One young social worker I know has scorned the ''singles

scene'' and moved to Lincoln Park, a North Side area that re-
tains a sense of neighborhood which makes it distinctive. She
lives in a small walk-up apartment above a drugstore and loves
it. ''The best part is the summer evenings,'' she said. ''I ride my
bike through Lincoln Park and everyone is friendly—an old
man will talk politics, a group of guys will ride along with me,
and we'll all feel great.'' Summer is a much friendlier time in
Chicago. The winters are so severe that there is little communication outside of homes and offices during the worst
months. Casual encounters are difficult. In the summer, just
strolling around the North Side is pleasurable, whether or not
you speak with anyone. There is an atmosphere of friendliness
and casualness that sometimes is all a lonely woman needs at a
given time.

In short, life for a young single woman living in a city with a
reasonably good job is neither as carefree and abandoned as her
parents may think it is nor as spontaneous as she would like it to
be. Many young women move in with an eye to meeting men
and find that all their neighbors are single women with the same
idea. Contrary to their expectations, most of their friends will be
found through their work. They quickly realize they can't rely
on the phony support systems offered by apartment-building
managers and singles bars, but must instead go about the same
search for friends that other women alone face—with the same
possibilities of rewards and loneliness.

A major problem for women alone is they have not been
trained to understand or accept the burden of responsibility.
There is no one else to blame for what they decide or do, no one
else to help make the decisions, and no one else with whom to
share the victories. A compliment, a promotion, and then home
to an empty apartment. A phone call to a friend to boast a little
is not the same as being able to rush in and announce an event to
a husband who will share the sense of achievement. A mother

alone must handle the responsibility for what happens to her children, protecting them through all the day-to-day crises that mark growing up. An older single woman may have to assume the burden of supporting or caring for an aged parent. One such woman who has taught many years, been single all her life, and is now in her sixties said to me, "The modern generation can't know what it was like to work in the Depression. I had a job and so I had to pick up the pieces for a lot of other people. When my father died, it was my job to support my mother; I became the man of the house, which is the story of women who don't marry. We are left to care for the parent or the retarded sister, or whatever the family responsibility might be."

But the greatest responsibility is personal. "I suffer the pangs of having choices and knowing that whatever happens to me, it is something I have done to myself," a leading woman journalist, who is single and in her thirties, has said. Within this responsibility for oneself is a significant freedom for women alone if they accept it and stand strong. It requires developing a kind of toughness; a denial of vulnerability. Most women alone do perceive themselves as vulnerable, but they can defend against this if they are able to accept responsibility for themselves and perhaps for other people.

I have found some women with few options, women who have been deserted, are on welfare, and are taking care of large families, who find a strength in endurance that is almost incomprehensible to middle-class women. It is their brand of toughness, this grim endurance that is often confused with apathy. But now some of these remarkable women alone are emerging from the ghettos to work in the new welfare rights organizations. They are women with the sharp-edged energy of militancy, out to change a system, often exhibiting more of an understanding of what society does to them as women alone than do their more affluent middle-class sisters. Working as welfare rights activists has given them increasingly positive images of themselves—and the more they are exposed to people who respond with attention and respect to what they say, the sharper these self-images become.

There are enormously talented women in the ghetto who have been exercising authority and ingenuity for years in holding families together under intolerable pressures. They are beginning to surface. And they will eventually write their own chapter to the history of women alone in this country. Yet they remain a minority. For most women "below the poverty line," as the expression goes, living means figuring how to get enough food for tonight's dinner; how to try to love your children when you are tormented by the need for money; how to try to love at all when your emotions wither in an environment where sex comes early and brutal, say, in an alley when you are eleven years old. "Coping" is a major achievement. "Building" is out of the question.

There are, of course, enormous gaps between women alone in poverty and women alone in the middle class. There is a striking lack of self-consciousness among poor women as they tell their stories, whereas middle-class women are more likely to see themselves in a social context, not in a vacuum. Perhaps for this reason, I have found the women who are poor often know themselves better; more directly, more simply, more clearly. They accept responsibility because they know nothing else. They have uncomplicated aspirations. They do not talk about wanting "meaningful relationships"; they say they want a man with whom they can live. Often they use the word "live" for "love," taking the abstract and making it concrete.

But these are simply random observations. I want to tell a little bit of what living is like for Diana Coratelli.

We visited at lunchtime, in her home, on a bleak afternoon just a few days before Christmas. Many blocks east of us, down on Michigan Avenue, the trees glistened with tiny gold lights and the mannequins in the store windows wore velvet hostess gowns and suede coats. Shoppers were dropping their quarters and dimes into the Salvation Army pots. (Why should their bells always sound so festive when they are meant to be a reminder of poverty?) Everything on Michigan Avenue, I knew, glowed with color and light.

I sat holding Diana Coratelli's baby on my lap. In the living room, the one herald of Christmas was an orange-juice can wrapped in aluminum foil with a fake poinsettia standing straight, bright red, carefully packed in dirt. Diana Coratelli smiled when I noticed it. "Tommy wanted something in here that looked like Christmas, so I fixed that up," she said. Tommy is ten; on the day I visited he brought a friend home from school for lunch. His mother looked worried for a moment and then said, fine, the friend could stay. But I noticed when she took a can of Campbell's soup down from the cupboard she thinned it out with two cans of water, not one. There was plenty of bread.

Tommy was filled with questions, fascinated with my tape recorder. We taped conversations through lunch, and it was clear Tommy was glad he had brought a friend home on the day something out of the ordinary was happening. His mother and I passed the squirming baby back and forth, a little bit of necessary business that helped us both feel comfortable, because she had been very shy and uncertain when I arrived. Her arms are long and thin; she wore a bright-red knit dress, and her brown hair was pulled straight back with a rubber band. She showed me Tommy's school pictures he had brought home, the glossy package that children are given with special offers that are supposed to be irresistible to parents, the kind that make it ridiculously expensive to order just one picture rather than the dozen or so you don't need.

"They want a dollar and seventy-five cents for these," she said. "Now why won't they let me get just one? For maybe fifty cents?" She was asking me a reasonable question, waiting to see if I knew why, her thin face puzzled. "I don't know," I answered. "It's stupid." She nodded as if that made sense, put the pictures back in the envelope and handed them to Tommy. "Take them back, Tommy," she said. He said nothing, just stared at the envelope with all those smiling images of himself that he couldn't have.

Diana Coratelli and her three children are on public aid, but that isn't what puts the strain in her face. Years of working as a housemaid, years when other people her age were going to school, and the knowledge she is, in a sense, on probation with the welfare department have etched the lines. Diana Coratelli once abandoned her children when she and her husband could no longer support them. The guilt has never left her. "I would die without my kids," she said. "I still dream about it."

The reason she is on probation is because of her husband. They are separated now, but he comes back periodically and they have bitter fights, the kind of fights that send the children into the bedroom to get away from all the hopelessness and anger. "I sit down and try to talk to him, but we just can't talk—we get mad right away and scream at each other, screaming and hollering at each other. My social worker told me I have to make up my mind, do I want to be together with him or just live by myself. But she doesn't want all the fighting all the time, or, she said, she would have to come and take the children and put them in foster homes."

Diana Coratelli shifted the now sleeping baby to her other arm, and we both got up and walked to the bedroom. She tucked the child in and we continued talking, both staring down at the crib. "Why do you let your husband keep coming back if you can't get along?" I asked. "Aren't you risking too much?"

"He claims he loves me, but I don't know, I don't believe him," she said. "I know I must still care for him but I'm not sure. I don't want to be all alone. But if the social worker says, it's your children or your husband, I'll tell him to go for good because they are more important to me. I just couldn't lose them again; I wouldn't have anything to live for." She looked at me with another question, this time anxiously: "I don't think she could just come out here one day and take them, do you? I think she'd have to let me know. I don't think she really wants to take them, do you?"

I shook my head. I knew the social worker didn't want to break up this family. "No, I don't think so," I said. "She knows you take good care of them." I told her she was admirable for her unique toughness, the quality that brought her back to claim her children again and assume responsibility for them.

For the first time, Diana Coratelli smiled. "The social worker, she's a very nice person," she said. "She just wants them to grow up and have a happy life. That's what I want too."

And what kind of happy life is possible for Diana Coratelli? That was my question, but I didn't ask it. I just took it with me in my head back down to Michigan Avenue and Christmas.

The stories are different in the neighborhoods where the rent is higher. And the quality of toughness is different. I have said that for some women, this involves a denial of vulnerability, but it can also mean the opposite. It means taking chances, not always relying on the safe and the planned. I know a young widow who deliberately married a man she loved even though she knew he was dying of leukemia. She has spent a great deal of time since his death evaluating the effects of the decision—what it meant to her then, what it means to her now. Not only does she not regret it, but she believes it made her more flexible, more receptive to new people and new experiences in the years afterward. "Right after he died was probably the loneliest time of my life, because I was uncommitted to anything except my own survival," she said. "And yet now I believe in more. I believe for one thing, that if you find love, in whatever form, it's wise to take advantage of it, because you might never have it again."

In her own way, she has found a method of reinforcing herself by asserting her strengths; she has turned the coin over and fashioned her toughness out of an acceptance of vulnerability. If all women alone could only find this vital balance between the two, worlds might quickly fall into place. To be tough is not to be hard, because hardness is an attempt at calcifying one's emotions. Women who try to do this usually succeed only in confusing themselves and everyone else. For example, a woman I shall call Donna.

The evening I spent with Donna was almost a primer in what can happen to a woman who isn't able to allow her ambition, her aloneness, and her sense of being a woman to exist compatibly. She has gone through two marriages and alternates between anger at "those weak men" and confessions of failure. She is both proud and upset about her success at work. "The only way I can make a success of it is being an absolute bitch sometimes," she said. "I call up a client and I say, 'Look, we were supposed to have this information half an hour ago. Get it over here fast.' Sometimes I'll be talking to the president of a company, sometimes the chairman. And I tell him, get me this information *right now*. I know I'm exercising my power legitimately, but sometimes I hang up the phone and I feel so bitchy."

As she grows older, Donna worries about her image as a feminine, attractive woman. "I used to be very fond of sex, but discriminating," she said. "Now I'm getting quite a bit less discriminating. I like sex, I want it, and I'll do things now that would have appalled me before. A couple of weeks ago I went to bed with a guy I had known as a business contact. A very attractive guy, but it was the first time we had gone out on a date. I would never have done that before."

The particular type of toughness Donna has shielded herself with isn't making living alone any easier, nor has it enabled her to reach the stage of self-acceptance that another woman, many

cities away, about the same age and comparably successful in
her job, has reached: "You have to be able to let go of things,"
this woman said. "That's when I began to feel my strength, when
I knew I could change a job or do something that risked some of
the gains I had made. And it was important to feel okay about
myself as a woman—when I knew I did, I realized I didn't need
other people's approval to feel good about myself."

Women left alone with children need more outside bolstering,
and they have access to such support in a way women totally
alone do not. And yet it is surprising how long both men and
women with families, divorced or widowed, were left to flounder
on their own without some organizational efforts geared to their
needs. It wasn't until 1958 that the organization now known as
Parents Without Partners was formed, an occasion marked by
the joyous comment of one early member, "We have built ourselves an Ark." There are now about 67,000 members in Parents
Without Partners—five women for every man. The organization in effect provides group therapy for individuals left isolated
from the world of marriage, and is particularly helpful in providing a group unity that children can appreciate and enjoy, children, for example, who otherwise have to skip events like Dad's
Night at school, because they have no father.

Parents Without Partners is not a panacea however, particularly for women looking for men. "All they do is talk about
making the kids obey and things like that," said one divorced
mother. "They have a special little clique. I want to have fun."
Organizations where women alone can "have fun" are few and
far between; and often they only compound the sense of being
alone because of their artificiality. As the singles bars have
shown, programming human relationships is awkward at best,
exploitative at its worst.

In general, then, women alone can expect little outside support. Differently equipped, differently perceiving, they cope or they build without much attention from the world of the marrieds. They live closer to loneliness than most other people in our overly busy world, but if they have a reasonably clear image of themselves, they steer around the easy routes leading to self-pity. This is an impossible bog. And it always breeds loneliness, the reverse side of appreciation of solitude, because it perverts a healthy process of turning inward into a process of carnivorous self-absorption. "If only people who are lonely would realize that all they have to do is reach out and someone out there is even lonelier": good advice from a woman alone who has learned to face it.

In its most positive sense, turning inward means being able to accept and live with oneself without fear. I particularly liked the way actress Helen Hayes explained what it means for her. Now in her early seventies, she was widowed over fifteen years ago. What is most arresting about this talented woman is her growing understanding of solitude, that peace with oneself that enables a person to live alone and make it a good and human experience —not a dead end; not a life of looking enviously through other people's windows.

One cold November afternoon we talked for hours high above the city in a quietly elegant apartment; at one point I asked her if she had ever been alone very much while married. She shook her head emphatically and said, "Oh no, never. But there were times, many times in my life—until I was left alone—that I wished for solitude. I love solitude, and we too often confuse solitude with loneliness; they are so different. I never had the blessed gift of being alone until the last of my loved ones was wrested from me. And now, I can go for days and days without seeing anyone. I'm not entirely alone, because I listen to the radio and read the newspapers. I love to read. That is my greatest new luxury, having the time to read. . . . But solitude—walking alone, doing things alone, is the most blessed thing in the world. And I think I am beginning to find myself a little bit. I never had time for myself before; I was busy making the acquaintance of other people, entertaining other people. Now I've learned I can live with myself. And I've learned to forgive myself for some of the mistakes I've made."

7.

Loving

We had reached the end of a long and painful interview. The woman across from me took off her glasses and carefully cleaned them, then wiped the tears from her eyes. For the better part of two hours she had been retelling the story of a love affair that had ended, and we were both exhausted. I felt deeply depressed, sitting there in her high-rise office, littered with the books and papers that told of the busy professional life she led as a lawyer. This was a woman lucky enough to live a life with multiple dimensions, not a woman helpless and destroyed without a man for self-affirmation. And yet she was totally bereft in a way I understood all too well.

I asked one more question, to me, an important question: "Marlene," I said, "if you had to make a choice, which would you choose—to love or be loved?"

She thought a few moments. And then she said, "I would rather be loved. It is more childlike, and less responsible. Anything you do is acceptable, and there is less burden to it." She thought again, then said with finality, "Yes, I would rather be loved."

Reflecting on her response later, I was struck by how many women alone have indicated similar reserve after a loss. They communicate a sense of emotional constriction and sometimes make deeply lonely acknowledgments of its existence. One woman, frowning in thought, her gray hair flying in the wind as we talked on a Loop street, said: "I was afraid before my divorce. I was afraid of loneliness, even though I already was lonely, and didn't know it." She shifted a huge carpetbag from one hand to another and continued, "Now I find myself having affairs only with married men, because I'm afraid of getting too involved again. It's safer that way."

Later I asked myself the same question. Which would I choose? After much thought, I knew that I would rather be the one who did the loving. Being loved is enormously satisfying for the ego; there need be no self-doubt or pain. But loving means feeling, giving, and without that what have you got but a reflection of someone's adulation that may mean nothing? The emptiness of adoration is nowhere so apparent as in the lives of women publicly worshipped as images, not valued as people, women like Marilyn Monroe. Beyond that, wouldn't there be at least a little longing, a little envy, felt by a woman who found herself the recipient of an authentic love but couldn't return the gift? Mightn't she feel cheated? (I thought also, perhaps I should have phrased the question to the woman lawyer differently. What if I had asked, would she choose being loved if the condition were she could *never* experience giving it?)

The fundamental human quest for all of us is our search for a love relationship. We want warmth and affection and companionship, all the things that are the antithesis of aloneness. For women alone the search is wider, and sometimes desperate, because there is no One. The challenge then is to underlay all rela-

tionships with what must be a base to any love, and that is tenderness—that compelling emotion which we privately cherish,
find publicly embarrassing, and are too often unable to express.
Little boys snicker if a mother kisses her son, and the son dies of
humiliation in front of his friends. A woman will draw back
from expressing tenderness for a friend, fearful of being misun-
derstood. A husband will reserve the words "I love you" for his
wife's birthdays and anniversaries, unwilling to appear too
demonstrative. She, in turn, finds it easier to be angry because
he hasn't mowed the lawn than to tell him she treasures the years
they have shared. And yet both of them will cry in a dark theater
when they view a moving scene between celluloid lovers.

For women alone, the obstacles to loving, to giving and
receiving tenderness, are everywhere, but particularly within
themselves: they are afraid of being branded lesbian, they are
disapproving and distrustful of themselves in groups, and they
are unable to establish relationships with men on other than a
sexual basis.

There are so many ways to love: man to man, woman to man,
woman to woman, adult to child. One of the warmest moments
of love for me was with my father on the evening he lost his job
at the age of sixty-five, before successfully making an entirely
new start in another business. We sat outside on the patio after
dark and he held my hand, telling me the private dreams and
disappointments of his life and the things that made him proud.
"I am glad you are here," he told me. And I was so glad that I
was.

And yet there are also so many ways we miss each other. I
have picked up my daughter's Raggedy Ann doll, holding it
close and feeling simultaneously a longing and a comfort, as a
child and yet not as a child, because in touching there is a yearning for a completeness which seems forever elusive. If there is a
loneliness most of us have at one time or another shared, surely
it has been reaching out to someone, physically touching, but ac-

tually passing that person by, unable to make contact beyond
the flesh.

I am told there is a painting in a Mexico City museum that
shows a man and a woman on a park bench holding hands, facing each other in a classic pose of affection. They are without
faces or heads; only mirrors, two mirrors reflecting blankness.
To me that means two blind egos feeding off one another for
gratification, but seeing nothing, feeling nothing. And when I
feel most depressed, I wonder, is that what love between a man
and a woman comes to? I hope not, because we cannot deny our
need for each other. There is a counterpoint, a tension, that adds
at least the promise of depth to the private experience of a man
and a woman. But a sexual relationship isn't the center of love.
There are so many dead people hanging on to each other every
night, hoping or pretending—or just not caring—and calling
the fact they lie in bed together an act of love. In one of his short
stories, Scott Fitzgerald calls success a "matter of atmosphere." I
like that description. And I think we too often have made love a
"matter of atmosphere," trading substance for illusion, holding
up our mirrors and hiding ourselves.

But for women alone without any kind of love the situation is,
at best, difficult and lonely; at worst, despairing. I can't speak
for men, but I do know that many women left suddenly alone
will throw off all common sense and reach out for a relationship,
any relationship, deluding themselves into believing they have
found fulfillment. A divorced woman described to me an evening spent in a bar with one of a string of men she had linked herself with after the loss of her husband. Somewhere in the depths
of the evening, after four martinis, she made her way to the
restroom. "How's this for a declaration of freedom into a dirty,
cracked mirror?" she asked me, her voice challenging. " 'I will
never again sleep with a man unless I want to. *Never*!' That's
what I told myself that night. And that's when I took control
over my own life. Finally."

The fear of total loss, of total isolation, compels many women alone to seek different relationships, even at the risk of pain and rejection. And yet I think part of the secret (if that is a fair thing to call it) of a woman standing free with individual strength is to be able to let go—to recognize and value the mistakes as well as the gains in a relationship, never forgetting that what dies is often what is held too tightly.

But what an impossible lesson to learn. I have tried to teach it to a crying child whose best friend is turning away, knowing all the while I haven't learned it myself; knowing that I too would cling, afraid and lonely. I have counseled children to pretend they don't care—trying more to provide a tool for their protection than a solution for regaining a lost friendship. We all care. And we pretend not to. How truly lonely we allow ourselves to be.

Without the richness of love relationships other than that between man and woman, we would be impossibly lonely. What, for example, would we do without our children? Or those few moments of closeness with a friend that make all the time we exchange chatter at cocktail parties less of a waste? Yet these are the relationships women alone will often overlook in their search for a man. We have a simple word in the English language to describe a legitimate form of loving, but we are uncomfortable in identifying it as such. The word is "friendship."

From childhood on, women lack the group unity common to men. They have not usually engaged in the type of teamwork that wins baseball and football games; rather, they have vied for the isolation of the post of Prom Queen. That particular goal is not so highly valued anymore, but women are always essentially engaged in a silent battle for men, and that unspoken but unceasing competitiveness is a formidable barrier to friendship. It isolates the young woman from her classmates, the housewife from her neighbors, the career woman from other women in her office. One would think the competitiveness would die away after marriage, but it does not. Two married women walking together into a restaurant with their husbands will silently evaluate each other in the foyer mirror, so automatically, so quickly, they are often not even aware of the coldness of their appraisals.

Authentic friendship between women is difficult when men are around, and so they content themselves with superficial substitutes. Housewives will gather together and exchange complaints about housework and their husbands, or confide their fears of getting pregnant. Young women will gather amiably in a sorority house and discuss the men in their classes. Old women will knit in their rest homes and sigh about their aches and pains and their ungrateful children.

A young woman, writing on her year in a commune, has described how this competitiveness affected her. "I was the only woman who didn't move into our commune because a particular man lives there," she declared. "But a good part of my reasons for moving in was the potential relationships I could have with the men. I certainly wasn't much interested in what I could build with the women." The women in her commune tried meeting with each other on Thursday nights, but with poor success. "We couldn't often maintain the support we gave each other in our meetings outside of them," she said. "Over and over our feeling together would evaporate when we were around the men. Looking back, the basic weakness of our group seems to be that we were together only because of and in reaction to the men."

Competition for men is not the only barrier isolating women from one another. Women also have a consistently negative image of themselves in clusters of more than two or three. Women in groups are not teammates or colleagues, they are the "girls" trooping off to lunch in a tearoom. We immediately imagine women in big hats and flowered dresses talking all at once and having a terrible time splitting the check. Somehow women in groups appear very unattractive to men and women alike. Yet women alone are not only relegated to such groups, they are expected to like it. As one middle-aged single woman has said: "We have to create our own social circles. And yet if we do, we are a bunch of old hens getting together."

Relegation to the group hits widows particularly hard. Helena Lopata relates this incident involving a newly widowed woman invited to attend a banquet given by her husband's company: excited and pleased, she bought a new dress and looked forward to the event with pleasure, believing it would be a chance to see old acquaintances and once again be part of the social life she had enjoyed with her husband. She showed up in her new dress, her hair freshly done, and was directed to a long table filled only with other middle-aged women in new dresses and with freshly coifed hair—a table set up solely for the company widows. I doubt if there could be many gestures toward women alone so callous as this twisted magnanimity of simultaneous inclusion and rejection.

Women commonly value men more than themselves. But who am I to criticize? For years I loftily announced to male acquaintances, "Women are all right, one or two at a time. But I can't stand a group of them together." I avoided clusters of unattached females at parties, particularly if I too was alone, deeply conscious of the wallflower image remembered from my youth, when groups of girls meant nervous giggles, hopeful glances, pretense. As adults, there were no giggles and the glances were far less obvious, much more controlled. But the sense of being part of a rather pathetic conglomerate waiting to be asked to join the party remained.

Friendship among women seems easier and most natural in youth and in old age, when the tension of competition is absent. But there are exceptions. A young woman, recently out of college, described to me an experience that had moved her for the first time in her life to think of deep friendship with another

woman. "It was one night around three in the morning," she explained. "My roommate was tossing and turning, unable to
sleep, and I felt so affected by her sleeplessness, I couldn't sleep
either. Then, in the dark, she held out her hand and took mine:
'Do you want to share a problem?' she asked. She told me she
was pregnant and she was scared. I lay there and held her hand
for an hour while we talked about what to do. I told her I knew
friends who could help, and we talked about abortion. It was the
first time a woman trusted me and cared for me enough to talk
so frankly. After that, female friendship meant something different to me. And it always will."

Years ago, I recall seeing a newspaper account of the suicide
of an old woman living in a New York City rest home. The
woman had jumped to her death the day after a long-time friend
had died. Neither woman, so the story reported, had family or
other friends, and they had been inseparable companions in the
rest home for years. In hearing of such a story as this, it is hard
to ignore how close friendship can come to love. At its best, isn't
that exactly what friendship is?

Some women have enriched their lives immensely with
friendship. Eleanor Roosevelt, for example, was able to expand
her loyalties during a lonely marriage to a number of close
female friends. She built a home near Hyde Park for herself and
two women, complete with monogrammed towels joining their
three initials. Such demonstrative affection was possible for
Mrs. Roosevelt, a woman insulated by her marriage and social
position from the type of damaging gossip which would have
been directed at an average woman alone in a similar situation.
Mrs. Roosevelt looked for warmth from other women, writes
biographer Joseph Lash, because "she needed people to whom
she was the one and only and upon whom she could lavish help,
attention, tenderness." Her needs then were not so different
from those of lonely people everywhere.

"Tenderness" is a word we hear often now, frequently in the context of a defense of lesbianism. There is a scene in Sylvia Plath's *The Bell Jar* where Esther, puzzled about lesbianism, asks her doctor, "What does a woman see in a woman that she can't see in a man?" Doctor Nolan pauses, then says, "Tenderness." This has a tempting ring to it, but it bears examining. Only women, runs the argument, have the emotional depth to feel and express true tenderness; men lack the capacity. It is true that men often do not expose their feelings, sometimes because of fear of appearing unmanly and sometimes, I think, because we put such emphasis on training men to be independent that we isolate them emotionally. But to deny men tenderness is to deny not only their warmth and humanity but to deny reality. Of course, men understand tenderness; ask any woman who has ever known herself to be loved by a man.

Placing the blame for frequently empty relationships between men and women is not that easy. The tragedy is that tenderness often exists in these relationships, but it is not expressed, so that eventually, without reciprocity, visible tenderness atrophies or turns in another direction. Rollo May, puzzling over the reasons for this, writes, "It is a strange thing in our society that what goes into building a relationship—the sharing of tastes, fantasies, dreams, hopes for the future, and fears from the past—seems to make people more shy and vulnerable than going to bed with each other. They are more wary of the tenderness that goes with psychological and spiritual nakedness than they are in sexual intimacy."

What then about friendship between men? Men are not restricted in certain displays of affection, particularly connected with sports (I've always been amused by the pat on the bottom given by one huge football or basketball player to a teammate who has scored in a game). But men are definitely affected by the same fears women have of expressing friendship and love.

An example of how this fear can become institutionalized is the phenomenon known in Catholic religious communities as "PF," or "particular friendships." Religious community members are expected to be very careful about their contacts with each other. "If I sat with another seminarian talking alone in my room, we had to keep the door open at all times," a priest told me. Priests have traditionally been discouraged from becoming close friends with any one person; if such a friendship develops, it is supposed to be broken. It is the same for nuns. "We were warned about talking too often with the same person," said one. "If we did, they broke us up—changing our seats at mealtime away from each other, and things like that." Apparently those who are to minister to the emotional needs of other human beings are expected to do so without experiencing the warmth of either love or friendship themselves.

On everyday levels, men are cautious of expressing affection. "If a man puts his arm around my shoulder, that's okay," one man said. "But only for a split second—I can't tell you exactly how long, but I know there is a point where, if he kept his arm on me, I would feel damn uncomfortable." There is much hearty cheer, genial insults, and slaps on the back that are often tentative expressions of authentic affection. But little more. Even though men apparently "bond" in group activities with other men far more comfortably than women with other women, they are reluctant to demonstrate tenderness. There is a moving scene in the film of D. H. Lawrence's book, *Women in Love*, that shows two men, friends for many years, taking off their clothes and wrestling each other. The scene is quite long and becomes something other than a traditional matching of male strength and wits, something much more. As I viewed the progression of the wrestling on the screen, it became for me a wordless expression of love between two men—a cinematic acting out of love that I had never seen before. I wondered what men watching that scene would feel. Repulsion? Understanding?

A few days later while riding to work on the train I told one of my neighbors, a cheerful man in advertising, about the film and about my question of men expressing their love for other men. He hadn't seen *Women in Love*, he said. But he became engrossed in his thoughts, and then told me this story: "I have a friend, a man I've known since we were kids. We've been to school together, gone on trips, played poker, done lots of things, even after we both got married and didn't get together as often. Last summer his little girl drowned. He was broken, and cried when I went to see him. I cried too. And I realized for the first time how much I love him. I told him so, but I didn't have to, because he knew it. I guess I always have loved him." My friend made no apologies for using the word "love." We rode in silence the rest of the way to town, a warm and comfortable silence, because it was an unspoken recognition of something shared in an unusual way.

But why does it have to be so unusual? Our concern about love is so fearful and limiting. Without marriage, the walls close in further. Who knows what might happen if two men or two women acknowledge deep affection and care? Social structures might collapse; institutions topple. Landlords would complain. The sun might not come up tomorrow. We fear "unnatural" sex relationships, because we have made what is natural a distortion, and so we deny feeling. But if women can't reach out for other women, nor men for other men, aren't we less able to realize love in a full sense? Haven't we, then, all lost something?

The question of loving a man—where to find him, how to keep him—is never far removed from the consciousness of most women alone, no matter how resourceful and self-sufficient they are, or how unneedful or undesirable they pretend to be. If they have no one to love, they also have less access to love substitutes than do men. When being alone gets too lonely, a man can pick up a girl in a bar to sleep with without necessarily risking his self-respect. It is a socially acceptable alternative. But a woman sitting on a bar stool obviously looking for companionship is typed immediately. Even if she has the courage to scorn the image, she also has to be aware of the practical dangers: picking up strangers is a risky business. In addition, work is not as absorbing a part of life for most women alone as it is for men, and is not therefore as helpful in fending off loneliness. Women look to the end of a day for what they value—not the beginning.

If a woman has been married, she may have her children and she may also have her friends, men and women, upon whom she has relied for years. But the transition from marriage to divorce is tricky for women with male friends. There is a latent sexual tension almost always present, a tension which had been repressed when a sexual relationship was out of the question, but which surfaces rapidly when a woman is alone. I have heard numerous laments about old friends coming to fix the boiler or mend the roof and being sent away, a friendship over. (On the other hand, a woman newly alone may be sending out "help me" signals that are honestly misinterpreted.) Married women feel cautious around a neighbor who has suddenly moved from marriage to singleness. "I know why, and I understand why, but it still hurts," said a divorced mother of two children. She continues to live in a Detroit suburb although she feels totally shut out of the social life of her neighborhood. "They think I'm something of a threat," she said. Again, the competitiveness is never far below the surface, and also the uneasy realization that destruction breeds destruction—and few marriages are totally invulnerable. This particular woman has tried, in her own way, not to back herself into a corner over the dilemma of friendship.

"The majority of women I meet I don't like, but I have to have a woman friend," she said. "There are just some things I can't talk to anyone but women about. For instance, I can't talk about my weaknesses and fears with men. With a good woman friend, I can let myself be vulnerable, if I trust her. But most women are so petty, just not honest. Like at work—if a man doesn't like what you are doing, he tells you. A woman will talk behind your back instead. I guess about 90 percent of the women on the staff of the hospital where I work are married. And they are very openly jealous because I am an available female. I'm free to have a cocktail after work with the men, and they resent this. But they don't resent the men, even when they're married.''

If a woman's friends are married, the relationships change slowly as she adjusts to a life totally different from theirs, and gradually a distance develops. She must seek out new friends among other people who are not married. Sometimes they are other women, and sometimes men—but again, a friendship between a man and a woman must survive the always present sexual tension. "I know a wonderful person who I care about deeply, but I don't want to go to bed with him. Yet it is always a question hanging in the air," said one divorced woman. She fears she will have to back away from something she both values and needs, or allow herself to move into an unwanted sexual relationship. Can a man and a woman be close friends when this tension is present? Many women alone say no. And in this realization, they find a particularly devastating loneliness.

But even more important to our need for whole relationships is this question: can men and women be lovers and also enduring friends? Consider the depressing example of an Israeli kibbutz: there, the children are removed from their families as infants and reared in a communal environment, developing great interdependence. Boys and girls grow to maturity as close friends, but friendship does not develop into loving emotional involvements and they rarely marry each other.

We have no comparable situation in our society, but we too

divide friendship from love. Anthropologist Lionel Tiger points to the kibbutz-raised men and women as examples of what he calls an "anti-bond"—friendship in childhood precludes love in maturity; one kind of bond precludes the other. If we are friends, we cannot love; if we love, we cannot be friends.

If this is true, we are indeed on opposite, lonely shores. One evening over dinner, I asked Tiger if he thought it was impossible to build man-woman relationships on both love and friendship. He shrugged his shoulders. He didn't know. We sat a moment, contemplating the implications. Then he said, in a 'let's settle for what we've got' tone: "Look. Most women will probably have men. With anxiety, with fear, with terror, with love, with brutality. They have men. Right?" He spread his hands, arms wide, eyes both answering and questioning.

Right. And something is all wrong.

The question of friendship between men and women is important to people alone; without it, existing in a society based on marriage can be intolerable. But because of the difficulties of establishing nonsexual relationships (it is so much easier to go to bed with someone than to work at understanding him), women alone tend to drift from one sexual involvement to another. On the other hand, there is a desolating loneliness attached to being alone without sexual love, or simply what some women have described as the comfort of being held in someone's arms. "My bed is too cold," one middle-aged unmarried woman said.

Almost without exception, no matter what their ages, the women I have met want the option of sexually loving a man. They may be sixty-five years old but after the obligatory "Of course, all that's too late for me," they muse over the possibilities. Being alone doesn't get easier as you get older. For centuries, novelists have eulogized romantic love as woman's highest goal and highest accomplishment, and many women alone pursue it with true determination. "If you're really serious about finding a man," one widow told me, "you have to approach it as if it's a task. You have to just weed through hundreds of men and discard them as soon as you find out they won't work. Don't waste time with the wrong man. That's silly. Use a pragmatic approach." She paused a moment, and a ghost of a smile crossed her face. "I talk a good game," she said.

The search can be a way of injecting purposefulness into one's life. But many women who have endured a painful loss lack the momentum to put together something new for themselves. Most widows, for example, say they have no wish to remarry. Sometimes it isn't a matter of conscious decision, it is the helplessness of women who had used their husbands' personal strength as a substitute for developing their own, and who now feel a vague, sometimes despairing, sense of having cheated themselves. Being alone is total confusion for them, and they would readily make the same mistakes once again if they had the chance.

Rollo May tells us that we can always depend on sex to give a reasonable facsimile of love. But used as a substitute for genuine warmth, it becomes a barrier to anything deeper. Love and sex in our society have been so thoroughly, so hopelessly mixed together that neither gets its due, nor does either have a chance to nourish the other.

How does this affect the woman alone? For one thing, she may seek her independence through sex, a time-honored tradition. William Bolitho, author of *Twelve Against the Gods*, was fascinated with the pursuit of adventure and the characteristics of those who dare try. One woman adventurer he included in his book was dreamy, romantic Isadora Duncan, a dancer of the twenties who died of strangulation when a long chiffon scarf wound around her neck caught in the wheel of a moving roadster. "The vast mass of men, then, have to depend on themselves alone," wrote Bolitho. "The vast mass of women hope or expect to get their life given to them. It is the first condition of a woman-adventurer to do as Isadora and bar from the beginning any such dependence.'' It was Bolitho's contention that a woman's one adventure is man, so her strike for independence can be legitimately made by throwing aside all rules and convention, particularly marriage. It is a route that looks so free. And at times in history it has been. The courtesans of France and the geishas of Japan, says Simone de Beauvoir, enjoyed far more freedom than other women of their time. And certainly the modern-day ''kept woman'' is a comfortable woman. But the route is mostly just well-traveled. A young woman working now as a cocktail waitress, who ran away from home and spent five years on sexual adventure, told me one evening:

''I have been with quite a few men, and my identity changed with each different man. Still I felt I was getting more sure of myself, no matter who I was with, not because of them, but I think there was something born in me that couldn't be kept down. I've been with about thirty-five men, and that includes about five or six who slept with me one night when I was passed out. From what I hear, that was about the number.'' (She laughs.) ''I don't think I'll ever live with a lot of men again. A lot of times I did it just for financial support. I got to a point where I couldn't stand to work, because I felt being a waitress was so degrading. Now I think living off a man is more degrading than being a waitress.''

Other women seek independence through the traditional jobs built on sex appeal—the films, the stage, the prize of becoming Hugh Hefner's Playmate of the Month. Sometimes they are successful; other times their self-images get muddled. I remember one Playboy Bunny, a beautiful girl with long red hair which she tossed in a graceful, artful gesture, a girl who has already learned to tilt her head up when she stands under bright lights in order to eliminate all shadows. The day we met she wore a tiny hot-pants outfit that drew all eyes as she strolled along, the shirt unzipped to her waist. She eagerly showed me her Playmate foldout, of which she was very proud. (How do you compliment a

Playmate? By saying the lighting was good?) At the same time she complained, "Men don't see me as I am. They're not interested in what I'm really like, only the fact that I'm a Playmate."

Sometimes a woman deliberately bypasses the traditional marital bargain of sex-for-support and instead chooses to have a child without the guaranteed support of a man. "What does a piece of paper mean?" an unmarried schoolteacher expecting a baby said to a reporter. "It doesn't guarantee a permanent relationship and it doesn't have anything to do with love. The most important thing is the way two people feel about one another." Still, old forms hold fast, and for every Lainie Kazan or Mia Farrow who poses proudly with what used to be called a "love child" (always worth a photo in the newspaper) there is the high school girl who "gets caught" and ends up an unwed mother in the maternity ward, hardly a gay, free experience for a sixteen-year-old.

Some women contrive a version of sexual adventurism that requires careful nurturing of a mystique of desirability. They are able to maintain the interest of a man by withdrawing periodically, playing on his jealousies by making him aware of how much other men are attracted to them. The problem is, their own emotions must remain under control if the game is to work successfully. And if a woman doesn't allow herself to be vulnerable, she runs the risk of becoming frigid. Surely it is no accident that some of the most famous courtesans of history were reportedly unable to enjoy sexual pleasure, only give it. "Such maneuvers are delicate; if the man sees through them, they can only ridiculously expose the servility of his slave," writes Simone de Beauvoir.

How, then, do women alone unmix sex and love and find some combination that provides warmth in their own lives? How do they explore the possibilities of love without heartache or misunderstanding? Erik Erikson, joining the ranks of those who have attempted to define love, has called it simply a process of mutual affirmation: two people, each acknowledging the worth of the other—no mirrors replacing faces. Simone de Beauvoir, on the same quest, has called love a mutual recognition of two liberties. Put them together: I affirm, I am free; you affirm, you are free. Add generosity and tenderness, and you have the best of what goes into both friendship and love.

Women who have moved far enough beyond the early years of their lives when men and women knew each other primarily in the unreal, dressed-up atmosphere of the "date," are revising their ideas of love and friendship. Sometimes the price they have paid is their marriage. "In many ways I'm less lonely now than when I was married, but more alone," says a divorced woman. And another, reflectively: "Isn't it a pity that we can't grow up and be married? Instead of having to grow up through a divorce?" Once alone, women have to be willing to risk additional loss and pain in order to overcome loneliness, unless they prefer to settle for a television set and a cat. Sometimes this means taking love or friendship in whatever form it comes, not wasting too much time carefully evaluating qualifications. "My feeling is, it may never come my way again," explained a middle-aged widow. It is true; it might not. And this haunts many women, particularly if the man who comes their way is already married.

An affair with a married man means much waiting. It also means uncertainty, because it is an unsatisfactory relationship built on surreptitious dinners and two hours at a motel; and it means jealousy of the woman who has the legitimate claim to him. Many women defend affairs with married men by pointing out that forty-year-old bachelors often are hung up on their mothers and divorced men or widowers are working out emotional problems of their own. "I like married men best," said one young single woman matter of factly. I also know a middle-aged woman of fifty who lives a quiet, realistic life as the mistress of a

married man and would have it no other way. But there is much
pulling and tugging in such an affair, and usually eventual loss.
Often the woman hangs on in the hope he will get a divorce and
marry her. But usually this doesn't happen, and how long does a
woman sacrifice her dignity for an elusive goal that is more of a
fairy tale than reality?

Eventually, there is an end of need. Perhaps it is simply a
great tiredness. Sometimes it means one or the other person
ceases to care. A question I have heard often from women is,
"Why is it, when I stopped caring, he began to care more?" In
the musical *Coco*, Chanel has a line that puts it beautifully.
"When I no longer needed, I was needed," she says sadly. The
mystique of unavailable desirability, in another form. There is a
special loneliness at the end of need, because a woman is aware
she must search once more, but this time uncertain of just how
fully to commit herself.

This uncertainty is experienced by many women in a variety
of situations, for example, the younger women who are in no
hurry to commit themselves to marriage. A serious-faced young
woman explained to me what it means for her now that she has
left the comfortable environment of her home and friends and
gone off to college:

"When you get on your own and you don't have your parents
to go to, you invariably find somebody to become involved
with," she said. "There is a person I've met who has really
influenced me. It's amazing how people outside your own family
can really get to you—he can make me tremendously happy,
like surprising me on my birthday when I didn't know anyone
knew. I've found I can have a life outside the sheltered little
niche I've been in for the last seventeen years, and it's a very
good feeling. But it's a scary feeling, too. I find myself depending
on him, and I wonder, can I really depend on him and ought I depend on him? There's a difference between needing somebody
and wanting to need them. One thing is certain—a lot of my

friends are fighting getting close to somebody or really needing them.''

Is this hesitancy reasonable caution or fear? Sometimes both. Unfortunately, in our solutions we often find new problems; fear of commitment is one of them. An interesting phenomenon bred by this fear is the ''people-renting'' services that have begun to attract attention, particularly in resort areas like Miami, which boasts ''Rent-A-Gent'' and ''Rent-A-Bird'' agencies. A woman who wants an escort tells the agency what type of man she has in mind—age, height, what color hair, whether he likes to dance or sail or ski—and she is provided with someone meeting these qualifications. A man does the same. He ''can take a woman out and look at her and talk to her and dance her around without actually having to put himself on the line,'' writes Peter Andrews in *The New York Times*. On the other hand, ''people-renting'' can be the only way a woman alone feels confident enough to go out to nightclubs and bars in an unfamiliar town.

The women who have the luxury to worry over fine distinctions between ''needing somebody'' and ''wanting to need them'' are usually young; when there is no dearth of young men. Older women alone are sharply aware that as they grow older the field of available men contracts; young men generally want young women, and older men are both married and fewer in number. For older men, the field of available women expands; their age is not a barrier. Sometimes these women deny worrying about loneliness. If they have never been married, they may wonder if they were too choosy. Some gain satisfaction from deciding they were. ''I could have gotten married, but all the men I knew were such idiots,'' one woman declared. Divorced women are more frank about admitting they want someone to love, partially because they have not built up the layers of independence, self-confidence, and rationalization that come when a life alone evolves rather than descends suddenly. Yet they will be tugged in two directions—wanting to throw themselves into a permanent commitment because they are hungry for love, and wanting to draw back into a safe world, alone, without risk, without gain. They chafe at impermanence and fear permanence.

Widows and divorcees are more likely to need other people to rely on than women who have never been married. Pauline Bart, a sociologist who has studied depression in middle-aged women, believes that marrying young often precludes success in living alone. "Women who have never married generally value privacy and independence above intimacy and companionship," she said. It is hardly surprising that a woman who has spent twenty years fixing family dinners, talking about the bills with her husband, hanging up his shirts, and living a noisy, full life will sorely miss it even if it was unhappy.

Marriage, somehow, is always the question. "Who needs it?" asked one young woman with a shrug. "It's just a psychological down for a lot of people. It's hard enough living with someone, let alone being married to him." Yet she acknowledged living with someone begins to look very much like marriage after a while. "That's the biggest down of all for any person trying to get out and not only discover who she is but try to do something constructive," she said.

Women who have lived all their adult lives as nuns and who are now attempting new life styles within their convents or leaving entirely are frank about evaluating what they see of women alone and cautious about how they see themselves fitting in. "I just went through with a friend the trauma of her second divorce, and I've decided I'm very lucky," said one. These women are, in a sense, out of step with the new "freedom" that puts such a high value on sexual expression. "I chose to be celibate because it's freeing for me," said a middle-aged nun who works on inner-city projects in Detroit. "I would find marriage very restricting." She has decided she can build a satisfactory, full life as a woman alone with friendships, but without sex or marriage. "I feel that way now," she admitted. "But if I were a twenty-year-old nun, I might feel differently." Is celibacy, then, a reasonable alternative for women to the unresolvable dilemmas of love and marriage? Are there any reasonable alternatives at all?

George Sand, probably one of the most famous of early divorced women, tried to answer this in a letter written in 1842:

> Now you ask me if you can be happy through love and marriage. I do not believe that you will be happy through either, I am convinced of it. But if you ask me in what other conditions the happiness of women may be found I should tell you that as I am unable to shatter and remold society entirely, and well knowing that it will last beyond our own short sojourn here in this world, I must place the happiness of women in a future in which I firmly believe, in which we shall go back to better conditions in human life, in the bosom of more enlightened society in which our intentions will be better understood and our dignity better established.

In short, she knows of none.

One final note on this: During an interview, after all the usual stock questions, a newspaper reporter said to a bored Lauren Bacall, "What can I ask you that hasn't been asked?" She immediately replied, "You can ask me to marry you, nobody's asked me that in eighteen months."

But there is a New Woman alone. Usually she is under forty, single or divorced, unhurriedly assessing the values and drawbacks of being single. She is a deliberate person in some ways, moving cautiously into relationships, questioning herself: "Is this what I need?" She is wary of fashioning herself to please the first man who demonstrates interest and affection, because she has done this before and found that attempting to please is no substitute for honesty. But most important, she has built something separate for herself that depends on no man: it may be her work, a life style, her children. In doing this, she risks losing the ability to take a chance on something new. But without it, she risks wandering through youth, middle age, and into old age still looking for a man to add a vital, missing piece of herself. She casts a clear eye on the marriages around her and resists the wishful hope that she too can conform, but more happily than everybody else. If she can find love and growth within marriage, that's what she wants. But if she can't, then so be it. She doesn't like the stereotypes foisted upon her, and tries not to be defensive about them. She is always looking for new ways to build independently. But not by closing off her emotions. She welcomes friends and lovers, but is often glad to see them go home. Yet she continues the most fundamental quest of all, to fulfill the yearning for someone to love truly, deeply, permanently.

A young divorced mother in her twenties said: "I have known a number of men since I've been divorced, and no matter how much I care for them, I would not want to live with any of them all of the time. Right now, I really prefer part-time relationships with men, because I was not happy in a twenty-four-hour-a-day, three-hundred-and-sixty-five-day-a-year marriage. Even though I have a child, I am far happier now. And yet I do need men—one man—to love and be loved by, in a lasting way. I want that."

I have thought often of the woman sitting in her law office who chose to be loved rather than to love, because, she said, it would be less painful. There are no easy answers for women alone. They have no ready security. Their relationships with men as lovers and friends hold no guarantees. But they have a freedom to explore that a married woman does not have, a freedom that could make aloneness more of an experience in living and less of an experience of isolation. It isn't sufficient to seek wholeness through men, it never was, and it never will be for any woman, married or single. The experience of love is far broader and richer, and to miss it is the deepest loss of all. Detachment and apathy are traps, the smallest boxes of life into which we can close ourselves.

What can love be? It can be a frightened woman holding the hand of a friend in the dark; it can be a man and a woman greeting each other as friends in the office for ten years—not acknowledging the depth of their mutual affection, but both knowing it is there all the same. Love in its many varieties can indeed be the key to the resolution of aloneness. And what can marriage be? It can be what I saw symbolized in a marriage ceremony where the man and the woman each held a lighted candle, then together lit a third: two individuals retaining their individualism while joined in one affirmation.

Storm Jameson, a novelist now almost eighty, has offered a lonely assessment of her own life that, I think, could be engraved on a multitude of tombstones: "Always," she wrote, "under different forms, the same failure—to love enough."

8.

Youth and Age

"The young are ignorant and stupid . . . and the old are unfortunate because they're old."

—Marlene Dietrich

In every department store there is a bright pink, perfumed world filled with middle-aged women whose job it is to sell the marvels of chemistry to women who want to be beautiful and young. No woman walks through a cosmetic department without wanting to believe; a child's faith in Santa Claus is nothing compared to a woman's faith in Revlon. I have stood patiently for five minutes listening to a woman whose face glows heavily with Sunburst No. 2 makeup (looking respectably forty-five or fifty), telling me the incredible results Sunburst can produce when applied to aging skin. Somewhere in the conversation she will casually let it drop that she is a grandmother and wait expectantly. I, in turn, will open my eyes wide and say, "Oh, really? I don't believe it; you look too young," when I do believe it, she knows I do, and we both know Sunburst No. 2, No. 3, or No. 4 won't push back the years. So I buy it anyway and we both are satisfied with that bright pink world for a few moments.

I doubt if many women are totally invulnerable to the promises of cosmetics. To be a beautiful woman in our culture is to be young; to be old is ugly. We have made youth and beauty so synonymous that one without the other is simply not presented to our consciousness: observe advertisements, films, television commercials. We see and we believe the chemical miracles touted in the media, then expend our energies in pursuit of a costly illusion that wipes off with cream at night. The process takes longer with each passing year. The vanity of the pursuit becomes transparent, so advocates are marshalled to defend it. Princess Luciana Pignatelli writes a book proudly telling the world she has had cell implants in her breasts, diacutaneous fibrolysis (small hooked instruments are put under the skin to dislodge fatty deposits of cellulite), silicone injections in her cheeks, a nose job, and surgical lifting of the eyelids and would be perfectly willing "to have my bottom lifted" if it would help the total look, because "I would risk taking any possible beauty cure." And then the magazines: a high-fashion model puts lashes in one by one in a tedious hour-long process and the fashion magazines call it the "natural look." And from cosmetics tycoon Charles Revson, this beautiful bit of palaver to make the hunt look like independence: women are divided into "groupies" and "loners," Revson tells us. The groupies are those women "who want that extra cocktail, who fill their afternoons with card playing because men are a very little source of pleasure and satisfaction to them, and who either neglect their appearance or do so much to their looks that they become unreal and overwhelming." The "loner," on the other hand, has "independence that comes from confidence. She does everything she can to attract without being a slave, or hysterical about the way she looks. It takes so little effort for a woman to taste and smell good. And the rewards are so enormous.''

Youth ordinarily ignores age. Old age is something that affects old people, far-away people. But there is a strong fear of it in women whose lives have been built on their beauty. A twenty-three-year old Chicago model who figures she has ''four good years left'' says, ''I like being beautiful. It's my whole life . . . That first wrinkle must be awfully scary. Why do you have to get all wrinkly to die?'' And yet, how much crueler death would seem if we did not physically age.

Most of us find the concept of death easier to accept than old age: we know at any time we can step from a curb and be hit by a truck; we know we can become ill with cancer; we know, in other words, that life is fragile and death can come suddenly. ''It forms part of what is immediately possible for us,'' says Simone de Beauvoir. ''At every period of our lives its threat is there; there are times when we come very close to it and often enough it terrifies us. Yet no one ever becomes old in a single instant.'' Instead, over the years, the lines appear around the eyes, the throat shrivels, the muscles slowly lose elasticity.

To be old. The ultimate nothingness, or so think the young. The magic year for old age is sixty-five, as the magic year for the end of youth is thirty. Women in the years between, the years when life has potential for the most fullness, run fastest after the illusion. These are the years of beauty parlors and lengthy shopping trips: women on a Monday morning in brand-new coats and shoes driving to Bonwit's or Field's to buy more coats, more shoes, keeping up an endless parade as they walk down Michigan Avenue with their packages, spending entire days looking for a dress or a sweater, joined at noon by the thousands of secretaries and clerks who have less time but just as much energy for the same pursuit. In dressing-room conversations, women discuss their figures (''I've *got* to go on a diet''), styles, husbands, parties. The saleswoman in an expensive dress shop

is the headwaiter of the female world—her feet may hurt and
her own dress may not be fashionable, but she can build a tiny
kingdom of loyal customers by building their egos, pouring her
energies into securing a special outfit for a special customer
from under the nose of an equally vigilant rival clerk. What
would the clothing industry do if women ever stopped buying
too much at too great a cost for the privilege of looking young
and beautiful?

And if anyone thinks this pursuit is not deadly serious, consider what a woman will undergo for a face lift. The skin is cut
from the face at the hairline all around the face to the ears, lifted
away from the muscle and blood and tissue like a flap of orange
rind, and pulled up, snipped all around and resewn. It may be
too tight, it may be too loose, the stitches may show; and then
again, after the necessary weeks of recuperation a woman may
look great, perhaps ten years younger, and that's why a plastic
surgeon is able to charge $1,500 for a face lift. Some doctors
perform as many as six of these a day, making half a million
dollars or more a year.

Beauty is big business. But the waste, the loss of self in pursu-
ing it, is not totally a secret from those who try. Not long ago an
old Los Angeles mansion was turned into a "bad-dream house,"
an artistic experiment by twenty-six women artists presenting
images and illusions of female experience. In one tableau, a real
woman sat before a mirrored dressing table in a bedroom me-
thodically applying and removing makeup; over and over again.
Said one of the contributing artists: "Old ladies just stood here
and wept while they watched her."

One factor that operates against the woman alone in the pursuit of youth and beauty is that she does not benefit from the social attitudes that tolerate a certain degenerative process of the
body of a married woman (who, after all, has reached her goal).
A woman who marries reaps babies and stretch marks and
security. Her ruined figure is her badge; she has paid her dues.
The married woman is more likely to spend excessive sums on

maintaining her face than her body, seeking the illusion that promises the most results by demanding the least effort.

The typical divorced or widowed woman must spend her money on the realities of rent, food, and clothes for the children. She is often depressed or resentful that she cannot spend more on herself. The young single woman will spend her money more lavishly than she can afford on cosmetics and clothes because she is still in competition with other women for a husband. If she succeeds in meeting the proper standards of beauty decreed in films, magazines, and on television, she becomes comfortably standardized. But there is a deadening anonymity to manufactured beauty. Try to differentiate among the models in a fashion magazine—with the exception of those few who have put together an individual, sometimes bizarre "look," they all look alike. The mother of the Chicago model proudly keeps a scrapbook of all the newspaper and magazine advertisements her successful daughter has appeared in. And each time the girl visits her mother, she sits down and weeds out half the clippings. They are not of her. Even among "ordinary" women, such is their sameness that as they walk down the streets they blur into one image: their hair is worn in the latest style; if eye makeup is "in," their eyes are made up; if bright lipstick is "out," they all have pale lips.

There has been a great fuss made over the emerging individuality of women because they finally have the nerve to wear their skirts at different lengths rather than according to the directives of fashion designers. But this "liberating" attitude has meant primarily that young women have not given up their miniskirts—a questionable liberation, since they wear them almost as uniforms, a proven part of a package of youth and beauty designed to attract the attention of men. A young woman who evaluates her success as a woman by the amount of attention she attracts from men does not consider physical conformity to one standard ideal of beauty too high a price to pay.

It is interesting that we do not demand such rigid standards of attractiveness in men. A man can be tall and skinny with an angular bony face and be considered good-looking. He can be massively built with a ruddy complexion and attract female attention. He can be sixty with white hair and be admired as "distinguished." The point is, a woman does not judge a man wholly on his physical characteristics even in initial contacts. She notes the way he walks, his confidence, his sense of authority, his interest in her, and it all is taken into consideration. Many times men have said to me incredulously, "I can't figure women out. They will call a man attractive for the darnedest reasons." Men will express surprise because many women are repulsed by the "Muscle Beach" stereotype of the beautiful man or find the perfect V-shaped male body only mildly interesting. But neither they nor the women question the rigid qualifications set for females.

The result of all this has been such an overvaluation of beauty, that young women will eagerly expend energy on improving themselves cosmetically while at the same time ignoring their minds. "Most women, given the choice between unusual intelligence and great beauty, would choose beauty," novelist Una Stannard has observed. Personality, character, and intelligence are willingly sacrificed. Too many women are not mutilated males without penises, but mutilated minds, and this mutilation consists of prefrontal lobotomies that leave them only their faces and bodies. But most don't lament the sacrifice, they value it. The loss to everybody, men and women, is incalculable.

Once a woman marries, if she is lucky or wise she can turn her energies toward enriching her own mind; if she is not, she can settle for old housedresses and bathrobes and occupy herself with toilet-training manuals and visiting with the neighbors while her husband watches television on the weekends. The race is over. In middle age the pursuit of youth may again become important to her; it may in fact become an obsession if she feels the security of her marriage is threatened by the loss of it. But for the woman alone, there are no periods of life when she is able to remove herself from her position in front of the judging stand. The unwritten rule is she is expected to look attractive, and everyone heeds the rule. (I recall one morning talking with Betty Friedan just before she went on a television show, and having her turn to me and say anxiously, "Does my hair look all right? Do you think I have time to put on some lipstick?" I would do the same.)

Most women realize they fall short of perfection and gladly accept whatever help cosmetics can give them, but they also accept as reality the image they see in the bathroom mirror at seven in the morning. But for some women, the born beauties, the mystique *is* the reality. Such a woman would have to be an exceptionally strong person to reject the attractive life offered her, which is filled with so much approval and so many rewards. She lives with a particular isolation from other women, because she is inevitably the object of their jealousy. A young woman whose best friend is very beautiful told me other people have suggested she must be masochistic to be involved in such a friendship.

Because of this isolation from her own sex, a woman whose life will be determined by her beauty is even more likely to want to conform wholly to what is expected of her by men. If she follows a career that trades in beauty, she may become depersonalized: her beauty is a commodity to be bought and sold. She bargains for the basic security of marriage with the same self-interest as she would negotiate a career contract.

It is fashionable now to talk of such women as exploited, but those who are the "exploiters"—the Hugh Hefners, the movie producers, the photographers—often offer what can only be called a fair package deal to those who accept it. Every day, everywhere, there are women who would gladly grace the centerfold of *Playboy* magazine, who would dearly love to be a "sex object." And some make it. Are they oppressed? Beaten down?

Unhappy? Hardly. Consider, for example, the life of this Playmate: "I have never felt so secure in my whole life," she declared. "It was never this good at home."

I will call her Tina. She is twenty-three with long red hair that glows in the sun. She pays fifty dollars a month for the privilege of living at the Playboy Mansion on Dearborn Street in Chicago, a formidable brick structure beyond black iron railings that looks as though it should house the president of a bank rather than Hugh Hefner and his Bunnies. Tourists often linger a moment or two on the sidewalk, peering up at the curtained windows hoping for a glimpse of a Bunny, somebody famous who frequents the mansion, or even the mysterious man who put the entire package together. This is the Playboy world, where life and youth, beauty and love, are imperishable, where age or ugliness does not exist.

It is easy to laugh about Bunnies with their little cotton tails and cantilevered breasts serving drinks to salesmen, but these young women alone are simply following one well-marked route to success. Tina, for example, has put in her apprenticeship, often working long night hours at the Playboy Club, part of the flash, the zip, the pow, the richness of the Playboy world. Sometimes she ends an evening nursing sore feet. But Tina is a Bunny who made good. A year ago she was tapped for the big honor: Playmate.

We met in an office at the Playboy Towers, the busy center of the Playboy financial enterprise, which is populated with former Bunnies and Playmates now working behind desks for the operation that brought them such fame and success. These women, "retired" as early as athletes, wear practical working clothes, their hair carefully arranged and sprayed; still beautiful, members of that rapid, strange world where old age sets in at twenty-eight.

Tina was obviously not one of them.

"It's a funny thing," she said. "You can't request a promotion here, and they never call girls in for interviews, nothing like that. Just one day, all of a sudden, I'm chosen Playmate." Her eyes were wide and pleased at the memory, her favorite spiky lashes almost touching her eyebrows. The lashes mean a great deal to Tina. She was happy with the photographs taken for the centerfold spread ("I knew they would be in good taste—I told myself if I ever do nude work, I'll only do it for *Playboy*") but unhappy when the photographer wouldn't let her wear the eyelashes. "I know the way I look best," she said, just a little upset. But her mood brightened as she told me of being picked as a Jet Bunny, the highest honor of all for the girls at the Playboy world. "Only twelve girls out of a hundred, a couple of hundred, get that," she said proudly. "I got everything: Bunny, Playmate, and Jet Bunny. Most of the girls never get beyond being Bunnies, and they only make one hundred and fifty dollars or sometimes two hundred a week."

But success, so Tina is finding, brings loneliness of a sort. Even in the Playboy Mansion. "I don't have many friends here," she said. "I guess too many girls living together isn't good. I think I could get along with any girl, but sometimes I am nice to them and they say "Hi" and act as if they like me, but as soon as I'm not there, they talk. It's the competition—I'm not competing with them, but they are with me. They are only Bunnies." Tina feels protected at the mansion, and life there has a rhythm, a security that she has come to count on. There is a house mother and the rules are strict: girlfriends can be invited to visit, but not boyfriends. Tina and the other girls often watch movies in the evenings at the mansion, sometimes until three o'clock in the morning, but they can sleep late. They live in a night world where work doesn't begin until six in the evening, and afternoon shopping begins leisurely at two or three o'clock. She and the others chafe a little at their lack of transportation, "We don't have a car to get anywhere, so we are stuck in the house. Just stuck, and some of us, oh, we'd like to go horseback riding or something. Get out of the city once in a while.''

It is, on the whole, a good life. And Tina and her friends could, of course, utilize public transportation or buy a car to do these things if they wanted to. But ''being taken care of'' becomes an easy way to live. Trips on the Playboy jet are frequent, and there is more money coming in now. It won't be too long until Tina can buy herself a mink coat—unless a man does so first, but she isn't counting on that.

Tina is already worried about the day when she may be asked if she would like a job working in the Playboy offices. ''Most of the girls get married or quit before they get too old, but sometimes one will stay on, and they will have to tell her—well, that it's time,'' she said. (A job in the office. The equivalent of a handshake and a gold watch?)

''I don't know how long I'll last,'' she continued. ''Most of the girls here last two or three years, some four years. I don't think they would even care if you were twenty-five or twenty-six, because some girls I know are really taking care of themselves.'' She fingered her long hair, combing it absently. ''How do I know how I'll look two years from now? As long as you look great, nobody worries about your age, and if they told me it was time to quit, I'd accept it. I think maybe, if I can look thirty-five when I'm forty, I won't worry so much about growing old.'' It was hard, looking at Tina, to think of her ever being thirty-five. She believed it even less. To be part of such a mixture of mystique and reality is to be left far from more ordinary shores, and that, as the saying goes, ''is the price you pay.''

I remember a few years ago meeting another Playmate: this time a bright-eyed woman with long brown hair, stepping off a night plane at South Bend, Indiana, to be greeted by three nervous, respectful Notre Dame sophomores, each with a copy of her *Playboy* centerfold in his pocket. She was there on a promotional tour, to be raffled off as a date for a Notre Dame student at the weekend football game.

She seemed unruffled at being the big celebrity, not even appearing to notice the rapid jockeying for position in the car which assured two of the students a place next to her, and left one in the back seat looking aggrieved. I was curious about her, wondering what it was like to walk around a university where all the men knew the size of your breasts, the shape of your buttocks, and the texture of your skin. "It doesn't bother me at all," she told me. "It was an honor to pose for *Playboy*, but I wouldn't do it for anybody else. And anyway, the magazine isn't me."

It certainly wasn't. After the end of that cold weekend, I had respect for her. During the football game a pouring, freezing rain emptied the stands of almost everyone—everyone except a dazzled-looking sophomore and this young woman, who hadn't even brought a pair of boots. At one point, when the rain became unbearable, he turned to her and said, "We'll go; it's getting pretty bad," looking as if somebody had offered him Christmas and then taken it away. She smiled and shook her head. "I'm okay." She was doing the job she had been paid to do. She knew the bargain, and accepted the terms. And I retain a clear image of those two lone figures under a black umbrella, his shoulders straight, hers drooping along with her wet hair as rain dribbled from the edge of the umbrella down her neck.

When does middle age begin? For a woman, it begins when she sees it reflected back to her through other people's actions: when the salesgirl calls her "Ma'am" instead of "Miss," when men no longer turn their heads when she walks by. A married woman moves toward this time at a slower, more measured pace than a woman alone. Her children grow and become teen-agers. She sees the passing of time mirrored in her husband's image; his hair thins as her gums recede, and she at least has the comfort of knowing she is growing older *with* someone else. Middle age for a married woman may actually have its compensations. She can afford a cleaning lady more often now; she has the new freedom of being able to walk out the door, be gone for the day and not feel guilty. Child care is a thing of the past, and financial security may no longer be something in the distant future.

But a single woman reaches her middle years with no such compensatory comforts. Unless she has had an unusual career, her pay has been much lower than that of a man, even doing a comparable job. She hasn't saved as much, planned as well. "Who will take care of me if I am alone?" said one woman now in her mid-forties. Her question frames the painful awareness that begins to haunt the middle-aged woman, the fear of growing old alone, with no one to care, no one to share the uncertainties with her. This is a difficult moment of truth for most women alone. It is not so bleak for a man, because there is a double standard operating in his favor.

A middle-aged man may be divorced or widowed and alone, but he is also at the height of his moneymaking abilities. He can afford to entertain a woman and offer her the particular combination of sex and power that is exclusively male, asking her only to overlook the fact that he is no longer young. Many women are more than willing to make such a minor concession; why should they not be? They need only provide youth and the illusion of love.

As she begins to lose youthful attractiveness, a middle-aged woman may seek to broaden her own bargaining base by becoming a "pal" or a confidante to a young man, and from there, establish a sexual relationship. She usually has no status to offer, no money and no power, but she does have more worldly experience than a twenty-three-year-old man—and the lure of "Mrs. Robinson" is not confined to wishful college students. This is not to say such May-September relationships cannot be both loving and lasting, because they can be and are, more now than ever before, as both men and women question the age taboos that have decreed a woman must be younger than her man. But a woman alone reaching out in this direction risks particular pain. Enter here a middle-aged English professor at a Northwest university, a brilliant and energetic woman I will call Barbara Leary.

We met only once, but had talked on the telephone a number of times first. I had expected to see a larger woman, a physical presence that would match better with the energy and authority of her voice and the impressiveness of her reputation. Instead I was met by a tiny, attractive person dressed in a bright red Mexican skirt. "I've invited over some people for you to meet," she said, with a smile and a forceful handshake. "Everybody's either divorced or single."

We were introduced all around—two middle-aged divorced women, one very thin and striking in purple pants who had just gotten her decree ending a marriage of twenty-three years; an older motherly woman, also recently divorced, sitting next to her protective married daughter; two bachelors; a divorced man. Most of the people present lived in the apartment building with Barbara Leary. She had sought them out and brought them together in an effort to build companionship on the fact that they were all alone. Life styles were an awkward mix, but she made it work with her enthusiasm and interest, an effort that I particularly respected because of what I knew about her life.

Barbara Leary has only recently begun to worry about having social contact with people. For fifteen years her teaching and her writing had been major enthusiasms, and she had felt no emptiness. But she is forty-two now, and not long ago the man with whom she had been living left her for someone else. "I thought I could hang on to him," she said. "But I couldn't. I guess this is one of the reasons why I've lost a little of my self-confidence. I used to feel that I was very talented and attractive, and I had all these attractive boyfriends and I was always able to hang on to them, but I've suddenly lost that ability." She stopped for a moment. It was a hard thing to be so frank. But I had the impression she found it a relief to speak her private thoughts out loud. She continued, "I'm worried now about growing old. You know, I thought that as an academic person I could transcend my culture, but I can't. I'm on the flesh market now. I don't like it but I'm on it. And given the market conditions, men are able to remarry much younger women than they did the first time around but women are not. I worry about my competition and I worry about lines in my face, and things like that. Not a lot, but the fact that I'm concerned about it at all bothers me."

Two years ago she would have challenged any woman who referred to single life as being "on the flesh market." But she is trying to face an uneasy situation as honestly as she can, and repeatedly referred to "market conditions" in our conversations. Barbara Leary feels her university work has put her in a different generation, both because she started back to school late after a divorce and because she identifies naturally with the more flexible attitudes of younger people. "One guy who was interested in me didn't speak to his hippie son because he was too dirty," she said. "That's crazy. I suppose most other women my age have the attitudes of men their age, but I feel much more comfortable with younger people in general—the man I lived with for nine years was much younger than I am." She smiled wistfully. "He was a rare bird. I'm still the most important person in his life, but he's able to get all the women he wants. That's the way the world is. Nothing is more ludicrous, I think, than an older woman forcing her unwanted attention on a younger man. It shouldn't be that way; it's an example of sexism that the situation is not parallel, but that's the way it is."

I wonder, can a man truly understand this very female, very private humiliation? Men have told me they too worry about losing their attractiveness, their sexual prowess, and in one sense I think they risk greater isolation because they often ignore the opportunities in life to be friends with women. But the line of demarcation between youth and middle age is much fuzzier for them than for women—their desperation can be masked, but a middle-aged woman's desperation is there on her face for the world to see. If she is the type of person who has been able to control the direction and events of her life, the desperation can be greater.

To ignore one's age can be to overcome one's fear of the loss of youth, but how, in this culture where the image of woman on every billboard, in every magazine, on every stage and television set is one of unmarred beauty, can this be done? Our cultural attitudes must be revamped to allow confidence and dignity in our transitions from one age to another. Unlike Europeans, we do not recognize mature beauty as something of value. But maybe this will change. A number of women and men have remarked to me at various times that viewing foreign films has helped them rearrange their own concepts of attractiveness and to look at women of different ages with a new eye. Unfortunately, the typical middle-aged American woman is no portrait of serene maturity; hiding herself behind too much makeup and too determinedly youthful clothes, she only looks tense. She is staring at old age, and she is frightened.

I hated the assignment that had brought me one snowy winter afternoon to a festive South Side apartment. I hated it, because the focal point of all the festivity was a tall, quiet woman with white hair who had just turned one hundred years old, and I never know what to say to people who are one hundred years old. Newspapers always like to run stories of such geriatric miracles, but I don't like covering them. The relatives are usually propping up the guest of honor with pillows and false

cheer (having ignored the old person's loneliness every other
day of the year), or treating her like a stuffed doll, yelling
simple-minded assurances in her face about how terrific it is that
she made this great event.

But on this particular day, it was different. I sat next to the
lady with the white hair, asked her a few tentative questions, and
received direct, simple replies. She was not senile. Nor was she
oblivious to the embarrassing hoopla going on around her. A
daughter handed me a family book that recounted this woman's
life, which I found truly engrossing. She had crossed the plains
in a covered wagon with her husband all those many years ago,
had settled in the West, endured the death of her husband, the
deaths of her children, and had then grown old quietly alone.
This day was meant to cap it all: in the kitchen, her grandsons
and nephews were gathered in a genial group drinking Scotch
and water; in the living room, her daughters and granddaughters
and nieces fussed over "Mother," covering her aged shoulders
with a brand-new shawl that looked out of place, non-vintage,
like green wood in an Italian cathedral.

All the usual questions seemed ridiculous when put to those
clear, sad eyes. I tried a new one, actually curious about how
this unordinary person would answer. "What would you like to
do most now?" I asked. She turned, fully facing me, a sliver of
bright light turning her eyes electric for a second. "I would like
to die," she said.

For a moment, there wasn't a word in the room. Not a sound.
She had spoken so clearly, and her voice had carried to every
wall. All I could do was look in those eyes and silently acknowledge the sensibility of her reply. Then every relative in the
room rushed forward with a babble of comforting words, and
our connection was lost. The lady with the white hair turned
away, her face still, and focused her eyes on some point above
the heads of everyone in the room, oblivious to the clatter she

had aroused by stating her desire to be released from the isolation of a life that had lasted too long.

At least she was able to state her preference.

The first time I stepped into the geriatric ward of the Norman
Beatty State Mental Hospital in northern Indiana I was overwhelmed by the stench of urine. Women sat in wrinkled white
gowns, some with their bodies only partially covered, their eyes
dead. Attendants rushed around with bed pans, everywhere the
smell of urine mixing with that of medicines and aging human
flesh. This is one reality of old age, the most unacceptable, most
unbelievable of all. I am convinced if there is an indictment of
our way of life, it is surely the way we treat our old people. How
stupid we are. We are only assuring similar treatment for ourselves.

That day at Beatty Hospital I remember most vividly a tiny
figure in a steel crib set apart from all the blank-faced women in
chairs. I walked over and saw a shriveled woman lying in fetal
position, the skin drawn as tight over her bones as that of a
mummy in a museum. I wondered for a moment if she was dead,
but then as I leaned over her crib she let out a terrible guttural
scream, never opening her eyes, producing a sound of such force
that I jumped back, frightened. One of the attendants stepped
forward and said, "Don't mind her. She does that every five
minutes or so." And she did. For an hour I was in that ward, and
every five minutes I braced for that terrible scream, the last in-
dication of life from a body already deteriorating. It was like a
final protest in the midst of the final indignity. Isn't it enough
that our bodies rot in the ground? Why is it that we must endure
rotting before we die?

These, of course, are examples of the end of life. But between
Barbara Leary and the old woman in her crib are many thou-

sands of women alone living within the years we define as belonging to old age. In this country, we say old age begins at sixty-five. That is when we observe the barbaric ritual of retirement for men. The arrival of old age is not so institutionalized for women; unfortunately, it is presumed to have taken place much earlier.

For most women alone in their fifties, old age has been decreed. If a woman looks attractive at this time of her life, we call her "handsome" when we are kind, "well preserved" when we are frank. She cannot enjoy Freud's fiction of being in maturity "the adored wife." She is caught in the irrational conflict of attitudes about her shadowy status, and is neither allowed to be considered attractive and female nor allowed to grow old "gracefully," as we like to describe it. If she works diligently to remain attractive, she is trying too hard to be young. If she gives the struggle up, she is letting herself go. She can escape the conflicting pressures by being very successful, very matter-of-fact, i.e., not very "feminine." If her work is indeed a substantial part of her personality, she is a lucky person. But she is in the minority.

Much as it might surprise the young, most aging women alone still see themselves as both sensual and sexual. Old age is not a giant leap; it is a series of small steps that connect us with our past and our future, lived day by day, an enormous passage of time only when viewed in retrospect. But a woman who shows too obviously the desire to remain attractive is viewed with disfavor. Both men and women laugh at old women in flamboyant out-of-date clothes who dye their hair yellow and wear bright red rouge on their dry cheeks. We dislike the fact they presume the right to still compete, because they no longer present the only acceptable qualification, and that is youth. Again, if they were married, our irritation would not be as great. I don't know why, but that is how it seems to me.

The result of all this is that we deprive ourselves of learning from older women, because we deny the value of their experience. An older man, being presumed to have accumulated knowledge during his working career, may be sought out for his wisdom. But an older woman who has spent years on a pension and before that, years in a factory or an office or as a housewife? Hardly. In my interviews with many of these women, they showed amazement that I was interested at all, that anyone would be interested. They have accepted as fact the image of themselves as tedious, unnecessary human beings who won't be around much longer anyway: even those who were once feted as beautiful, desirable women. They are perhaps especially alone.

One evening I sat down on an old wicker sofa with a little woman in her late sixties who had once been a Ziegfeld Follies showgirl. I was the only visitor Linda Lee Fentyn had had in a long time. She was at first a little defensive. "Were you expecting a raving beauty?" she said with a bright smile. "That's all gone now." It took some urging on my part, but finally, half reluctant, half excited, she brought out a thick batch of old photos and clippings in a standard dime-store binder. For three hours we went through that book, starting with the early photos of a pretty blonde with wide, startled eyes, dressed in dark satin, large red satin flowers pinned to her shoulder. "My sister did a fast job when we came over from England," she explained. "They gave me a Dutch bob and fixed my blond hair. I had such mousy-colored hair, but my sister renewed me, you might say. She made me a picture of something. I was so pleased, because my grandmother had always said I was too ugly for the theater."

Linda Lee Fentyn was fourteen when her sister first took her to Ziegfeld, and it is apparent in her early photos how fresh and young she was, qualities that must have appealed to the showman. "They called me the baby of the Ziegfeld Follies," she laughed. She remembers those years as the happiest of her life. "It was so natural to be on the stage. I knew just how to make it all work—I used to pick out one person in the tenth to fourteenth row back, and I would give that one person all that I had. I would think, 'I am going to charm *you*.' '' Linda Lee Fentyn glowed, remembering, and it was such a jumble of image and time, watching and listening to this woman in her print housedress and white bobby socks talk about the stage. She still talks with an English accent (which she thinks is gone), an unaffected accent, with a lisp caused by two slightly crooked front teeth. Ziegfeld had wanted to have those teeth pulled, she told me, but she refused and likes to think now that but for that, she could have had a longer and brighter career on the stage.

We looked through all the publicity photos of those brief years, pausing at one in which she wore a long white wedding gown and veil, a beautiful picture that didn't look posed at all. ''It wasn't like that,'' she said sadly. ''When I did get married, it was just a little runaway marriage; you reach a certain age, and your body starts talking.'' She left the stage after her marriage and had a baby, embarking on a long line of rough years with an unemployed husband, trying to earn a living for her family by working in a machine shop, wishing she could enjoy once again the excitement of the stage. ''If I had only saved my money and gone on,'' she said. ''But you need clothes, you need to keep attractive, you have to pay an agent whatever he wants . . . And to tell the truth, I was afraid to go back again. To use the common word, I didn't have the guts.''

At one point I asked if she had ever loved someone else after her marriage and she blushed, then got up to hunt busily for something she told me would probably answer my question. It was a cartoon of a little man with palpitating hearts drawn around him, and under it was written, ''Gosh, Lin Fentyn is a dandy girl!'' The cartoon had been ripped into pieces and then carefully glued together on a piece of cardboard. I recognized the work—it was that of a cartoonist well known in the twenties and thirties. ''He came up to me in a restaurant and drew this and gave it to me,'' she explained. ''I tore it up right there, and said it wasn't him at all. But it haunted me for years.'' She added proudly, ''He had a crush on me, I know. I kept the pieces, as you can see, and I've kept it all this time.'' She took the treasured bit of cardboard and carefully replaced it in a box she kept behind her books in the bookcase. It wasn't much as illusions go perhaps, but it had sustained her for many years, a symbol of what could have been, a reminder of youth and beauty long gone, of the bright life that had once been hers.

We are very selective in our memories, and what would we be without them? They give us a sense of ourselves we can believe in privately, with no one harmed if we color the truth. For Linda Lee Fentyn, the realities she remembers are harsh enough. And the realities of being alone and sixty-six are to be dealt with now. ''I wonder, how am I going to go?'' she said to me later in the evening, just before I left, musing, not despondent, but wondering. ''I am worrying about it a little bit lately. Will I go fast? Or will I have pain?''

As we slowly turned the pages of her book, she pointed proudly to the press clippings, her name carefully underlined in each one (''Appearing in the show was a charming little comedienne down in the program as Miss Linda Lee Fentyn, who is given not nearly enough to do''), and described for me minutely the colors and fabrics of clothes she had worn forty years before (''I'll always remember that dear little green velvet; it had gold braid woven in the sleeves'').

Near the end of the binder of clippings was a photo of two middle-aged women sitting in a restaurant. They were both facing the camera, grinning and holding aloft steins of beer in mock salute to the photographer. They looked like women who had worked hard, factory women, their hands roughened, their faces ruddy. ''Who are these two people?'' I asked. She put a finger on the figure at the right of the photo. ''That's me,'' she said. We both sat through a moment of confused silence. I hadn't recognized a photo looking almost exactly like the woman sitting next to me. For three hours I had been with her back in the illusions and realities of another time.

I told Linda Lee Fentyn how much I had enjoyed our visit; I told her it had been a privilege. She smiled and told me she had not shown her clippings to anyone else in twenty-five years. "I probably won't again, I suppose," she said. We closed the book.

The experience of aging for women alone is as varied as the women are themselves. For example, women closely bound in an ethnic neighborhood are spared much of the isolation. Their husbands may die, but their families are geographically close and they are part of a unit, not cast adrift. I recall the comfortable sense of community I observed on a special Polish holiday in South Bend, Indiana, a day known in town as "Dyngus Day." All through the West Side there was dancing and drinking and picnicking, and men and women and children of all ages gathered together in the halls for the celebration. Old women alone mingled together or with the young, obviously part of the group, not separated; they danced sometimes with each other, sometimes with their sons or grandsons. They were not set up at a widows' table.

For some women, particularly widows, church activities become a focal point of interest and a source of companionship. Catholics, with a less gregarious custom of socializing, are not so lucky. But for most widows, those without close family ties or without the comfort of church contacts, the ability to find a niche in society after the death of their husbands is severely restricted. Sometimes an older woman's health is uncertain; perhaps she cannot take long hours standing behind a sales counter or waiting on tables, two occupations open to women without training. They retreat into their age, and no one much cares.

Professional women nearing retirement age face the same

uncertainties and fears involved with the loss of a lifetime's pattern of work that are faced by men. A professional woman on the East Coast made perhaps one of the hardest adjustments for an aging person to make: she deliberately perceived the end of her usefulness and made the break by herself. "I think the critical point for me came about five years ago," she said. "One of the men in our organization who really should have retired decided to hang on for one more year. Everybody agonized over it. You know, we can't turn him out to pasture, and all that stuff. So the day we decided, okay, we'll humor him for a year, I was driving home and I said out loud, 'By God, that's not going to happen to me. I'm going to pick the date of my retirement, I'm going to announce it and I'm going to fix it so I can't change my mind later.' " She did. It wasn't easy. "I wanted to retire while I was making the decisions, and I wanted to retire while I was on top," she explained. That, as many men know, is one of the hardest things in life to do. It takes a type of courage, a flexibility that many aging people do not have.

Are there ways to assure oneself of retaining qualities that can make old age something reached and entered with one's head up? I think so, because of people like the woman above, who perceived reality as it would be and acted on that perception.

If only young women could develop a similar clarity about their lives. I am not profoundly impressed by the young women who declare, "I never intend to get married, and if I do, it'll be a long time from now." I would like to be impressed, but I don't see them deciding what else they might do. They are satisfied with the enjoyment of their youth and see their freedom as being part of their youth. What happens when it is gone? If I ask, most of them shrug and dismiss the possibilities. They do not expect to be old.

There have been recent experiments in pretesting one's ability to adapt to age that are intriguing: young people were put in accelerated work environments that would handicap them in the same way that old people—who characteristically become slow—are handicapped in normal environments. The subjects were given work tasks to accomplish in a given period of time; these tasks were repeated, each time with a faster tempo required. The researchers found that most of the subjects responded in ways commonly associated with the aged: some became anxious and fumbling, others just gave up, and most settled on one routine—one rigid strategy they refused to change, even when it didn't work. As the time pressures increased, only a few of the young people tried shortcuts or learned from their mistakes. It appears, concluded researcher Robert Kastenbaum, that "some of the psychological changes that eventually become conspicuous in the aged actually begin years ahead of time, when a person is considered young and flexible."

If the patterns of adapting to age are set early in life, it would seem the young might well view aging as more than a process of hardening arteries and withering skin; it would seem women alone who fear aging might better concern themselves with the loss of imagination and flexibility, with the loss of vision in adapting to the future that would sacrifice the joys of being human and alive in the futile pursuit of the unsalvageable pleasures of youth and beauty. Women alone need to pull themselves away from their mirrors, whatever their ages, and face down the cultural attitudes that decree old age at fifty-five and a rest home at seventy. No one will do it for them.

9.

Power and Powerlessness

It was Easter Sunday, a dull, cold day. Looking out the window, I watched my younger children hunting for their Easter eggs in the back yard. Monica was running around the yard, spotting the bright-colored eggs one right after another, dumping them into her basket and yelling happily. Maureen, her arms swinging aimlessly, her smile self-conscious, was wandering around, looking—but not really looking.

"Maureen," I wanted to call out, "you are right next to the eggs. You are almost staring at them!" But she had her thoughts scattered across the yard, her eyes watching a self-confident Monica yelling, "Here's another one! And another!" At one point Maureen came to the woodpile, which hid half a dozen eggs, and stared right past them. She glanced down into her almost empty basket, then over to her sister running with one piled high, and began to wander anxiously to another spot.

I watched my child and wanted to help her, but there was no way. The eggs were there. Maureen was next to them. And all

187

she had to do was *believe* she could find them and she would see them. How simple. How frightening.

Is this where it all begins? None of us, men, women, or children, can accomplish unless we believe in ourselves. But mustn't there be something before believing, something that gives reason for it, that convinces us we are worth believing in? Isn't there a key or a lever to break through the lack of self-confidence which produces patterns of uncertainty that particularly affect the lives of women?

I knew I could help Maureen break through her sense of inadequacy, her powerlessness. Why had it been so hard for me to do it for myself? Because at no point could I go back and change the social structures that decree from childhood that men will have the social approval and self-confidence that gives them the power to direct their own lives and the lives of others, a power that is not accessible to women. I couldn't go back and change the fact that when I climbed a tree as a child and tumbled out, I got a lecture on being more careful; for the boys on my block, a fall meant mothers shaking their heads and saying, "Boys will be boys." The boys moved toward self-confidence by developing agility in climbing those trees, even though they fell out of a few. They took risks. I played mostly with my dolls, building childhood worlds of interpersonal relationships of the kind so familiar to women, so alien to men.

And that is how we grow, men and women. In maturity, a woman takes on the identity of her husband and builds her social relationships around his life. It can be a comfortable existence. The woman who becomes president of the League of Women Voters need not spend much time thinking she was elected because of her husband's political connections; the woman appointed to a mental health board doesn't have to dwell on the fact she was chosen because her husband's name would add prestige to the organization's letterhead. She can be and often is a competent person with talent and ambition, but the fact is she has access to power and prestige simply because she married well.

Women do not have power to change society. They may exert great influence over the men who do, but they do not order the armies to war. They build different power bases, in the home, on a personal level. The word "power" is strangely charged when discussed in connection with women; it is an essentially masculine word and most women do not feel comfortable using it—partly because they do not have access to it, partly because they either do not understand the concept or distort it on the interpersonal level.

I think it is particularly crucial for women alone to undertand and learn how to use power. It is part of the circle of believing and accomplishing, part of the process that can give a woman on her own the ability to decide her own destiny—the ultimate use of power. Women alone should at least have the power to set their own life styles in terms of who they are, to choose what their relationships and opportunities will be rather than being told what they will be.

Partly, that means finding ways of exerting power to change existing structures that discriminate against women. But only a few people can have the opportunity to do this. How do you direct a frightened widow, a woman on welfare, or a divorced mother with little money to go out and fight a war against social attitudes without a weapon?

This is a simple point that escapes those who would be the movers and shakers. "Women are forever bitching about not having any chances," declared a single, successful businesswoman impatiently. "But it's never good, constructive bitching. They become their own worst enemies when they fuss over everything instead of figuring out a situation and doing something about it." It is true that many women left alone without even elementary control over their lives—they cannot afford to keep their homes, they cannot find decent jobs, they cannot freely choose their friends—will sink into total help-lessness.

"No health, no money, kicked out into the streets without a dime to my name," cried one woman. "Now I'm supposed to be a man and support two children after slaving and taking all kinds of abuse and everything else from a man, an animal! What can I do? Where can I go? I was forty-seven years old last November, and I don't have love or faith or anything left, and nobody, nobody cares."

Sometimes women will react with bravado or defiance, par-ticularly if they have been left suddenly alone by divorce or death, but it is usually a sudden flare and then confusion. "I felt like I hated the world and I could use my fists on it if I had to," a middle-aged widow told me. "But then I just stayed home and cried."

For most women alone, finding the power to control their own lives won't come from shaking their fists. Nor will it come from wishful dreams of being elected to the state legislature and putting together a coalition to change, say, discriminatory em-ployment laws. They need instead to change their relationship to society, to recognize the options that singleness can pro-vide, to set out to change what they can change—be it where they live, who they know, or how they equip themselves for work. There are some women who are exerting power over their lives, and yet they don't see it in terms of exerting power—again, because of this very alien word. These women are more likely to describe what they are doing in terms of how they feel. "There is something inside you that is nudging you, and then you look back on it and realize it has become a pat-tern," said a divorced woman with two children. After years of clinging to a marriage without love or stability because she was afraid to be alone, she finally got a divorce, moved to a strange city, and began her own business. At first the guilt and regret and uncertainty pressed down hard. "But finally I realized I could do things in my own way," she said eagerly. "I finally realized I didn't need somebody else's approval for everything I did. Then I was okay."

Believing in oneself does not come effortlessly for anyone, but how much harder it is for women who are alone without support structures, who never learned to feel good about themselves if they took chances, and how much easier for men equipped with education or training, who can bluff their way as they collect more experience, more understanding, gaining confidence as time goes by. Women left suddenly alone must take a giant leap to a larger world, without the series of small steps that build self-confidence.

Inevitably perhaps, they make many mistakes in trying to tackle the intimidating world. For one thing, they take too literally the promises of achievement if they play by the rules. I have met many women who decided the answer to all their problems was to go back to college and get a degree—and then found they had bought a symbol of status and power, but not the reality.

"I was a good student," said a divorced woman bitterly. "I studied, I did everything I was supposed to do and I got good grades and I graduated, and I was not able—not able at all—to get a good job." Women who go back to school invest time and money they cannot always afford, faithfully conforming, reaching for this route to freedom without understanding how the system can do them in. Many find they are not considered serious students, nor are they given intelligent counseling. They find out, often too late, that winning doesn't mean being a nice little girl; winning means testing the limits, pushing. It means challenging, not just working harder than anyone else.

In my own life, it meant getting a degree in journalism—not striving for a Phi Beta Kappa key in English. When I went back to school, even though I had no concept of power, even though I had no clear idea of how I intended to get from where I was to where I wanted to be, at least I knew I had to have a goal to be taken seriously. I do not mean that women in English are necessarily making a mistake—what I do mean is that too many women choose a traditional female field because they can't think of anything else; they choose it not because they wish to teach but because they like to read novels.

Women are often intimidated by employment directors, college professors, landlords, social workers, all the people who are in positions to exert control over them. They smile and acquiesce instead of challenge and question. (Why do women smile so much more than men? Why, even in business situations, are their smiles so often stiff and constant?) In order to have a comfortable self-image, they set out to please—and in so doing, they avoid taking chances that might elicit disapproval. But so long as women who must take control of their own lives don't take chances—in the sense of doing something on their own, that they have both decided upon and carried through—they lose the opportunity to break into the circle of believing and accomplishing. If they cannot exert power over their lives, how can they expect to accomplish anything? They are merely reinforcing society's expectations for them, and they are bound as tightly as Gulliver by all the fragile Lilliputian threads that together produce immobility.

Women who must strike out on their own often undervalue themselves monetarily—and in our culture, that is a sure way of decreasing one's worth. A woman goes out to apply for a job and timidly accepts the first thing offered, at the lowest pay. I recall when I first began working, I was offered a job as a reporter at $105 a week—this was in 1966, and most other beginning reporters at the paper made more than that, as I later realized. But at the time, thrilled that anyone would even *want* to hire me, I accepted, voice shaking, fearful the personnel director would change his mind. I at least got the job I wanted; I did not have to search the want ads looking for "no experience required," as so many women alone must do. But it is not just the beginners or the women left stranded without training or education who undervalue themselves in this way.

Recently a personnel director told me of a woman who had applied for a position as head of a particular division in his company at a salary of $15,000 a year. After her first interview, there was a corporate decision to divide the top job into two jobs. The woman, who was considered highly qualified, came in for a second interview.

"I offered her half the job at a lower salary, and told her it would be on a one-year, renewable basis," he said. "She sat there, nodded, and never asked why. She accepted the job without a question. The thing that bothered me was, if she had been a man, I would have been challenged. And I expected to be challenged. A man would have said, 'Why less money?' And he would certainly have asked, 'Why the one-year contract?' " He shook his head. "Women are like that," he said.

It is true that women often want the chance to prove their abilities so much that they will accept inferior positions or inadequate pay in order to have that chance. But it is also true that women often do not fundamentally believe in their own abilities. They expect failure. "I'll never be able to handle the clerical work, I just know I won't," an older widow said after starting a new job with an insurance company. "I'm not smart enough."

The reverse side of this is the woman with a keen appreciation of her intelligence but who has been trained from childhood to underplay her abilities. She may have a good job, but she fears exercising authority because that means public demonstration of her ability, and that makes her a "castrating bitch." Perhaps this is why women in America not only fear success, but that the fear increases with their ability. And the greater the fear, the less well they do in competition with men—a classic Catch-22 for women. I have sometimes thought back to my own education and been grateful for the convent-school environment. It gave us a chance to use our minds and to compete freely, because we were not in competition with boys. Of course, sometimes the boys we dated realized this, although we usually managed to hide it. And, I find, so did other people at other places. "I always resented Radcliffe girls," a man once told me. "They had a sense of knowing too much—they used to analyze a movie after a date and drive me crazy, particularly if I hadn't thought of it from whatever angle they did."

Perhaps the most damaging mistakes women have made in their attempts to exert power have been in personal relationships. Women traditionally have been manipulators, not of systems, but of people, and their manipulation has given us the sad-humorous image of the henpecked husband. Domineering wives concentrate most of their energies on establishing a pattern of ascendancy, a pattern that leaves a man quietly behind his newspaper at home and freed only at work. They handle the money, rear the children, make the decisions and their word is law. They "rule the roost." And sometimes their sons grow to manhood fearing or resenting women in a vague way they cannot articulate, the result of which is another generation of men dedicated to keeping women down outside the home. Often the domineering mother is a frustrated woman who, helpless to channel her energies into expanding her own life, settles for controlling the lives of her children. And she can leave her husband and sons frustrated too, because she doesn't play by male rules of the power game. Does it seem so strange, then, that many men view their mothers with ambivalence or even active dislike? When such a man marries, his wife may acquiesce to the absurdity of pretending to be the child, easily done in a culture that assumes the daughter-in-law should take over the responsibility of family communication. The letter from daughter-in-law to mother-in-law goes something like this: "Dear Mom, everybody here is fine and Joe says hi. He's pretty busy lately and hasn't had time to write . . ." But of course it isn't a matter of having "time." We always manage to find time for people we love and respect. The truth is, a son has been lost, and a daughter-in-law's correspondence has been gained.

Women are rarely able to exert social power directly, although I can think of one example: the women members of a Santa Fe, New Mexico, commune who became angry with the men and walked out, taking all the goats and effectively destroying the commune. But usually women have forced change through manipulation, traditionally through sex. The women of Greece in Aristophanes' *Lysistrata* provided perhaps the first case of this on record—and certainly the most direct—by denying sexual favors to their men until they agreed to stop waging war. Through history, the courtesans of kings and statesmen built themselves formidable personal bases of power. They did not issue the commands, but they could persuade the man in power to do so. Or, like Mata Hari, they could coax from a man what they wanted to know. A woman's using sex as manipulative power is not only tolerated but often enjoyed by men because it comes wrapped in a velvet glove of feminine wiles. Bonnie Swearingen, wife of the president of Standard Oil of Indiana, is a frank advocate of pussy cat techniques: "It takes a strong woman to make her man think she's weak," she has declared. "In the Orient, where a man has many wives, the favorite is always soft and feminine, but still very powerful. We can learn from the geishas and the wives in a sheik's harem."

Some young single women I have talked with frankly admitted they were interested in capitalizing on their sexual attractiveness because of what the "right man" can do for them. "I want money to travel, a house in the country, and lots of status," said a typist. "And the only way I'll get it all is to marry it." For these women, marriage is not so much an expectation as it is calculation, again an acceptable manipulative use of sex.

This single woman has another perspective: "It's very sexy being a woman lawyer, I find," she said. "And I'm sure a lot of other women lawyers find that true, too. There are men around you all the time, always being very nice and respectful of what you have to say and appreciative of your femininity, but not in a demeaning way.'' She added, ''One way I have of suppressing my anger is, I cry. Don't take this too seriously, but it works fine in court. I don't usually use it, but I also cry when I can't help it. When I'm very angry and I can't do anything else.''

A woman who ''uses'' her tears is justifiably criticized if she is trying to melt the opposition, unfairly using her sex to her advantage. Although it is true that men unfairly use male attributes to take advantage of women, this is not nearly so stigmatized. A very simple example comes to mind: in a press conference a male reporter will sometimes take advantage of his louder, more commanding voice and cut off a woman in mid-sentence in order to gain the floor. And yet women do find it difficult to control their tears in stressful situations, because they feel helpless or immediately interpret criticism as an accusation of inferiority. I recall one day when the city editor criticized me roundly (and justly) for an approach I had used in writing a story, I had a difficult time keeping from crying. I forced myself to rewrite the story and deliver it to the city desk, then walked to the women's restroom where I finally shed a few tears. But not many.

Women who take their work seriously resist this temptation to self-indulgence, not only because they are aware it reinforces a stereotype but because they realize it keeps them from being considered reliable and valued as competent. This is very important to a woman alone who cannot rely on someone else to be the breadwinner should she get laid off or passed over for promotion. ''I can't afford to play female games,'' said a middle-aged divorced mother of three working as a secretary. ''These young girls can throw crying fits or moan about their menstrual cramps, but I cannot afford the luxury.''

In addition, most single, widowed, and divorced women do not enjoy the luxury of manipulative power over men. They have no men. Their concerns are strictly practical, with lack of money usually in the forefront. "Men think they get taken by a divorce? Well, let them come and see me," said one embittered woman. "I don't even feel like living any more, because me and the children just can't exist on one hundred and sixty dollars a month. I'm in debt up to my head and I will be buried with it."

For a man earning an ordinary income, there is no possible way to split the family into two parts without hardship on both sides. Most divisions please nobody. A typical divorce settlement means straining the husband's income to an unendurable state—and yet the wife has no extra money to allow for teen-age sons eating more than daughters or to buy corrective shoes for a child who needs them. The money she gets is arbitrarily set and usually inflexible, as arbitrarily set and inflexible as it is for the welfare mother who is supposed to buy a child's winter coat for four dollars. Without sufficient money these women cannot freely choose a neighborhood, or even maintain the standard of living they enjoyed before their divorce.

It is not just the lack of money that impedes women alone, it is the *fear* of the lack of money. "Nothing is coming in from anywhere else for me, just what I produce myself," said author Marya Mannes. "I worry about when I won't be able to work. Will I have enough?" Most women alone worry about being sick and without money, even the young women, because they cannot conceive of a worse state of helplessness. The basic fear is they will lose dignity. I have talked with women living alone, sick and old, who have existed on minimal amounts of food for weeks because they were too proud to ask for help; not only that, they were often confused as to how to go about getting help. Often it was a neighbor who finally called the hospital, the newspaper, or the public aid department.

Job requirements present another barrier to dignified self-sufficiency for an older woman suddenly divorced or widowed who has no professional training or education. Even is she is personable and "gets along well with people" (the usual requirement listed in the advertisements for receptionist jobs) she has neither youth nor beauty to offer and is quickly passed over by a personnel director.

The inadequacy of child-care help can be an enormous problem. Women alone with children almost always have nightmare stories to swap with each other about trying to work and at the same time provide decent care for their children. I came home one day from school and found that the baby sitter had walked out, leaving my children alone, huddled and frightened in a corner. No amount of money a mother can pay is insurance against this type of incident, because there are no qualifications, no licensing, no way to guarantee that someone you hire to care for your children in your home will do so properly. I do think that if we truly valued our children in this obsessively child-oriented society, we would officially recognize the fact that 50 percent of all mothers work and that they must be assured of decent, dependable care for their children.

But perhaps the most formidable barriers to women alone gaining power over how they live their lives are psychological, and the worst of these is the inarticulateness that frustrates and impedes accomplishment. Women often have a serious inability to present themselves clearly, confidently. So many puzzled women have said to me, "Why can I talk so easily right now? As soon as I try standing up for my rights at work I stumble all over myself."

Psychologist Erik H. Erikson has seen this as clearly as anybody. "It still seems to be amazingly hard for many women to say clearly what they feel most deeply, and to find the right words for what to them is most acute and actual, without saying too much or too little and without saying it with defiance or apology," he writes. "Some women who observe and think vividly and deeply do not seem to have the courage of their native intelligence, as if they were somehow afraid on some final confrontation to be found to have no 'real' intelligence.'' I recently reread that passage in *Identity, Youth and Crisis*, finding I had underlined it so heavily in black ink that I obliterated some of the words. When I first read it I had wanted to cry, because it was personally so true. I wonder now only that Erikson observed this with such surprise.

Is it so hard to understand? Women have spent their lifetimes acquiescing to a man's presumed prerogative of not only making decisions, but also of setting the tone of a marriage, a friendship, or a business relationship. They adjust as easily as chameleons and have lost the ability to speak for themselves in any significant way. Ironically, many of them conform to the stereotype of the chattering woman who exists, in the thousands, in the millions. I have listened to these women in restrooms on their coffee breaks, overhearing variations on their basic monologue: "And *I* said to her, look—and then *she* said to me, and *I* said to her—" But this nonending substitute for conversation is not an exchange of ideas, it is an exchange of complaints, of gossip, of domestic minutiae, and bears little relation to speech as the expression of larger worlds of work and ideas.

I sometimes have felt painfully inarticulate in work situations, usually when they are of particular importance to me. One day I went into my editor's office with an idea for a story, first carefully preparing what I wanted to say, defensive about how good it might be and afraid he would think it was terrible. In the midst of our understandably stilted conversation a male reporter strolled in, greeted the editor, and casually talked about a project that interested him, throwing in a request for time off. The two men, both outwardly relaxed and easy, negotiated a bit and settled the problem within a few moments. I sat there, my speech out the window, envious and frustrated, wondering why that type of encounter came so easily for the man and so hard for me.

David Riesman has suggested that a basic problem for working women is they do not know how to make use of the informal structure that men use in the process of advancing their careers.

Women are not and never will be casual members of the un-
definable but always present male circle, whether in the office,
the city room, the factory, or the university, which is why, if they
want to achieve, they must work twice as hard as their male
counterparts. Men no longer believe in Horatio Alger, but it
seems many women do, and they have forgotten he was a man.

Because women alone are dropouts from society of sorts, they
tend to overconform in order to be accepted. But precisely because there are so few options open to them, they have the
chance to make their own. They do not have to build friendships
and life patterns around a husband's life. They do not have to ask
for anyone's permission to, for example, move to the city, where
being alone is not considered unusual or strange. They can go
out and find supportive people and build supportive relationships, even build a community of their own. (In a sense, I am
part of a community of two in the city room, sharing and gaining
self-confidence with another woman reporter.) They can form
organizations of widows or divorced women and shape them to
be what they want them to be—not settle for groups of lonely
women consoling each other. They can form and join summer
communes where women and men alone can share with each
other what they wish of their lives. They can choose jobs, not for
security, but for challenge and supportive atmosphere.
Women alone could learn a valuable lesson from the ghetto
women who spend lifetimes managing large units of people in
chaotic situations. Some of them have raised families of brothers and sisters from the time when they were barely past childhood themselves, then had their own babies as teen-agers, and
were deserted while still in their twenties—and they held it
all together. The ghetto of course isn't Hollywood, and nobody
walks off into the sunset, victorious, after conquering insurmountable odds. The usual story is a life alternating between

fierce fighting and lassitude, a downward spiral accompanied by the slow deadening of emotions that comes with poverty. Yet the women who have put their energies into the organizations designed to pressure the system into legislating welfare reform are experiencing what power can mean. They are not buying the image of themselves as dregs of society; they are not accepting this psychological barrier. Because they are not accepting it, they see the social absurdities more clearly. "Everybody's hipped up about being taxpayers," one welfare mother observed. "I'd really dig it, if I didn't pay taxes too, on everything I buy. There's no such thing as a non-taxpayer in this country."

Women alone will sometimes deny the need to exercise power over their own lives, because they fear they will be considered too aggressive. They fear they will be passed over by an interested man if they appear too self-sufficient, too competent, or even too happy with themselves. "I am a female, feminine thing," one woman has proclaimed, "only one of thousands in the female silent majority who adore being protected, loved, cuddled, and spoiled by the master of the house." Most women alone would choke a little on that statement, but still they carefully step aside for men and let them take care of the details of life. They want them to make the dinner reservations, open the door, or hail the cab. More important, they step aside in discussions or disagreements on the job even if they believe strongly in their own position, rather than risk disapproval or dislike.

Ralph Nader was once asked what type of person functions best in his consumer protection investigations. He answered that the one absolutely necessary trait is "not wanting to be loved." Unfortunately, most women want to be loved more than they want anything else—including respect.

Our social structures are so weighted against their performing with full competence in their jobs that it is not surprising few women have social power. (Many women are in positions of authority, but that is not the same thing.) But is it more power that women need, that any of us need in this way, in this world? To be powerful is to be disliked, sometimes hated. Our image of the powerful man is the ruthless man; our image of the powerful woman is the emasculating bitch. Power can be corruption and war; pleasure for a few and misery for others. "The only difference between women and men," Gloria Steinem has said, "is that women have not yet been corrupted by power." For men and women to face off against each other in a struggle for power to direct *each other's* destinies is not to solve any of our existing problems. It is instead a sure way to increase tension and hostility. There are middle grounds; we only have to agree what they are.

10.

Beyond the Cardboard City

It was a beautiful spring morning. I awoke before the alarm went off and lay in bed a few moments longer, listening to the street sounds outside the window, looking around the narrow confines of my room. I had then lived at the McCormick Y for almost six months, a good, peaceful, exploring six months. But suddenly I felt restricted, restive, ready to move on. I decided that morning it was time to leave the Y. For months I had felt the decision to leave would come quickly when it came, and so it did.

I checked the morning paper for apartment rentals, circled two or three, and went to see one that afternoon. It was a small place, decorated by a bachelor teacher with things like a hanging fishnet and wine bottles with candle drippings; but there was a rough brick wall and a Franklin stove. I liked it. I had been apprehensive coming up the dingy, dark stairway of the second-floor walkup, which was over a storefront building in Lincoln Park. My apprehension must have shown because later he told me, "The day you came up those stairs, I figured you would never take the place. You looked too timid for this neighborhood."

I was, of course. And that is why I wanted to live there. But it was a struggle. Before signing a sublease, I told the teacher I wanted to walk around the block and think it over. Actually, I wanted to worry a little longer about the crime rate and duck into the corner drugstore to phone and check out another apartment. I put my dime in the phone, and started hunting in my purse for the number. Then I stopped, hung the phone up, and thought, don't be a fool. It was time for this move; I was ready. I went back to the apartment and rented it immediately.

The move to Lincoln Park was my last in the experience of living alone, and in some ways the best. I was not fifteen stories from the ground in a high-rise building, nor was I encased in a fortress; I was living for the first time close to the cement of the city.

One of my neighbors, a social worker, told me cheerfully one evening that there had been a few burglaries and assaults within the building in the previous year. "It's not so bad now," she said. "The landlord finally put better locks on the doors, but people are always forgetting to close the one leading to the street." She shrugged with the air of bravado city people adopt, and I allowed myself to be worried without dissolving in panic. But when I walked back into my apartment I inspected the fire escape outside the window, and hammered in two nails above the half-opened window so it could not go any higher. And then I slept soundly.

I was learning how to be alone without fear, that familiar fear I had lived with most of my adult life as a housewife and that had kept me huddled sleepless in a chair with a butcher knife all night in a house alone only a few years before. Most housewives I know have a deep fear of being alone at night. They speak of prowlers and rapists and worry about inadequate locks and open windows, all in suburbs where the crime rate is negligible. Then their husbands come back from their business trips and they feel secure again.

I do not mean to imply I had suddenly become very brave and self-sufficient because I was living alone. But what I was learning were the differences between handling the physical realities of being a woman alone in the city and handling the emotional fantasies of being a housewife alone in a house with four children. I had grown to adulthood in a state of constant and automatic dependency. Even in the years when I returned to school and began working, my total reliance upon my husband continued, a situation not at all uncommon among married women. A woman who has learned she can lean on someone else does not easily develop emotional independence, the kind of independence that can make possible a mutual exchange of affection and need—not a constant dumping of one's helplessness on someone else's shoulders. Her inability to feel self-sufficient in this way leaves her vulnerable to fantasies of disaster, fantasies that married women don't like to talk about too much, but which keep them awake at night all the same.

The woman who comes home every night alone to an empty city apartment cannot afford to see shadows in every corner. There is no husband to disperse those shadows if she allows them to overwhelm her; she must muster her own strengths to deal with reality. And reality is the issue. Who kills the spiders when a woman lives alone? Who takes the garbage out on a dark night, puts the car in the garage, or hunts for an absent building superintendent when all the lights go out? These are the realities that, once faced and dealt with, could never feed my fantasies again. Learning to feel in control of the physical realities of life also helped me understand, for example, the enormous relief and sense of achievement a divorced mother feels when she no longer collapses helplessly at the prospect of unclogging a drain or fixing a fan belt—little things that seem trivial but loom before most women like insurmountable barriers. Women who have told me of their success in overcoming these barriers exude a new confidence, and this in turn makes it easier for them to look ahead to the big problems, easier to transmit to their children an aura of self-reliance that will make them more confident. And most of all, easier to put their aloneness in perspective as part of their lives—not an engulfing, consuming thing that will destroy them.

I walked around Lincoln Park many evenings that summer. It was a vital, interesting place to be, and I enjoyed for the first time the variety of a city neighborhood where you can eat a Japanese dinner, buy a purse at an Indian import shop, and finish off the evening with a Baskin-Robbins ice cream cone, all within one or two blocks of where you live. I found this part of the city a comfortable place, a place where violence and crime were not really on my doorstep every moment. The potential was there; I was aware of it, and I was reasonably careful. I did what anyone else alone living in the city must do, and that is, took my precautions and then accepted and enjoyed where I was.

It was a summer for reflection. Originally the decision to leave my family had been with a question mark on the timing of my return; the decision never had been intended as permanent. And yet I knew almost from the beginning I could never live in South Bend again. I enjoyed my work in Chicago and felt a part of that city in a way I had not felt part of a place since my marriage, and one of the things I wanted in my life now was a chance to choose where I would live. I could never again try to be the biblical Ruth, following unquestioningly in her husband's footsteps.

The summer before, my husband and I had tentatively planned to move to a suburb between Chicago and South Bend, even going so far as to negotiate for renting a home. One day we visited the suburb. The children ran around the house, excited, exploring; the couple who owned the house were genial and smiling, the house beautiful, the neighborhood perfect. And I was miserable. Frightened, panicked in a way I could not understand or explain. I felt something precious would slip away if I lost the privacy of living alone at that point. And so we did not move. The children began another year of school in South Bend, and I moved to the YWCA.

I am not quite sure just when I knew I was ready to end my life alone. My husband and I had agreed during the spring, before I moved to Lincoln Park, to schedule a change by fall. But it was an arbitrary decision made more with our minds than our hearts. It was a decision that meant another experiment—this time, we would move as a family to Evanston, a town just north of Chicago, and he would commute to South Bend. At times I worried that if I went back prematurely I would lose the value of an experience not yet totally finished, not yet totally understood. During that summer in Lincoln Park, though, I felt increasingly sure it was time to take another chance. I knew I would never be totally ready. I would probably always reserve a part of me privately now, almost jealously, because it was so newly discovered and valued. I knew then, and I know now, I will always want a separateness, a psychic "room of my own," a freedom that is perhaps too much for an enduring relationship within a marriage that has already borne such heavy strain.

No decision could be perfect. But I realized also that being alone just for the sake of being alone was no longer necessary. I had learned something of the limitations of life alone—both for myself and for the many women I had met. Alone or with someone, we all build in patterns and limitations to our lives, and there is no way of living that is "free" by definition, with vast, wide-open horizons. When I first went to Chicago, I anticipated opportunities to make choices on my own for the first time in my life without consulting or deferring to anyone. I had these op-

portunities. What I did with them had permanent effects on my
life. Yet I was not doing all the things I had once yearned to
have the freedom to do. I did not go to the symphony in the
evenings; instead, tired, I would have a drink with friends in a
bar or go home to read. I did not visit all the exciting places and
meet all the exciting people; I did not take an excursion boat out
onto Lake Michigan on a summer night, as I always intended to
do. I had developed habits and timetables as restrictive as the
ones that had held me as a housewife at home—not the same
ones, to be sure—but habits and timetables all the same.

I was beginning to understand the siren call of "what might
have been" that tempts so many women and men. It allows people to ignore walls they have built around themselves and en-
courages them to blame their inability to break free on something, someone, anything else but themselves. At first this was
depressing; then exhilarating, because what it meant for me was
a reconception of aloneness. I began to see that I could take
aloneness as solitude, as self-communion, with me wherever I
went, however I lived. I had not found definitive answers for the
problems of my life, but I had found a way to know myself. I
knew now I had inside me the energy, the discipline, and the
motivation to continually challenge the arbitrary restrictions im-
posed by society. This was a key to freedom that no one could
ever take away—because I controlled it. It didn't matter if I was
alone or not any more. What mattered and would always matter
was resisting the temptation to settle for less than I wanted to be.

It had been almost two years since I left my family in South
Bend. Major changes had taken place in my attitudes toward my
children, other women, men, and myself.

I longed for my daughters. I wanted again to kiss them good-
night every night, see them off to school in the morning, and
show them I would love them always. I no longer felt the world
had passed me by while I stood and folded diapers; I no longer

resented being a mother or suffered from guilt for feeling that resentment. I wanted the children to be part of my daily life, and I wanted to be part of theirs.

In those months away, their perceptions of me and of themselves had changed. Much of this was inward; deeply thoughtful, sometimes positive, sometimes troubled. I had expected and was ready to deal with these changes. One positive example: Margaret, always a loving and generous child, had moved subtly from being a little girl to being a sister-mother to the younger children. She would scold and console, generating warmth that touched and benefited us all.

What bothered me were the uncertainties other people generated. For example, the subtle attempts to erode what was not understood by neighbors who would wonder aloud, "You *poor* children. How can you stand having your mother gone so long?" What hurt was a short note written by a concerned second-grade teacher: "Maureen is doing beautifully, but I think she misses her mother very much."

And yet I also saw my daughters consciously expanding their ideas of who they were and who they could be. I have since realized it wasn't all bad for them to sense my uncertainty, my search for focus and direction. They felt more free to ask me questions about what I felt and thought, and shared willingly with me their views on our unusual life as a family. In the process, these four young girls grew in a way that makes me proud. Not in my way—but with new ideas, new plans.

Someone has said that we consider our children successes if they perpetuate our own neuroses, if we have instilled in them the same worries and fears, the same self-doubts and limitations. We may want to reject such an assessment, but I think there is truth in it. When I was a child, if I had ever announced I wanted to be President of the United States someday, my parents would have laughed indulgently, patted my head, and told me to go play with my dolls. (I don't fault them for that—they could transmit to me only what they perceived to be reality.) When my eldest daughter Marianna announced this same intention a few months ago at the dinner table, she was serious—and so was I upon hearing it. Both Marianna and Margaret have grown with clear images of themselves as young women, unrestricted images that allow for more in their lives than dolls and early marriage. They will of course accumulate their own problems, but narrow vision of what they can do and what they can be won't be among them. I feel partially responsible for that.

One evening recently I was talking with Marianna about this, and told her I wanted to discuss it in my book. "If you're going to say I want to be President, Mother, you'd better also say I want to get my nose fixed," she said. "Because I still have ambivalent feelings—I want to become famous and powerful in politics, but I also wish I was beautiful." It was so familiar: the pull between achievement and the wish to conform to what a woman is ideally supposed to be. I doubt if it will be resolved in my generation or hers—but at least the dilemma is identified.

As for my attitudes toward other women, the change can be stated simply: a joining of experience. I have had the privilege and good fortune to meet many women whom I otherwise would never have known; and I have spent hundreds of hours listening, realizing how most of my life I have not listened—only talked. We all do it; we stand and hear words only, not absorbing what they mean, not caring to, waiting for a break so that we can toss words out at other people, strangers whom we want to think well of us. A cocktail party, I believe, is one of the loneliest places in the world.

The realizations which strike us most deeply, most profoundly, are usually simple. For me, the realization that many women feel the same emotions at the same times, only from different perspectives, was of this category. The old women, the young, the ones living in expensive high-rise apartments, the women who would feel rich if they could only pay the rent on time. And the lonely ones: the young unmarried mother who held her baby long enough to name it Alisa ("That's Welsh for 'fair of skin,' " she told me), and then walked out of the hospital without her child, telling no one; the prostitute who advertised for friends, received a dozen replies, and happily told me she was inviting every one of them to a party; the old woman on welfare who bought a book at the grocery store entitled *Women of Courage* and read it and reread it, gaining comfort from reading about Susan B. Anthony and Jane Addams. "*I* never had any courage at all," she said sadly.

I have seen what being young and alone can be like; I have shared the memories and fears of the aged. In one way or another, I have been drawn into the lives of all these women alone, hardly as an objective reporter, but then objectivity—as any reporter knows—isn't an ultimate criterion for understanding.

And men? They look more vulnerable to me now, and I like them better. I used to demand that they always appear to be strong, without realizing I was doing this. Absurd as it may sound, I feel more aware of their humanity, not as people who are stronger, wiser, and more powerful than myself, but as people who, like women, have been bent to the restrictive roles society demands of them. In other words, men are not enemies. They are common sufferers, and the fact many of them don't realize that yet is an educational problem.

Not too long ago, on my way to work, I idly watched a well-dressed young businessman boarding the train. His briefcase was expensive, his expression firm, his movements sure—the standard successful young man. Then he tripped. He had just greeted someone apparently from his company, all poise and self-assuredness, and his embarrassment was obvious. Ordinarily I would have felt a remote kind of irritation with him for breaking his image so awkwardly. I would have felt like laughing. Why? Because he had an image to live up to and had failed to do so. Instead I felt sympathy, knowing how embarrassed I would feel—have felt—in a similar situation.

Again looking in retrospect, I think I can see how I have changed. My restlessness has eased, although what may be a permanent conflict remains between my desire for freedom and my need for security. But I feel better about myself now. For years I drifted, cut off from the only concept of morality that had been familiar to me. I could not please other people first and please myself last. I could not whisper to a priest in a confessional that I was "heartily sorry" for offending God with my sins unless, first of all, sin offended me. And finally, slowly, I think I have found a deeper and more personal understanding of my own moral sense—this is mine, carefully and painfully reached, and it depends on no one else's affirmation or interpretation. And because of that, I will have it always.

On September 1, 1971, we moved from South Bend to Evanston. The children said good-bye to all their friends and their home, not without tears. "You'll love Evanston," I assured them, assuring myself I would make it so, but feeling uncertain. This was more than taking responsibility for myself. This was taking responsibility for a move that would affect the future of all of us. It was taking responsibility for the inconvenience to my husband, who would spend the next year commuting three days a week to the University of Notre Dame. Who did I think I was? But don't husbands do that all the time?

I felt overwhelmed by the packing details, so overwhelmed I just shoved clothes and belongings into boxes at the last minute, much to the irritation of the friends who helped us move. When we drove away from the house, I never looked back. Somewhere out on the toll road, I began to feel relieved and heartened. I had not solved the dilemmas for my family; I had merely resolved them, but I was finally convinced this uprooting was not wrong. For my husband and myself, it was another risk. But I had now the chance to pull together the elements of love, freedom, and responsibility in my life in a way never possible before.

This book began with a dream. I remember that dream mostly for the deep sense of desolation and loneliness that descended on me when I found it ended at a city made only of cardboard, a city reached with a crowd of people who knew and cared nothing about what was happening to me and about whom I knew and cared nothing. I dreamed that dream at a point in my life of impending loss, when I knew I could no longer live through the Catholic Church or through a man, when neither any longer had the power or responsibility to tell me who I was or what I could or should do.

What, then, is the cardboard city? I see it now as a jumble of self-deceptions. It is the loneliness or disillusionment at the end of false hope or unrealistic expectations; illusion instead of reality. It is what we all march toward when we are unable to make contact with each other, when we can't make what we have work or grow, when we cannot even find a way to try. It is the pursuit of happiness and not self-knowledge.

The cardboard city can appear to be a place of freedom, as it did to me in the dream. I was lost and totally self-absorbed, and I wanted the comfort of predictable solutions. Most of us hope at one time or another for what was symbolized in that dream by the sunlight and the gaiety of the Ferris wheel, the sense of being children, of waking from a bad dream to a good world. But Ferris wheels with streamers are only for children, not for us. To go on, we must give them up.

I realized this last summer on a grassy bluff above Lake Michigan where I had joined friends for an outdoor celebration of the Mass. The altar was a card table; a nun with an orange bow in her hair sat cross-legged in the grass, strumming a guitar. How different this was from the churches and cathedrals I had knelt in each Sunday for so many years. No incense, no vestments; just a sunburned priest in casual clothes, myself and my children, and a dozen friends. They take it so easily, I thought, this incredible change in the Mass.

Marianna, my eldest daughter, was offered the chalice of Communion wafers to pass among the group, and she solemnly offered one to me. It had been eight years since I received Communion. I thought, "Why not?" I no longer believed I was so evil. I took the wafer and remembered the reading from Hebrews, particularly the line: "They did not obtain what had been promised, but saw and saluted it from afar." Then I drank from a silver chalice, the first time I had ever taken Communion wine. No one did that eight years ago in the Roman church. And I felt an overwhelming, final sadness, because I did see something and it was too late to do anything but salute it. From afar.

There is a strong temptation to stay in one place and flail our lives away, to become so absorbed in personal pain or anger that everything else fades in comparison. I have met many women who are unable or unwilling to move on alone. We are all incomplete people, and I have not forgotten for a moment that men march in tunnels too. But women are far behind men in realizing that the only true progress is that achieved by self-reliance. Single or married, a woman must be able to stand alone.

Women fail to move on in a variety of ways; for example, they will join a consciousness-raising group but, instead of making it a forum for individual realistic efforts to break patterns that impede their lives, they allow it to deteriorate into just a new stage for old complaints. "I have become so depressed with some of the women," a divorced woman told me, after quitting in frustration a group she had sought out for help. "Each meeting came to sound like the one before, always the same anger, the same complaints. Last time I said to them, 'Let's quit this; let's *do* something, and quit talking about how rotten we have been treated by men.' And they were angry—at me." Her voice took on an edge of bewilderment. "Somehow I'm supposed to be selling out, and I don't see it that way. I think they are selling themselves short, and they don't even realize it.''

A consciousness-raising group is valuable to women just learning to understand who and where they are. Not only does it give comfort, it breaks through the traditional barriers that isolate women from other women. But those women who simply wrap themselves in isolation once again as part of an angry little group that doesn't want to hear or do anything that might dilute their anger are also part of a tragedy. They are afraid, still uncertain of how to go about actually changing their lives after defining the problems. This makes them little different from the ''totally unliberated'' women who are too timid to take the chances that could mean widening the scope of their lives. Rejecting whatever hopes or ideas that might take her too far from familiar moorings, a widow will cling to her children or the family home; a divorced woman will work as a file clerk and complain bitterly about her wasted life with the wrong man; a single middle-aged woman will pass up a chance at a better job because she doesn't want to risk her pension. Take a chance? ''I can't,'' they reply, each one echoing the other, and not even knowing it.

''Trying to change a woman's long ingrained self-image,'' wrote one woman wryly, ''is like telling a three-year-old dog she is really a cat.'' But psychic confusion or not, a woman left suddenly alone has to see herself differently—everyone else does. If she insists on sticking with only the familiar, she will harvest only the familiar. If she accepts her status as a nonentity affirmed by a society that doesn't know where to fit her in, she will be a nonentity. There are no slogans or groups or friends that can make the transition any easier, a fact which women find particularly hard to face. Elizabeth Cady Stanton, weakened by old age after years of proud and militant feminism, warned women in 1892: ''We may have many friends, love, kindness, sympathy and charity to smooth our pathway in everyday life, but in the tragedies and triumphs of human experience each mortal stands alone.'' For a woman alone, accepting this fundamental fact of life is of itself a significant triumph. But still there must be more.

A man can choose to avoid certain hard realities of singleness. He may fear being alone when he is old, but he can take comfort for many years in the mystique of bachelorhood that puts him high on the list of most wanted guests at a dinner party. An unattached male is desirable by definition unless he is both illiterate and eats off the floor. Any morning he can look at himself in the mirror and, if he chooses, see reflected a dashing man-about-town—whether it is true or not. (I recall a long-ago song sung by a male chorus about the joys of singleness: "I've got spurs that jingle, jangle, jingle . . . and they say, oh, ain't you glad you're single . . . and that song ain't so very far from wrong . . ." There's more, all about Lulu Belle and Mary Ann and others, but most women wouldn't be interested.)

Even temporary refuge in such a comforting mystique is not available to a woman alone. Whatever her age, she is on a search for something better than she has, something more complete than she is. If her hopes are illusionary rather than realistic, she may wander all her life. "I want to find someone better than I am in every way, someone wise and large," said a single woman wistfully, voicing an almost universal yearning of women alone.

Someone wise and large. How to find him? (And women do mean "him.") Search frantically through a series of loveless sexual relationships as one would search through a stack of file cards? Sit and while away the years waiting for the perfect man to come along? Decry the callousness of this world of pairs we live in and retreat? Or perhaps—as rarely happens—look for that "someone wise and large" within oneself?

The results of the search in this last direction are unpredictable. How do women learn to trust and take comfort in their own sense and sensibility? There are no guideposts. They only know when they get to where they want to be. "I've learned," a divorced woman told me triumphantly. "I can sit home alone and be happy with myself now on a Saturday night. I can read a book, have a drink alone, and live inside my own skin. I've found real security, and I can't imagine being a Mrs. Somebody giving me security I can't provide myself ever again."

On the other hand, there is a woman I shall call Viola, a woman who pursues wisdom at a run, eagerly reaching out for it through new experiences. At twenty-one she was married to a drug addict; at twenty-three, she is one of William Bolitho's most determined adventuresses. Viola is everybody's lost child, and she can still proudly say, "There is something in me that can't be put down."

"I was a prostitute," Viola told me. "I was stoned all the time, but I had to pretend like I wasn't, otherwise I wouldn't be asked back. The men were mostly rich and we got fifty dollars for ten minutes." She paused and added, "I didn't really enjoy it very much, but I needed money."

"My life sordid?" she said in answer to a question at one point. "I don't know what the word means. Jaded? Scummy? I don't think so. Everything I've done has been for reasons that were pure, I thought. I wanted to find out what life is all about, to experience a lot of things, so it would make me wiser."

I looked at this earnest woman, her owlish eyes. "Wiser?" I asked. She leaned forward. "I've always been trying to acquire wisdom," she said. And then, with a shrug: "Whatever that is."

To be wise. Is that to understand oneself? Or to clearly view the world outside? For some women, it is simply to view oneself with dignity, to live prudently in a small private place. I remember a woman whom I met one lonely night years ago in Oregon while I was out selling cosmetics as an Avon lady. Divorced and in her early fifties, she lived with a teen-age daughter in a small, somewhat dilapidated apartment on the less affluent fringes of town. She invited me in when I delivered her order, something few people ever did. And for a special hour I was privileged to

visit with a truly curious and interested person eager to meet
new people, to discuss new ideas. Her daughter had the same
gift.

In the strange way coincidence works, some three or four
years after that time we moved to an apartment and found this
woman had also moved and now lived above us with her
daughter. I will call her Harriet Stone. She was a bank clerk, but
that was only how she earned the money to pay the bills. She was
a painter. All through her apartment hung the results of years of
painstaking work—each oil or pastel was intricate, carefully
planned and executed. We formed the habit of running up
periodically to view her progress and offer praise, which she
delighted in receiving. One day I found Harriet in her bathrobe,
depressed, unhappy. She looked at an unfinished painting and
said, "I'm no good, you know. I have no talent. How I wish I
did." I protested, but she was weary and sad. Her daughter was
going to be married and would soon leave for a state thousands
of miles away. The companionship of the two women, mother
and daughter, had a beauty and a dignity that I find difficult to
describe. And now it was to be lost to her. Harriet was a timid
woman. She never attempted to sell or show her paintings. She
had gained solace from the presence of her daughter during
some fifteen years alone, solace that made it possible to have a
special self—an artistic self—away from the anxieties of pleas-
ing a bank supervisor who didn't have much patience with older
women.

"I have no talent," she said. Of course she had talent, but I
was too inarticulate to tell her what it was. Was she a good painter?
I don't know. I only know I have a pastel she did of Marianna
when she was in kindergarten, a drawing that was strangely
unlike my daughter at the time, but which Harriet did with patience and care. I pulled it out of a box only recently, wrinkled,
never framed, and there was my burgeoning young child-
woman. As she is now.

Sometimes for a woman alone, to be wise means simply to endure. An old-fashioned word, "endurance." It means living within the confines of one's life as well as one can, going from day to day, buoyed by the knowledge of one's responsibility to a person, a job, or to one's own philosophy and ideals. It is this last that sustains women like Sister Barbara Jean, principal of a Catholic grade school in a changing West Side Chicago neighborhood.

A cordial, plump woman wearing a short blue veil and a business suit, Sister opened the school door after I had knocked repeatedly. She was apologetic. "I'm sorry," she said. "We keep all the doors locked because we've had so much vandalism, and I'm afraid the bell isn't working." We went into her office, a large barren room with whistling steam pipes. Sister Barbara Jean was nervous and sat very straight, her hands folded. Behind her, over her desk, was a sign that read, "Every human relationship is an eternal responsibility."

We talked about the changing character of the school. A school administrator for over twenty-five years, Sister Barbara Jean is worried because the rules don't seem to work very well any more. The transition is hard, and it means learning new ways to deal with angry parents, uninterested children. "But I'm still the authoritarian here, and they're still afraid of me," she said with some pride, drawing up even straighter. (It struck me how the new habits take away dignity from an older woman. Knees, roughened and chapped from kneeling, are exposed for all the world to see. Loafers and snagged stockings rather than black laced shoes. Woman instead of nun.)

Sister Barbara Jean is tired, and knows her authority is eroding. The children yell back more defiantly than they used to, and the sense of community in the neighborhood is tenuous. "People won't come out for meetings or school open house after dark any more," she said. She wishes her order would give her a transfer. "It's time for something different, but I don't think they want to transfer me." Sometimes in her mind there is a larger, wordless question, but she has a firm answer for herself. "There are other things a woman can do today, and sometimes I wonder. But I've been living this life for so long, it would be very difficult to change."

She doesn't mix with the other nuns in the convent too much. She is their superior, and total relaxation after work is not always easy because a distance must be maintained. I had the impression of a very conscientious but lonely woman sitting across from me, who is fully aware that endurance may be the one virtue she needs to keep on in work that is increasingly confusing, uncertain, unrewarding.

In the middle of our conversation, a nun rushed through the door. There was a problem in the lunchroom. Sister stood up to go, looking very tired. "I've been doing this too long," she said abruptly. We shook hands and I followed her out into the hall. With each step away she looked a little more vigorous, and I had a sudden memory of a long ago similar indomitable figure. ("The *principal* is coming!" we would whisper, and the classroom would subside in awe.) No more, I thought. Things are different. But the principal is still trying.

For over a year and a half, I have been talking with and thinking about the problems of women alone. To say attitudinal and institutionalized prejudices against them should be changed is akin to saying it would be a good idea to eliminate poverty, war, and unhappiness and then everybody would love one another—true perhaps, but unrealistic. Attitudes toward singleness *should* change, and I think they will do so slowly, as marriage becomes less of a universally perceived goal.

But in the interim, I offer these few observations: Why can't job training for a woman be included automatically as part of a divorce settlement? This would ease her past her initial fear and helplessness so she needn't flounder at facing her first job application. In conjunction with this, why couldn't there be employment and counseling services geared to the needs of women alone? Such agencies could offer a mother information and access to jobs that are available on a part-time basis or point her in the direction of companies that offer day-care services; the same guidance would be available to the widowed older woman whose timidity keeps her from knowing there are jobs that could make use of skills she doesn't realize she has. Also, there are organized groups for widows and for unwed mothers; why not decompression groups for divorced women? "Some women need the protection of a temporary one-sex world," Caroline Bird has said. "Women can learn from each other many things that can't be learned in a dating factory." Such groups would be temporary, designed only to help women through the jarring transition of divorce.

Expansion of the social world for women alone is badly needed, and that means something more than Parents Without Parners and dating bars; it means perhaps experimenting with the cooperative living patterns used in Sweden, where people alone join together in apartment buildings, sharing meals and baby sitting and developing living patterns that do not isolate them one from another. There must be societal recognition of the awful loneliness of people who are alone, particularly the old. A Chicago woman saw this as a base for a new service industry: she began a telephone calling service to check up on the aged for their children, to remind people of appointments or to take medicines, and just to say good morning or good night. Churches could provide much more help to single people than they do now. The first church for unmarried people was opened recently in Orange, California. "Traditionally, churches don't know what to do with singles and remarried people," the pastor said. "The person who needs help comes away feeling like an outcast and often leaves the church altogether."

Federal and state programs that utilize older people are also needed, similar, for example, to the federal Foster Grandparents program, which hires men and women of retirement age to work in institutions with the sick, the retarded and the handicapped. They are not volunteers; they have both the dignity of a paycheck and the knowledge they fill an authentic need. I stood at the doorway of such a day-care center with a supervisor one afternoon, watching an old woman talking with a four-year-old child, both earnest and absorbed, sitting together on the edge of a cot. The supervisor nodded in their direction and said, ''They need each other. Could anyone doubt it?''

And finally, if there is one attitude that women alone urgently need to change within themselves, it is their presumption they will marry and stay married. Women should plan from youth as if they might never marry; they should see this not as a bleak fate but as an expansion of possibilities that opens worlds, not closes them. If indeed maturity can be measured by the degree to which one attempts to perceive reality (a definition that appeals to me), then most women who stay deliberately blind to the possible prospects of divorce or widowhood have not yet moved out of their cradles.

We have lived now for one year in Evanston. I have not regretted the move or yearned for a life alone; I have rather found substance and deep pleasure for the first time in my adult life in the plainness of everyday living and sharing within a family. I now value croquet on the lawn, chasing the ice cream man, neighborhood softball games and candlelit dinners with the children, sitting with a book, reading during a storm while they play beside me.

But when that long-ago train pulled out of South Bend for Chicago, the things that began and ended did not begin and end only for me. They began and ended also for the man who turned back into the station alone, my husband John. We have grown differently, perhaps too differently. Even though two people may try hard for a blend of mutual love and independence, they may not manage to find the right balance.

Sometimes I wish I could go back and change some of the things that happened, but I know, given the opportunity, I would not change the fact that I had to learn to stand alone, to take risks and make decisions, in order ever to be truly free. I don't think other women should necessarily try it my way, but I do think they must try—and I believe there are as many hopeful ways as there are people with the courage to search.

What I would hope for now, what I think I now have and can hold, is what Abigail McCarthy so beautifully described in a short epilogue to her book: "a sense of the past, its continuity in the present, and a sense of identity stemming from the past which enables each one of us to withstand the assault of change." I would only add, an understanding and acceptance of the pain of that past and an eagerness for the future, even if it means going on alone from here.

That, to me, is what moving beyond the city of cardboard is all about.

Voices: An Epilogue

Many of the women I interviewed spoke eloquently and revealingly of what life alone has meant for them. In this section, some of them speak for themselves.

Most of these interviews are edited from tapes of two- to four-hour conversations with each woman. They are not included to prove any particular point; I chose them simply as random, dissimilar examples of the individual experience of being alone.

Some of the women are identified by their real names: Helen Hayes, of course, and also Helen Sewell, Martha Stewart and Peggy Terry. The others, real women all, preferred pseudonyms.

Martha Stewart

I'll never forget Sally's face when I told her her father and I were getting a divorce. Anybody who says it wasn't hard for them to announce a divorce to their children isn't admitting the truth. It was very difficult for her and her brother, partly because they sensed the disapproval of other people. Somehow their mother was suddenly a woman somewhat strange and slightly off-color. It seems to me that it is more immoral to stay married to someone you don't really feel good about. To go to bed with that man is immoral. Many a woman does, because she is trying to maintain a family for her children. But the children know it. It's very hard to be saying one thing and feeling another without children being aware of what's happening.

I was married in 1952 and we separated about ten years later. I'm awfully glad we didn't have children for the first four years, because that's when I started to work. It gave me confidence, something that lasted through the years when I had babies. I got into public relations work for a television station, and I was able to arrange it so I could work the hours I wanted to work. It was a very lucky job with much responsibility that helped me later when I went to New York.

I was afraid, terrified, really, when it looked like we were heading for divorce. We were driving each other nuts, two people growing in different ways. I have trouble ending almost any relationship, even a conversation. Two hours at the end of a party, and we're down to the last minute, and I just have to say one more thing. That's the way it was, and it was particularly hard on people who didn't know what to make of the ambiguity of it all. You're expected to do what is thought to be right in St. Louis, Missouri, whatever might be right for you.

Friends weren't much help. I wasn't an individual in most people's eyes when I went through that divorce. To them, I was Martha rejecting her husband, even though many of them were living with men they were not happy with, but they had decided to continue for one reason or another. It was, "I've decided I can do it, so why can't you?" That game. And the rumors that began circulating. When our friends got a hint of trouble coming, they

began passing this big rumor around that I was having an affair
with a doctor in town. A friend of mine who had been divorced
herself told me how it went around. She was at an investment
group meeting one night, and a girl came in and said, "Guess
what? Martha's having an affair." Everyone talked about it for
the whole meeting, dissecting my marriage, my personality and
speculating on what came next. At the end of the evening, the
girl who had walked in the door with the juicy rumor had second
thoughts. "I think I was wrong," she told the people there. "I
guess it isn't Martha—it's the girl who lives next-door to her who
is having the affair."

This kind of thing made me feel very lonely. I felt so fragile,
like an open, walking sore. Before we finally decided on the
divorce, we separated and my husband moved to a nearby town.
This was when we were thinking it over, but people couldn't accept the fact that we were trying to decide carefully on whether
or not we should get a divorce. At parties they would come up
and say, "Oh, you two haven't found a house in Akron yet, have
you?" That's the fiction they built to explain why I was still in St.
Louis and he was gone. I remember one dear friend who cut a
conversation on that line short and said, "Oh, just be glad she's
here and don't look for reasons." Then he pulled me away from
the group. He understood.

The problem is, people who don't have many choices in life
don't want you to have any choices either. They feel if they can't
have options, why should you? Particularly women. My pending
divorce just brought into their consciousness something they
didn't want to be conscious about. I wasn't an individual to
them, because they weren't individuals to themselves. All
women are the same.

After the divorce, I took my two children and moved to New
York. I didn't have any contacts, but I had this tremendous confidence I could eventually get into my own communications
business. I was lucky. The World Fair was here, and I knew I

could get into something connected with that, because I had worked on expositions quite a lot. There were gobs of interesting jobs connected with these expositions. One I worked on in Oklahoma City became kind of famous, because it actually made money, which is unusual for fairs. People were nice to me and things just moved. It was scary but I was deep into the "I can do it" sort of thing, and I wanted to make it in New York. Partly because I knew it would be a city where a divorcee wouldn't be something odd.

In this city, I can choose to be alone where before I didn't have any choice. Rejecting a marriage is a very scary thing and very lonely. I think divorce is a growing-up process for many people. Seriously. It certainly was for me. What should have happened when I was an adolescent happened after I got married. We married young, and in a sense we used each other, no doubt about it. And I felt so lonely afterwards—no husband, and no support from people who understood. I'm very lucky to be in this city, where everybody is perfectly able to cope with me walking in at a party alone. It's not a place where everyone is expected to pair off. For instance, New Year's Eve is a time to be concerned for your friends when you live in New York. A bachelor friend of mine called last week and said, "Martha, you just absolutely have to come to the commune for New Year's Eve. You just cannot stay in New York." People just sort of take care of each other in that way here. But I didn't need to go—I would rather be alone in my apartment, which I really like, than I would in a sort of make-shifty thing where people are trying to be happy or, you know, not really enjoying each other. On New Year's Eve, you really have to be with someone you like a lot or forget it.

I should explain about the commune. It hasn't been too meaningful for me personally, but it has been for my children. A group of men and women with children who are widowed or divorced got together and took this house on Long Island, mainly for summers and weekends. Most of us lead unusual lives, and aren't home a lot. So it's been a nice thing for my children to be with the children of other people who lead unusual lives. For example, my daughter and Betty Friedan's daughter loved each other right away because their mothers were such anomalies, even in New York City. A little bit different from most people's mothers.

Children get a little jealous if they know you are wildly committed to something. They have to somehow figure out where they fit in. They don't want to be different, and they don't want their parents to be different. They want their mother to do all the ordinary things other mothers do, like fixing peanut butter and jelly sandwiches and complaining about dirty floors. And they want their fathers coming home after work, taking their shoes off and reading the paper. So it's hard if things aren't that way. My children are learning. Sometimes I feel just really great and I'll start to sing, and my son will say, "Mama, I think adults who can't be different and express themselves just haven't grown up." That's important to me. His best friend's parents are divorced and I'm sure it's an unspoken bond between them. A lot of kids' parents are divorced in New York and it's not such a big thing, but I know he feels a little more support because of that friendship.

My children and I really have a very lovely time together and do very lovely things, but for me as an adult woman, that's not enough. The loneliest thing is going to bed by myself. Making love is just the nicest kind of communication that you can have, a woman with a man. There are some things that simply don't happen without another person, without someone to love. It's terrible not to share things, and it's terrible not to be making love all the time, literally. I don't care so much whether I ever marry again, because I don't want the state involved in my business again in any sense of the word. Never again, ever. If I marry, I'll make my own contract. And again, I'm lucky to live in a city where that type of thing would be easily tolerated.

My love with the children is a good kind of love. But it doesn't get back to you except when you say something nice to them or they say something nice and hug me. Like my son, on my birthday last month. He is twelve, and not all that enthusiastic about demonstrating affection, but he said, "I'm going to give you forty-two kisses because you're forty-two today." That was a very special moment. But still, it isn't the kind of long, equal caring, the process of making something new out of each day that comes with loving a man. I think it's nice to be married. It's a way of saying, "Look, we've made this commitment to each other." And it doesn't have to be some kind of trap if two people want to share everything together.

I don't know what makes me different from other women. Something inside nudges me on to do more things, to try new jobs, to make new contacts. And then I look back and I see a pattern, something progressive. I love my work and throw myself into editing tapes for television and arranging all the details for a show.

What is it that makes human beings expect a happy life? Why do we find it so hard to make our lives what we want them to be? We are raised to expect happiness, but Mother never defines it. It's "All I want for you, dear, is that you be happy." No one ever talks to children about reality. Instead they talk to them about concepts such as "happiness."

I think that usually the person urging a child to "be happy" hasn't found it himself or herself, and they're hoping the children will find it. But if you can build something calm and easy, something without a hidden agenda between yourself and a child, well it can be incredible. It shouldn't be always this process of looking for happiness, but just taking pleasure in being where you are and what you are about. You can't pursue happiness. If you get it, you're lucky; that's what I consider a little fun in my life.

But I can't count on it, so it's important to look in other directions. For instance, one of the better substitutes for a real relationship with a person is making something happen. Changing things is exciting—like creating. I feel that way when I edit a tape for a show. What stays in and what goes out is up to me. It's a lonely thing, really, but lonely in a good way. It gives me time to think and work through things in my own mind and my own feelings, which is something I don't usually have much time to do. It's an artist's sort of aloneness which I choose. It's creative, a completely different thing for most women. But it is a kind of aloneness, and many women are beginning to move into something like this. Then I get so excited, and I want to share everything. It's a whole concept of freedom where there are minimum limitations. There have to be boundaries. Like the children coming home from school, or something. We have to create some kind of structures or we can't survive.

But I don't think there are very many men who can really enjoy a free world, you know, cross this kind of threshold and feel vitality. Instead they want and expect to be happy, with a really easy loving relationship. The kind that doesn't happen. Isn't it a pity that we can't grow up first and then get married? Marriage is probably the largest single thing that holds women back from doing things they can do and being what they can be. It's beginning to change. The difficult thing is, women have to get out into the battleground if they want to grow, and most normal married women don't want to experience that battleground. They're afraid they'll get out there and find they now live on different planets from their husbands.

I feel guilt still about my divorce, but I know it wasn't wrong in the same way that I know it isn't wrong to send my children to a progressive school with ungraded classrooms. A risk maybe, but not wrong.

I ran into a friend of mine the other night on the plane, and he told me he and his wife had just separated. His youngest daughter is fifteen, my daughter's age. I told him to come for Christmas. For the last five years I've had a Christmas party for everybody I know who is divorced or getting divorced, and they all bring their children on Christmas day. I do that because I want to help them realize that divorce is an okay thing, and things are going to be okay for their children and for them. I want to help them realize that divorce is a learning process, even though your own life is without any anchors any more.

I had to experiment with what was right to do, and that has been very difficult. I think the hardest thing is to be surrounded by people who disapprove, people I suspect who are very lonely and who don't want to face their own lives. They don't feel separate—alone, in a good sense—and so they feel they are like everyone else. It follows that everyone else has to be just like them—so that means they don't want you to have any choices. All the things I knew were right weren't happening in the places I lived. But they were happening in New York, and the best thing I ever did was to come here. And here I'll stay.

Helen Hayes

Sometimes in the morning I pretend I'm still a great star of the theater and very carefully carry my breakfast to my room on a tray, using my best breakfast china and my best tray cloth. Everything is exquisite. Then I put it on the little table by my bed and crawl in, putting on a very pretty bed jacket, the tray on my lap—and I'm a star in bed having breakfast. It's fun, and it brings me back into the old rhythm and feeling. But usually I don't sleep late. I don't want to miss too much of the days that are left me—it isn't as wistful an idea as that—it's just that I love to be up and about, seeing the morning. I do bits and pieces

around the house that need to be done. I do some writing, letters
and things of that sort. That's another hour or two. Then in the
summer and autumn, I have much to do in the garden. It is a
very beautiful garden which I very much love and work in a lot.

As a matter of fact, since I've been alone and had fewer
responsibilities and since I have, for sure, left my profession, I
find the days are too short for me. Funny. Once in a while, I do a
little television. When you've had a very active life, it is frightening to try to be inactive all at once. But being alone has its good
points. I like coddling myself, thinking about me first, before
anybody else. I don't know that I ever did that before. But it is
pleasant, and aside from a few twinges of conscience—which
happens once in a while—I'm living with that very well.

There were many times in my life, until I was left alone, that I
wished for solitude. I now find that I love solitude. I never had
the blessed gift of being alone until the last of my loved ones was
wrested from me. Now I can go sometimes for days and days
without seeing anyone. I'm not entirely alone, because I listen to
the radio and read the newspapers. I love to read. That is my
greatest new luxury, having the time to read. And oh, the little
things I find to do that make the days, as I say, much too short.

Solitude—walking alone, doing things alone—is the most
blessed thing in the world. The mind relaxes and thoughts begin
to flow and I think that I am beginning to find myself a little bit.

I never had time for myself. I was always busy making the acquaintance of other people, and entertaining them in my home
or in the theater . . . Now I have that time. I've found that
though I have a lot of faults, and I am aware of them, I can live
with myself. I've learned to forgive myself for some of the
mistakes I've made. I've learned to tell myself that when I made
mistakes, I had a good reason at the time, or thought I had, and
that there couldn't have been any other way than the way it was.
For instance, I've refused plays that I didn't like and they've
turned out to be great successes. Instead of mourning that and

blaming myself for having missed out, with another actress achieving that success, I say to myself, but it would have been so terrible not liking that play or that role if I had done it and it had been a success and I had been forced to play it every night for months.

Unfortunately, I know mostly women now. I like men better, but I am very happy with my women friends. One of the proud things in my life is that I know two women who have been my friends over sixty years. And I spent my seventy-first birthday with one of them on the tenth of October in New Hampshire. She also is a widow. My husband died fifteen years ago, and for two years I was just about as crazy as you can be and still be at large. I didn't have any really normal minutes during those two years.

It wasn't just grief. It was total confusion. A woman who loves a man, who has had the good fortune and good sense to marry a particularly bright one whom she trusts—I think she feels very helpless when he dies. I did. I've known other women, like Mrs. Wendell Willkie, who were terribly thrown by that loss when it came to them. I was frightened and alone. I felt unable to decide. Decisions were terrible—Charlie had always been watchful and supportive and protective about me in the theater. We don't all have a gift for being alone, living with ourselves. Some of us are afraid of ourselves. I don't know why. It must be something that goes way back, deep-seated in childhood. With some people it is so bad that they cannot trust themselves to be individuals and can only live as part of a group.

My great advantage was my career—it was there to protect me like a wonderful life preserver keeping me on top of it all, keeping me from sinking. A career is a good tranquilizer for the spirit when a woman is alone. I think it is good. But I've seen other women, without the advantage of a job or a career—the tranquilizers they choose are the more obvious ones, like the bottle or the bridge table.

After Charlie died, my friends finally persuaded me to do a picture, *Anastasia*, with Ingrid Bergman and Yul Brynner. I said, No, I can't, I haven't the will to do anything at the moment. They were so persistent, and they didn't realize I needed time to mend. I needed quiet time, apart time. Grief is a very feeling thing. If I had had a chance to sit still and indulge in grief, I think it would have made my time of recovery much quicker, shorter.

Instead I went over to England to do this film, and found myself doing the oddest things. I had always been so reliable and dependable, always on the job—a real trouper, they called me. Well, one time I took off, went to Brighton with a friend. I just took a fancy to go to Brighton and I went, and left no forwarding address at the hotel where I was living. Heavens, the picture company was beside itself. I had completely put it out of my mind that I was making a movie. Curious, isn't it?

That's a time I look back on and flinch to think of, because I was most unattractive. Unreliable and erratic. I squabbled with directors—I had never squabbled before. I took umbrage at nothing at all. I gave rather pompous and silly statements to the press. I was nutty, and that's the truth. How did I come out of it? I don't know, because I didn't know when I was in it that I was in it.

Now I look back and can see how my self-image had to change. Until Charlie died, I was pretty darned arrogant. There was actually a time when I felt, why did God give me this gift of being so right so much of the time? Why should I be the one who always chooses the right play, the right line of action? I literally felt infallible. I don't any more. Unfortunately, today you have to be courageous to the point of audacity in the theater. It's one of the reasons I wanted to get away from it, get out of it, because I became too nervous and too frightened of my decisions. I told you I relied on Charlie. Really, he was making the decisions, but I wasn't recognizing it or acknowledging it to myself.

I think the problems of being an actress and finding myself alone have been no different from the problems of anyone else widowed or divorced. My private life has been far removed from my theater life. It was different for Katharine Cornell—at the time Guthrie McClintic died, a good ten or fifteen years ago, Kit walked off that stage and never walked on a stage again, never wanted to, never had the nerve to. And truly, I've been marking time since Charlie died. I haven't wanted, really, to be an actress since. Without his judgments.

I'm such a compulsive planner, now. I really bore myself with the way I fuss over plans. Every once in a while my companion will say, look it's six months off, Miss Hayes, can't we just wait? And I say, no, no, no, we have to straighten this out. It's a little crazy, I think, to make all these picky plans. I do it more than I ever did before, but of course, I depended on Charlie to do a lot of that. Not that he was much of a planner, but I would go along with him, and then we would just plunge ahead with whatever was to be done.

I'm seventy-two now, and I have to face up to some of the things that happen with age. I suppose I've tried to prove to myself and the world that I'm not getting old and deteriorated. My mind is as sharp as ever. I *can* remember things. I *can* think of the right word that I want to use. I *can* converse. The effort to prove all this makes me apt to overdo—trying to prove myself a little more than when I was young. It's nervousness about the deterioration of time—talking too much, trying to be funny too much. You have to face the idea that others have of you. As a dried-out lemon.

Oh, well, you just have to roll with the punches, to use the vernacular. For one thing, I used to take it for granted that if you were a celebrity, a star, you just walked into a room and things would happen, simply because it was you who walked in. Now I don't feel that. I take the back seat a lot, and that's a hard transition for someone who's been in the driver's seat through life.

Little things keep happening, and I'm startled. For example, there is a film I was asked to do by a producer recently. He and the writer were in love with it, and they were so eager for me to do it. They spent a year trying to raise the money to do that film in which I would have been the star. And they couldn't raise the money. That's a new thing for me—they couldn't raise the money for me to star. That means something extraordinary has happened. What do you do when you face that?

Well, I just told myself, all right, no more trying for star roles. If I want to be in the theater or films, I will play character roles, with young stars. There is nothing wrong with that. It's the general pattern of the great all-time stars. Youth should be served by age always. This is as it should be.

But this isn't the route for everyone. I remember Booth Tarkington years ago telling me about how he tried to get Maude Adams back on the stage when she had been gone many, many years. He wrote a play about an actress who was getting on and a young man who had a great feeling about this actress—two people, young and old, who come together. In the play, she taught him not to think of her age and he taught *her* not to think of it . . . but age, with capital letters, was the subject of the play. Poor Mr. Tarkington thought that was a graceful way to bring Maude Adams back. But she had been Peter Pan—how do you bring Peter Pan back as a middle-aged woman?

Well, she went to stay at his house, and he gave her the play in the evening to read. The next morning she came down and told him, "I don't understand this play at all. I couldn't possibly be in it, because I can't understand it." Puzzled, he said, "What's unclear about it?" And she said, "I have no realization of my age, I never think in terms of age. In going through this play, it is all about age. I have never aged."

And there it is. She was a little dumpy, she had lost a bit of her shape, but as far as she was concerned she had not aged. And she wasn't about to let anybody impose it on her. I wish it were possible for most of us to feel that way. Not that we would go gamboling about like lambs, but that we could stop trying to pretend we are young.

It's awfully hard to keep on remembering that I'm old. I'm as capable of romantic dreams as I have ever been in my life, but here in this country we have a sense of embarrassment about older people trying to enjoy some of the things they enjoyed in their youth. I knew a brilliant and attractive woman with money, widowed, very bright, and she was over sixty. We had supper one night in London, and she told me why she had moved there from the United States. She said, "I would have been covered with shame to be seen going out to dinner or to dance with a young man, but no one thinks anything of my doing it here in London. I don't have to be scorned for taking on a gigolo, as they call it." They were not gigolos, they were young friends. She likes to dance with young men, to be surrounded by young people, and she particularly likes having an escort.

There is nothing wrong with that woman. Her taste is impeccable. But here in the United States it would have looked atrocious, so she moved. It's almost an Oriental attitude. When I was in Korea I used to look at those elderly couples in their kind of uniforms—a gray Korean coat, the national dress, made exactly like the gay colored ones the young people wore, but gray. And their hats—the men look like old mother witch with those high-pointed crowns. All that gray stuff. They put on those uniforms when they reach a certain age, and that's that.

So here, women my age try to do the twist. Or they did—going down to the Peppermint Lounge in New York, trying to learn the twist. Why? Everybody over forty-five has a touch of arthritis and it must hurt to do the twist. That isn't natural. And it isn't natural for women whose shapes are changing—one's shape does change as one grows older—to put on miniskirts and try to wear the things youngsters look so adorable in, with their coltish figures, and their long, straight, beautiful legs. Women my age, we should wear the things that look best on us. And stop carrying on like crazy. How silly it is—but it's the philosophy of this land, I suppose.

Helen Sewell

My husband had his stroke in 1955. We were just sitting pretty, getting ready to retire with a real nice business built up, and ready to sell. I've had my hell on earth, believe me, during those three years when I took him everywhere for treatment, to Mayo and Massachusetts and somewhere in Canada. We went through everything we had, every dollar, and when he died we had three hundred and sixty dollars left in our account. But I still had my work. I was sixty years old then, but I went back to it and kept it going, and now I don't have any financial worries.

The loneliest, hardest part of my life was when he was sick. He was alive, but not there. And I had leaned on him so much, this brilliant, brilliant man, so loving and understanding. When I would worry about something he would be quiet and in the morning he would say, "Well, now that you've worried all night, I guess everything is all right." He just never worried about anything. He felt things would take care of themselves, that this was the way of life itself. He used to say to me, "Helen, when you lose your head, you lose your case." He was a great man, and from him I learned about so many things.

Going out to that final hospital was just hell on earth. I can't believe in this idea of purgatory or this hell deal. God in his mercy couldn't do such a thing. I would go there and see all those helpless men, and he would come and sit beside me and put his head on my shoulder. He couldn't talk, wouldn't talk, yet in the back of his mind he knew me, but didn't know why. Then all of a sudden he would bounce up and run away from me, and that hurt. Two years and eight months of that, two and three times a week, and then he died. And I would be less than honest if I didn't say I was grateful to God, because he was no good to himself. He died. And all I could do was watch him. I knew he didn't suffer. I prayed so very hard while he was sick that God wouldn't let me go ahead of him, leaving nobody to take care of him. I prayed that He would give me just one hour after him, but that is the only time in my life—before or since—I've worried about age or death. I don't know why, maybe I should have, now that I think of it. But it never does any good. I live from day to day, and frankly I don't feel my age . . . I don't know where I lost all the years in between now and when I was young.

When Harry died, I had already become accustomed to being alone, accustomed to being able to do things for myself. I knew if I couldn't carry on, I would have to give up and I wasn't about to give up. So I kept working, and I've traveled, done things. I've always had this sense of independence—a sense that God will take care of things. I still feel that way; whatever is to be is to be and there's nothing I can do about it.

What made me tough was my family. My father ran a small tobacco farm and we were very poor. My mother was very strict, very independent, and she taught us that we were born to handle our own way of life. She was very religious herself, but she never pressed it on us. She always used the expression, "If you dance you must pay the fiddler." It's up to you, she said, because it's your life and forced prayer is no devotion. But we were raised Catholic, and if we didn't go to church on Sunday we didn't go out to play. That was it. Everybody had rights, and God created us equal, but life wasn't a playground. Mother drummed that into our ears from the time we were knee-high to grasshoppers. She was the boss; she was the queen. She never weighed over a hundred pounds in her life, unless she was having a baby—there were nine of us. Out of those nine, there was only one Catholic wedding, only one.

When I was really young, I remember mother had a sealskin

coat that I admired. At Mass one morning I saw a woman with a big hat made of sealskin and I thought, I want one of those. So I went home and took Mother's sealskin coat and put it down on the floor and cut a big circle out of the back . . . that hat was so tempting. It was wrong, but Mother didn't punish me. Yet I felt guilty and confused and scared. I had a fear of God punishing me. But then I thought, why should I be afraid of the church? Why should the priest control me? I was supposed to have done something so dreadfully wrong, but if I hadn't gone to church and hadn't seen that hat, I wouldn't have done it. Mother always drilled into us that the priests and nuns are human, they make mistakes. We had then, as now, a few people talking out loud about the priests and nuns, and we would ask questions. Mother said everybody makes mistakes and they must not be judged by you or me. God will judge them. Anyhow, that coat deal was the thing that changed me, and made me decide it was important to think for myself.

In high school I saw my life as getting married. And that was it. I didn't go to college, so after school I went to New York and worked as a switchboard operator at the Astor Hotel. I met my husband through friends while I was there, during the war, and we were married in 1919. I knew him five days and married him the day he sailed for Europe. I had a little money. So I worked. And when he came back we moved to Northwestern so he could go through law school. We bought a furnished apartment house with what I had saved. It was money-making, and as soon as he graduated he said he wanted to go to work for somebody. And I said, "No, you don't work for anybody else." You can't fire yourself, so we both started in, he in law and me in the millinery business. I opened a shop on Sheridan Road, sold the first apartment and bought another one, a nine-room apartment, and took in seven roomers. How I worked.

We had no children, but we tried to adopt a little boy in 1921. We had the child for twenty-eight months—his mother had deserted him and at first she was perfectly willing that Harry and I take over, but the very day we went into court for the final adoption papers, she showed up. Right in the courtroom. She demanded the baby back, and it was awful. The judge told her, "All right, take him home," but she would have to bring him to me for forty-eight hours every week. I couldn't have stood that, to love a baby as my own and be allowed to keep him only two days each week. So I said, "No, Judge, I won't take that arrangement." And I cried. That was the turning point for me, in how my life would go. Harry and I spent the entire night after that agony in the courtroom walking up and down Clarendon Avenue, walking all night. How strong he was, and how I needed him then.

Afterwards when this youngster grew up, after World War II, he called me up on the phone. And he said, "Why did you let me go?" He told me how he remembered crawling under the dining-room table when Shirley—he wouldn't call her Mother—came to the house once. How could I answer? He was just five years old when they took him away.

I had a bad breakdown after I lost that child, and went to visit friends in New Jersey. By the time I got back I decided to throw myself into my business, which I did. And I was successful. Then the Depression came, and that's when I got first into volunteer work and then into politics, through the American Legion. My husband was the most active man in the Legion, and it was from him that I learned about the needs of child welfare, disabled veterans, veterans unable to find work—he told me about this, and I decided I cared and wanted to help. So I got into politics from that, and never stopped. Always had confidence. God gave me my life and I answered only to God, and God alone. When I got pushed around a little in politics, I fought. Would I have done the same things without Harry? I wonder. But I can't really answer that.

I've always remained religious, though Harry was not a Catholic and we were married outside the church. I wasn't afraid to do it, because I was head over heels in love, no doubt about that. I tried after that, and Harry was very understanding, but the church saved me the trouble. You see, I was barred from everything. I couldn't go to confession, I couldn't receive any of the sacraments. I became very, very bitter when I saw prominent people getting dispensations when they had barred me. Funny, my husband's parents were Mormons, and narrow as a half-inch ribbon, terrifically narrow. But my father-in-law thought there was nobody on earth like me. They didn't have trouble accepting a Catholic. We were led to believe there was a Catholic God, but my mother always said there is only one God for everyone. Yet the nuns and priests pounded into our ears that we controlled God; he was ours and nobody else's. My mother never believed that. And I don't believe it.

I think Harry would have converted, I don't think there was any doubt. He would go to any affairs the Catholics had that I could attend, right along with me. But he had parents of his own, he was raised differently. Wouldn't have been right.

Harry and I would have been married fifty-two years in March, and forty-five years with him were the happiest of my life. We never went to bed—I know we didn't—without saying good night and God bless you. Mother taught us as kids that we never went to bed without saying that. Harry felt the same way, even if we had had an argument. He would say, ''Well, how about it? Is it good night?'' It always was, and I only knew him five days before we were married.

I guess I was an early liberationist, though I tried not to be obnoxious. These ones now, I can't stand them. I just did things my own way, and if people didn't like that, that was it. But I wouldn't fight. Just go ahead and do what I wanted to do. I don't believe in fighting, but I do believe in being firm. The thing I don't like is these liberationists getting out in the picket lines and so forth, even though I'm very active in the labor movement. It sort of cheapens them, and I don't like being cheapened. It could be done in a different manner, but how? I'm at a loss to say.

We always worked together, Harry and me. If a case of his went wrong he would come home and say, what will *we* do about it? And when friends of mine would want him to draw up their wills or do their probate work, he would get their check and bring it home and lay it on the kitchen table. "Well, this is the fee," he would say. And I would always get half—split right down the middle. I never threatened him by being so independent, and he made sure I had money so I could have my own bank account. Otherwise, I don't know how I would have handled things when he passed away, I really don't.

I had a very bad temper—red hair, freckles, and O'Connor as my maiden name, and what have you. Harry was easygoing. He would just look at me when I got mad and kind of grin, and I'd be kind of ashamed of myself. I never could have loved anybody else. I don't know what's wrong with young people today, I think they expect too much. We didn't. Marriage won't die out, even with all these new ideas. If only people didn't expect so much.

After Harry died, immediately after his death, I received the sacraments. But that was the last time, frankly. After all those wonderful years, I found I didn't really need them. I did it to see exactly what would happen, and there was no change. No feeling. But I will always be a Catholic, even though I don't like what I see happening. Again, it is God's world, and not for me to say.

I have no regrets, none at all. I'm sorry only that my husband didn't live longer, because there is so much in life he would have enjoyed. A lot of things would have hurt him that are happening—he was an American from the word go, and that was his creed. Apparently it was God's will that he not be hurt. Nothing in the world like being an American. Anyhow, no regrets.

I'm blessed by being a very independent person and I always will be, and I'm blessed with my work, which keeps me from being lonely. I'm not afraid of anything.

Pauline Mason

My husband was a dealer in a gambling joint and then a bookie before I finally realized he lacked any ambition to better himself. I was working on and off at various things to keep some steady money coming in for the family. After about ten years of marriage, I reached a point where I was earning more money than he was. I'm restless, independent. I didn't like having to go to my husband for every nickel I needed for a package of cigarettes. Since it wasn't a good marriage anyway, I just decided that if I was contributing the major amount of money to the household, I didn't need the aggravation that went with it. So I got a divorce, and was awarded a big, fat fifteen dollars a week child support. No alimony.

I had to do it. It was traumatic for him and our son, but as far as I was concerned the only trauma was the way he fought it and made divorce such an ugly thing. He was accusing and jealous, and refused to understand the business that I was in. If I had to work seventy-two hours around the clock in order to complete rehearsals for a play, that was what I had to do.

I'm an actress, and I love my work. I started doing bit parts in the theater because it was cheaper than therapy. I never dreamed I would enjoy doing a long run, but when it's there and you're doing it, you enjoy it—even though it means eight performances a week, with two on Saturday and two on Sunday. On Saturday night I get through the last show at a quarter of two in the morning. And by the time I get my street clothes on and unwind for a few minutes over a glass of wine or a drink, it's close to

three in the morning. I have to be back at the theater in the afternoon for a matinee and then again at seven in the evening. So
that's bad on a marriage.

It's been a constant struggle since the divorce, particularly to
pay for college for my son. But I've done it now. He graduated
last June with a Master's degree in physical education and he's
teaching in a Milwaukee high school. I'm satisfied on that score.

I dated a married man, a marvelous man, after my divorce. I
didn't feel I was breaking up a marriage, just that if I wasn't with
him somebody else would be, so why not? If his wife doesn't
have anything to offer, it's a man's prerogative to be out looking
for companionship. I'm just accepting what *he* has to offer.

I'm looking for a replacement for that man now, but I find
too many men bore me. I don't have time to sit around patiently
listening to things I already know. I don't even have time to sit
down and read the newspaper any more, because I'm busy with
the theater day and night. I sometimes go with papers stacked
this high and I haven't even read a headline. I would love to
marry again, but in a way I like being alone. There's something
great about crawling into that big king-size bed alone every
night. Don't misunderstand, I'm not knocking sex. It's very nice
to have that thrown in, but honestly, if I could find a man kind
and thoughtful, understanding and communicative, sex would
be the last thing in the world of importance to me.

Climbing into bed with just anybody is great for the teen-ager
or career girl in her twenties or early thirties. Marvelous. But
I'm sorry, I just can't see getting into the sack with a boy every
time he buys you liquor. Fortunately, I'm in a good enough
financial position that I don't have to depend upon anybody to
buy me a drink or take me to dinner, figuring I have to pay them
back that way. I don't know if that's pride or what it is. I won't
even eat alone in a restaurant [either]. I think women who do
that are far more lonely than I am. They're seeking atmosphere.

Pretending. I don't need that. I don't need guys coming up to me in restaurants and assuming I feel like talking to them because I'm alone.

When I'm traveling out of town alone, I tell the bartender, "I'd like a Scotch on the rocks, please, and I buy my own. Pass the word." Every bartender I've encountered has been very understanding. Once when I was changing trains and had a layover in St. Louis, I went into the bar and ordered a long, cool drink because it was so hot. I passed my message to the bartender, and after a while he came back to me and said, "The gentleman over there wants to buy you a drink." I shook my head and told him, "Thank the gentleman very much, but tell him I buy my own." I didn't even know who the man was because it was crowded, and I always seat myself at the very end of a bar if a stool is available. "No strings," he said. "The sender is anonymous." I took the drink then, but not until I told the bartender, "Let's keep it that way." That's important.

I met a very attractive man, really attractive, a few years ago. It was a chemical something. I dated him a few times, and we had dinner together while I was on the road. He traveled too, and sent me postcards from all over the country. He'd do little things that were so nice, like calling from O'Hare Airport and saying, "I'm just passing through and thinking about you." Kind, thoughtful. Anyway, so I thought. One night he asked me to meet him in a cocktail lounge, a place where a lot of my friends hang out. So he walked in with some guy he worked with, the two of them just delighted with a new restaurant they had just tried out with great Mexican food. I was polite and smiled, and said, "Oh, you liked it?" But if a man has dinner with a guy and asks me to meet him later for a couple of drinks, who needs it? Every time he comes to town now, I manage to be busy. He doesn't come that frequently, so there's plenty of time when I don't have to worry about what my next excuse is going to be. I can laugh it off now, but it hurt then. Last time he called, I told him I only have Monday nights free and they're pretty well filled.

I'm not lonely as long as I'm working. Last summer I was supposed to have minor surgery, which was canceled after I had arranged for a replacement in the play I was in then. I insisted the woman they hired play the part for two weeks anyway, in case I ever needed her later. And I want to tell you that in those two weeks I thought I would lose my mind. I found things to keep myself busy, like seeing which clothes weren't wearable any more. Mostly I sat and watched television, which bores me more than anything.

I'm not afraid of being lonely. I don't think I ever will be. I love people. Even during those two weeks, I would go out late at night when everybody else was through work and meet them for drinks, just to be with them. We have such a terrific rapport. Most of them are some twenty odd years my junior, and I find it flattering when they beg off late evenings, saying they just can't go out after the show because they're too tired. So I tell them, "When you get some years on you, maybe you'll be able to keep up with me."

It isn't that I don't want to go home. I'm not fighting my four walls. I love my home. It's very comfortable and I'm happy there, but I miss my dogs. One died and I was very attached to the other one when I started this show, but you can't have a dog when you're gone all day and night, so I gave him back to the original owners. I adored him. But I don't really think I miss him now.

Alice Bowen

When I'm seventy and rocking in a chair on the front porch, I'll remember David, even though I know I'll never be able to marry him. I don't feel guilty, and I never will. I've caught glimpses of his wife, once shopping downtown and once in a restaurant, and I feel sorry for her. What I have could have been hers. She's very nice looking, but one of the things she did wrong was in becoming too much of a mother and not enough of a wife. And she loves his money. She enjoys having it and spending it and she is so devoted to her children, it's unreal. Now she has grandchildren, and she's right in there.

I appreciate the fact he never discusses her with me, none of that phony business. He's not like other men I've known, particularly one who succeeded in making me feel cheap with a single stupid remark. We were coming out of a restaurant after lunch and someone asked him—he didn't know I heard—who the babe was that he was with. And he smiled widely and said, "Gee, I don't know her name." He didn't want to take any chances his wife might know he was dating someone else. I realized then why we went to some of the stupidest, hole-in-the-wall restaurants in town, and his furtiveness shamed me.

Since my husband died five years ago, I've traveled a great deal in connection with my work and I've met many men. They've all been married, and I'd say 75 percent of them play around. I don't find that shocking, in fact I think it's perfectly normal. Some of them play in a nice way, and some of them don't. If I ever marry again, one of the requirements would be that the man would have personal strength. And this wonderful person I'm seeing now exudes self-confidence and is never unpleasant about it. My work and my success don't intimidate him, even though we are diametrically opposite in every way. I think he could be married to the most famous movie actress in the world and never feel threatened. He would be fine and strong, in every way. To me, that's one of the most beautiful things in any man, that he knows he's all right.

We met through a blind date, when a girlfriend called and asked me if I'd be interested in going out. I'd just gotten a little dog and I told her I was thinking of going to a dog-training school that night, but I never did. She said, don't do that, come meet this man. I asked her, "Is he married?" and her exact answer was, "He's got problems." Anyhow we went out to dinner and he was very quiet and charming, and he asked me out to lunch. So time went on, and because it was a place close to my work, I often saw him at one particular restaurant, always eating alone, until I joined him. I asked myself, "What are you doing?" I knew he was married. But I was planning a trip to Europe and, you know, figured I could make a total escape.

The night before I left for Europe he asked me to dinner and gave me the most beautiful jade ring. He said, "Here, take this, I want you to have something to think about me when you are in Europe." The restaurant was dark, and I couldn't see the ring too well but it looked very nice. I thought, "What is it with this guy?" And then he took me home, said good night, and didn't ask to come up. I closed the door and went over to the light to see my ring. It was really gorgeous—jade surrounded with opals. I called him at his office the next morning, trying to be light about it, and said, "I'm really glad I don't have to square this ring with my mother." He laughed. Then I went to Europe, and all the time there he kept going through my mind. I would look at the ring and wonder what was going on back home.

It was shortly after Christmas when I came back. On purpose. All holidays are awful when you live alone. I walked in the apartment and found the manager had placed all my Christmas cards in a bowl, waiting for me. And there were eight or nine cards from him. So that's when it started; evidently he had made up his mind before I left.

Two years, and it has been a gorgeous relationship. There hasn't been a bad moment in it. All the bad moments have been private and my own, all because he's married, never because of anything wrong between us. I'll tell you, he's just made a career of not hurting me in any way, and trying to make me happy. And no one has done that in a long time.

When my husband died, things were terrible. The first year, I'd come in the door at night and make it to the hall bench, and just sit there for about an hour, crying. And freezing. I hadn't known how to put up storm windows, so just to make me feel more sorry for myself, I was cold. Little by little I came out of it, and little by little I met people. I adore men. I really do enjoy myself more with men, and I don't mean just a male-female sex thing. I've met many wonderful people through my business relationships, traveling and so forth, but this man is the first person I've met I would live my life with.

Not too long ago, I had to have an operation; a hysterectomy, nothing serious. But it wasn't very pleasant and I was in the hospital for seven weeks. And you know what I found out? He's more distressed about the fact that I'm alone than I am. When I came out of the operating room, I found myself attended by private duty nurses and getting all sorts of special care I could never afford by myself. I knew how much I loved him then, because he gave me that very real sense of being there when I needed him, really needed him, not just offering a weekly candlelit dinner for two.

I would love it to be marriage, but not at the cost of his marriage. Their children are grown, but she is very dependent on him. Sometimes I have to watch myself because I find myself wishing his wife would die. That's awful. Pretty natural for a woman in my position, but I shouldn't do that. I don't mean it personally, because of course I don't know her as a person. She is the woman married to this wonderful man who doesn't even know how lucky she is. He never pulls that old stuff of "My wife doesn't understand me." Never. But without his saying it in just those words, I get the feeling he believes she sees him mainly as a meal ticket. If he didn't show up for a week, about the only concern would be that he was inconveniencing her. That's very foolish. But she can be very sure of herself, because he's never going to go away. She's missing something and she doesn't know it, that's the sad thing.

He comes to see me about once a week in the evening, and I count the hours of the week. It's scary. I'm not dating any other men, and it isn't as if loving him is holding me back from something, when I'm realistic. But at the same time I think, boy, now any man I meet I'm going to compare with him, and that's making it harder for other men all the time. Occasionally he's able to come up for breakfast before he goes to the office, or we meet for lunch. The important thing is, we see each other regularly. What should I do? Quit seeing the most important person in my life because he's married? What could I say, don't come around any more? That would be like saying, look, I can't stand being happy, I'd prefer being miserable.

I don't feel satisfied with this arrangement, what woman would? I don't want to be a mistress. I want to be his wife. The funniest thing about my feelings concerning his wife is that I feel sorry for her. She could have all this that I have with him. It's hers, by right. Last week she went downtown with her daughter, to buy her a mink coat. They found one, and she saw another one that she fell in love with and went off and bought it on the spur of the moment. Do you know what I felt? Thank heavens, she bought it. She recently bought a new blue Cadillac too. So now she's got the Cadillac and the mink coat and I know it makes her happy, and I'm glad. I'd rather have Saturday-morning breakfast; that's the prime time. It helps my guilt a little if she gets a mink coat. She's getting what she wants, and evidently she doesn't miss what I've got.

Of course, I would love to marry him. But he's been married for thirty years and we could never survive the break-up of a home that has lasted that long. But I'm glad I'm more particular now than I was during the time after my husband's death—I know all the things that aren't good, and I know the things that are. And I'll tell you this, if I ever marry again, I want to hear that key in the door with the greatest joy. Otherwise I don't want to hear it at all.

Marlene Hinchman

A friend of mine referred a fantastic murder to me once at a cocktail party. It was a lovely case with lots of potential; someday it's going to be heard by the U.S. Supreme Court because it's that kind of a case. And you know what I did? I walked right over to my boyfriend and said, "Here, this is going to be a great case. You take it." I actually felt compelled to give it to him. At first he wasn't enthusiastic about it at all, I suppose because it had been offered to me first. But I didn't think of that at the time. I kept arguing with him, thinking, "He just doesn't understand the issues." It was so fantastic. Finally he said, "Okay, I'll do it." And I gave him that wonderful case.

I've wanted to be a lawyer since the sixth grade. Lawyers seemed so well educated, so verbal, and I wanted to be able to express what I thought—you know, one of those childhood fantasies. School was easy for me, so easy I finished high school in three years, graduating with extra credits. At one point—when I was president of the Student Council, as a matter of fact—I was suspended for "aggressive conduct." That meant I talked back. I was always terribly aggressive as a child, outspoken in my ideas and all that, although I never got into real trouble, except for being suspended.

I went to the University of Chicago and finished in three years and was all ready for law school, ahead of time, but it was the wrong way to do it. I've always felt too young, always felt that other people doing the same thing I'm doing are a lot more mature than I am. I wish someone had told me while I was racing through school, "Do something else for a while. Go somewhere and think about something else besides school. Forget about rushing so fast." But no one did, and it seems so ridiculous now. I get angry thinking about it. I wanted to be a lawyer and that meant a long time in law school, and I didn't want to be old when I finally got out. I'm not sorry I'm a lawyer, just that I hurried.

I love my work and I feel much luckier than my father. He's a successful corporate lawyer, but he does it without enthusiasm. Sometimes I think he just likes to bitch, and other times I think he is really unhappy with his work. It wouldn't have been that way for my mother if he had let her go on to graduate school. She finished college while I was in high school and studied psychology with great relish. But my father didn't want her to get too well educated, and he wasn't very subtle about it. Actually she has been a greater influence on me than he was, probably because I'm an early war baby. I was born in 1942 while my father was in the service, and he didn't come back until I was four years old, so he missed that influential growing-up period when I was just with my mother. He had some influence, of course. But I think some of my problems are the result of not having had a father in those years. I don't remember missing him, but we've never had a warm relationship. My parents have terrible arguments to this day, but when I was a child they were really bad. It was just my brother and me against them. At least I felt that way. I wish there had been more of us, and then Dad would have had to consider us more.

I got to law school when I was twenty, and everybody else was a couple of years older and had considerably more savvy than I felt. Most of them were married too. I was terribly naïve, but got over it in a year. You just have to adapt, and when I finally did, things weren't too bad. I didn't do particularly well academically, which was shocking, but I adjusted to that too. I thought I'd still be a pretty good lawyer. And I had met a man and begun to live with him very happily in the last year of school.

I had an offer from a pretty good firm, a major Chicago firm. Maybe not *the* best, but one of the best in town. I was pretty surprised, and felt terribly fortunate. Everything sort of fell together, and I decided I would work for them. At one time I had thought of going to graduate school in philosophy, because I had done some graduate work in that area between law semesters. But I was disenchanted with philosophy by the time I graduated and I thought, well, I'll go with this law firm for a while. And that was six years ago now. I haven't thought about it much since.

I'm not all that pleased with this firm any more. I do a lot of real estate, which is interesting, and mortgage work and appeals. It does have freedom and variety to it, but it isn't that stimulating. There's no relevance. The mortgages I'm dealing with could have been written in the twenties. I'm not sure what type of firm I would like to work for. Maybe in civil rights or something. I don't know. I've done some political work, but I get so personally involved it becomes a great emotional strain.

What bothers me is that I'm without interests. You know, real sincere, outside-of-work interests that I know some people have. One of my friends plays in a string quartet and belongs to a math club and does all sorts of creative and satisfying non-vocational work. I wish I were more in a position to do things like that. I'd like to develop other interests, but they have to sort of grow. You can't force them. I think I would be a little interested in graphics. I don't know. Graphics are very big, and people are always talking about graphics these days at cocktail parties. There are a lot of interesting things—I have kind of an interest in art history. It's not all that relevant, but it's amusing and would be fun.

I don't know where to start. In a way I feel I could stay with this law firm for the next forty years and professionally be somewhat content, but I'd rather have a vocation—vocational expression of what I think is more my entire personality than this is. I don't know that I can find it. Really, what it is is a dichotomy between my professional life and my personal life. In law school the environment was more entire, and I have no other working experience to compare. This is a "business only" firm. You can tell. Look around—no one's here tonight. Where are they? People who love their jobs work a lot. Some law firms are classified by outsiders as high-pressure places, but the people who work there love their work.

It's my fault too—I haven't been willing to really scrounge around and find one or two jobs that exist that would mean all the things I want and need. I've told my parents—they think I'm really weird in wanting to give up the establishment aspects of the practice, but they're not too concerned. They're not altogether convinced women should work. I don't think they're even pleased with the fact that I'm practicing well and successfully. It just doesn't matter whether it's State U. or Harvard. I guess they think working as a salesgirl or an attorney is about the same. Just different places to be waiting for marriage. But I'm not so sure any more that I want to get married.

I've had a series of interesting relationships, one in particular which is hard to talk about because it's over now—he got married—but I'm afraid it's still not over for me. It was the closest relationship I've ever had with a man. I met him when I was nineteen and lived with him until I was twenty-six.

I thought it was a very good relationship while it lasted because of all the things we shared; the way he would deal with me and talk about things that interested both of us. But if it had been really that good, he couldn't have walked out quite like he did—by calling me in the afternoon one day at work and saying, "Listen, I think it would be a good idea if we didn't see each other for a while." So he got married four months later.

It was such a bad experience, I still can't handle it. After he disappeared from my life, I started thinking about the demands I had made on the relationship and how I was treated by him and how I treated him, and oh, just everything. I still haven't figured it all out, but I know one of the problems was that I come from such a damn traditional sanctimonious family. Instead of saying what I was thinking, I would act, you know, in a way I thought appropriate, instead of acting like I felt. It's hard to give examples, but I'll try.

We met in college, and afterwards he went with a brokerage firm. It was good in the beginning because we were both lovers and companions. It had all the warmth of a good human relationship, and the physical part of it was great. There is nothing like living with people. I just wouldn't have it otherwise, if I could help it, but I wouldn't live with anyone again until I feel better able to get myself together. My shrink says I have a real need for a certain amount of male approval, and that's why I want to live with a man on a permanent basis. What he doesn't understand is that I get a lot of male approval anyway. It's very sexy being a woman lawyer. And I'm sure a lot of other women lawyers find that true, too. There are men around you all the time, always being very nice and respectful of what you have to say and appreciative of your femininity, but not in a demeaning way. But I suppose I probably do have a certain need to live with others. I don't know. By comparison, living alone isn't as much fun. You have more freedom coming and going, but you have a lot of freedom too in a good relationship, planning and things. I don't know.

I've never been married, but I don't think there's much difference between being married and living with someone for over six years. We lived in the same apartment, entertained, went everywhere together, and all that. There was, of course, never any social designation of me as "wife" only, because I was a lawyer. A person. Living together is a marvelous experience and

certainly ought to be a prelude to being married. I can't understand how people can marry without having lived together,
though I'm sure they do. I have a good friend and his wife who
got married after living together for only two weeks.

It was nice not being defined as a "wife," but after a while I
got tired of all the necessary sneaking around. He was concerned about traditional people, at his firm and mine, and with
our families. In fact, our families never knew we lived together.
It was easy. We were so good at faking it, no one knew for sure,
except the people we wanted to know. After a while, that's what
began to really irritate me, and now I get angry when I think
about it. I would rather have been married. He wouldn't have
left so easily. But, hell, if the relationship was so bad from his
point of view, or so unsatisfactory, or whatever it was that made
him leave . . . (Cries.)

I'm sorry. One way I have of suppressing my anger is, I cry.
Don't take this too seriously, but it works fine in court. I don't
usually use it, but I also cry when I can't help it. When I'm very
angry and I can't do anything else.

Anyhow, we lived in a great apartment, high up with a terrific
view, and it was so much fun. We had lots of people over often. I
entertained all kinds, from business cocktail parties to times
when he would just bring anybody to dinner. I liked it in a sense
—the spontaneity of it. What I started to resent horribly was
having to work so darn hard and never getting help from him. I
should have spoken up, but I thought, well, this is my job, I have
to do this for him. You know—lover, cook, cleaning
woman—I'll never make that mistake again. I could have been
more assertive. I could have said, "Listen, I need some help.
You can't just bring over four people for supper and expect me
to make it when I've worked all day. You just can't do those
things to me. It's too unfair."

But I never spoke up. The irony of it is that later he complained I hadn't been professionally active enough.

Things got worse in the last two years we lived together. For one thing, our financial arrangements were poor. It seemed I ended up paying for almost everything. Rent, food—I paid all the bills, which I thought was appropriate because we were saving his money so he could have the freedom to change jobs at the right time, take a cut, and in the end get way ahead of the game. That's actually the way it worked out, but I wasn't around to share the success. It never occurred to me that he damn well should be sharing the expenses. In a way now, it's almost funny. But I learned a hell of a lot. I made about $17,000 a year, which isn't all that much money in law, but this firm is tight. So it got to be quite a financial burden and completely ridiculous. I'd have to remember not only our expenses, but his mother's birthday and his sister's anniversary, her birthday, the baby's birthday, and Christmas presents for the whole family. I enjoyed doing it to a certain extent, but after a while I never had any money.

And I was getting more and more irritated with all the secrecy. I had to be so careful, and I learned you don't have to let anybody know anything, which enabled us to do anything we wanted. It was quite a game. He had another address, which he convinced all his business associates was the place he lived. After he left, one of our friends said to me, "You mean all those stories Phil told about his apartment, that we all laughed over, you mean they weren't true?" They weren't. Just fabrications. Very convincing young man, in a way. He was brought up strictly in a religious Catholic family, and you just don't live with someone when you're from that background. I wanted everyone to know, but I was afraid to tell my family, and how could I start telling everyone else if I didn't tell them?

I kept saying, "Let's get married. I want a bigger apartment, I'm unhappy here. I want a bigger bed." He wouldn't respond, because he didn't want to get married. I knew that, so why was I so stupid? Marriage was the end of things for all his friends, and he had a real fear of it. He would argue, "We live together very well and very happily. We're not confined, we're growing and it's good." And it was. Oh, it was.

Finally he got this terrific job, with lots of opportunity for doing what he wanted to do. He came home one afternoon, feeling great, and said, "Let's take a vacation." And I said, "I'd rather get married first, and then take a vacation." He said, "Well, I don't want to, so let's take a vacation." I said, "Okay, okay. You get the tickets." He never got them. We had a terrific argument, and I ended up begging. I told him I was really sick of the way we were living, that I couldn't understand why he was doing these things to me. I told him I could get a better job, that I thought we should get married. And you know what he said? He told me, "I don't want to get married and I don't want to marry you, because you're overly domesticated. You depend too much on me." He said I was too insecure in my own identity. After hours of this I got so fed up and tired I just said, "Fuck you," and turned over and went to sleep.

He left the next morning before I was up and I heard nothing from him until the end of the week, when he called and said he didn't intend to see me for a while. So then he went to the Virgin Islands.

I saw him only once again, about three weeks before he married another girl. He came to the apartment at midnight, about three months after he had left. I opened the door, and there he was. "Why did you do this to me?" I asked him. "I don't understand." He just shook his head and answered, "I don't want to get married." Why couldn't I have picked up the signals? Why couldn't I understand why things had gone wrong? I had heard he was dating this other girl, and I told him I was fantastically jealous. I asked him, why? We got nowhere. After half an hour he left. I guess all human bonds are frail, but that one meant everything to me. If he had just once said, "Look, I don't care for you and I don't want to go on with this because of that." But he never did. It would be easier to be told you aren't loved.

I've been very lonely since, even though I've stayed busy. It's hard to cope with any loss, and this one still hurts. I missed his family too, and the friends we mutually shared didn't know what the hell had happened. So they didn't know what to say. Some of them were very dear and made a lot of effort to include me in things, and so forth. But it was hard to participate, and that was really feeling lonely—when all these kind people were around and caring. This has been like a death. I'm sure death is much worse, but I don't know.

I've known a number of men since Phil, and sometimes it has been great. But most of the affairs have ended because I'm supposed to be so independent. I'm not all that independent, really. I like male companionship. I'm not all that dependent either. I'm sure that—oh, I'm not sure of anything. My shrink keeps saying, "You've got to have a peer relationship if you are going to feel mutually equal, where you can demand a certain amount of respect and affection equal to what you give." But that's what women are trained to do—give a hell of a lot more than they get. It seems to me that we are expected to settle for less affection than we give, and that's ridiculous. With Phil, it got so I reached the end of my usefulness to him. It was time to get somebody else who could do more—like a girl with a rich family that's well connected. Which he did. My shrink says, "Look, if he went right quick to another relationship, that means he must have enjoyed the one he had." That infuriates me. I can't tell you how mad that makes me. But what do I do? Women aren't trained to deal with their aggressive feelings very well. I wasn't, and I'm an aggressive person.

A lot of women choose to be alone, even though it's difficult for them. In law there is a generation of old women, some of them lawyers and some legal secretaries, who are terribly bright and very professional, but they are such stereotypic old-maid, spinster types. I see them walking around, and I wonder about them. They've never been sexually realized. Our generation is going to have a different kind of woman who chooses to live alone, and it isn't going to be because they're afraid of sex or because they fear men, which I suspect is part of the reason so many older women are alone. It's going to be for other causes. I don't know. I started talking with my psychiatrist when I really got miserable. He's a male chauvinist, which he admits. He tells me to remember that women have a biologically motivated set of drives and he says it's too bad, but some of them aren't what I want them to be. He says I can't be totally aggressive, that I'll be happier if I try to satisfy some of my maternal and caretaking and those kinds of drives.

I don't want it that way. But the way our society is set up, it might be easier. There are certain benefits to a legal relationship like joint tax returns and potential tax exemptions, but particularly the ability to have children without attaching some stigma to them. I would really like to have children, but I would like to be married when I have them because it would be nice for them to have a father. I didn't think much about it in the past, but now I've seen people I know with real hangups who grew up without their fathers. However, I intend to have children anyway. I refuse not to enjoy that aspect of life, but I'm not quite ready to do that yet, without more time to think about it.

If I had to make a choice between someone whom I loved or someone who loved me? I'll tell you which I'd choose. It's more fun to be loved, it really is. It's more childlike and less responsible. Anything you do is acceptable, and there's less burden to it. It's best not to have a relationship where there's an inequality, but if I had to choose, yes, I would rather be loved. It would be more fun.

Sheila Farrow

Saturday night I was lying in bed, thinking, that phone's not going to ring, nobody's going to call me. Nobody might call me for a month. Where is everybody? I'm really alone a lot now—I suppose I could die up here and nobody would know it for a week. And other times, when people come up, I think, gee, I wish they would go home. It was so quiet. Why don't they leave me?

I live in what could be called a romantic situation—a summer home on the lake, no neighbors, way out in the country. A perfect place to live, though at first I was afraid. At night every owl, every twig that snapped, was a footstep. For a while I was sleeping with scissors under my pillow. I have to think of those things, because if I yelled, there's no one around to hear me. But I've rationalized that if I have to go, I'd like to go from here.

I'm the youngest of four children and we were raised kind of like, "Kids, go play in your room." We were allowed to do almost anything we wanted, as long as we did it alone and separated, so it was natural for me to want to live alone as soon as possible, which I did when I was eighteen. In a really crummy neighborhood. I lied and told my parents I had a roommate simply because they felt more secure about it, but I wasn't afraid even at night up there. I could come and go as I pleased. No one around to listen to the stereo when I wanted to take a nap. I hate being in those kind of conflicts, because I end up saying, "Listen to the stereo," and then I don't get my nap and I hold in the hostility.

I moved here when I started medical school, and I love it. I go to school during the day—there's only one other girl in medical school—and I spend my time, peacefully, up here in the evenings. I don't know many people at school, but that doesn't bother me. I'm a great fantasizer—I was Annie Oakley until I was about ten, with Indians behind every hedge and that type of thing. I never wanted to be a nurse or a teacher, but rather figured I would be either a doctor or a ballerina. I used to watch the old medical shows on television and I just told myself, that's what I want to do. If I can get over my nervousness. I'm very nervous, with knees shaking, stomach—the whole thing. If I can get over that, that's what I would like to do.

I go through periods of trying to decide what my mental image of myself is. Am I going to be successful? Am I doing what I want to do? If the slightest doubt comes into my mind, I get very upset and depressed and I think, this is really stupid, why don't you get a job and make money and forget this career stuff? I remind myself I can always wait on tables. A lot of this is fear of failure. When I first started med school, I told everybody that I was just trying it out to see if I liked it, mainly to keep them from putting pressure on me.

I see these guys in school now whose fathers and grandfathers have been doctors, and if they don't become doctors they might as well forget their families. It's a do-or-die proposition for them, the worst possible way. The other girl in my class, I swear she will have a breakdown before March. She studies so hard, and doesn't allow herself a minute of relaxation in a day. We are in class until about two o'clock, and everyone lolls around the coffee machine after and just talks. But this girl will not permit herself to do that. She studies. And if we have a five-minute break in classes, she's got her book open. The pressure is weighing on her, and it's going to kill her.

It's strange, but I don't consider myself a Women's Lib advocate particularly. I don't think I've ever really faced up to the fact that I'm a woman working in a man's world or a man's profession. I just feel I want to be a doctor, as much as my next-door neighbor might want to be a doctor. The sex angle hasn't come in, as I suppose the real implications of a woman in a man's world haven't hit me yet. But I'll feel it when people in my class who aren't doing nearly as well as I am get better internships because they are men. I'll feel it then.

I never told anybody I wanted to be a doctor. Not anybody, and I've known what I wanted since grammar school. Have you read some of these books about it? Professional women are always supposed to be a little weird. Little girls get funny ideas. But I didn't want to be a housewife or a teacher.

I'm pessimistic about marriage. I run into a lot of married men who want to fool around. I've had more propositions from married men that I either dated before they were married or have met since. Some of these guys think that if you are not married, you are ripe for them. They say, this is perfect. You pursue your career, and we'll fool around. I'm not into that at all. It's dumb. One of the best things about any relationship is to be able to call a man at any hour of the day or night and say, hey, what are you doing? Come over, or something. But when he's married, it's so stilted. You've got that "other woman" image.

People don't really accept a single girl for being a single girl. They always figure there's something wrong somewhere.

I moved to this house far from everywhere last winter because I was completely fed up with the city. A man who lived with me had left, and as I look back on it now, I can see it was kind of a dumb affair. We had nothing in common. I wanted to be a doctor; he wanted to live on top of a mountain. It was no good, and I wanted no more of the city and all it meant—fussing with clothes and dates and schedules.

Now I spend a lot of time still figuring out where I want to go and what I want to do, but peacefully, in the evenings, with a fire in the fireplace and no one around for miles. Having a choice—that's important. I can invite people up if I wish. This man I lived with, for example, as much as I thought I loved him, I was very glad when those hours of the day came when we were separated—when I had my freedom. I loved being with him at any hour. I loved him caring and I loved caring about him, but I still enjoyed too much my own freedom. That meant I could say, don't come over tonight. You can't say that to a husband. You can't say, hey, don't come home, because I want to take a long bath and I don't want to talk to anybody. But when you are just living with someone you can say, hey, go to your own apartment tonight or go out with the boys or something. There is so much that marriage is supposed to mean that it really doesn't deserve.

I don't think he and I could have made it. Neither of us could have given the amount of time we wanted to our careers, and it would have been a life of compromise. In a sense, that's good, but I would rather marriage were a constantly mutual thing, where I wouldn't have to give up something that meant a lot to me and he wouldn't have to give up something that meant a lot to him.

My life up here isn't totally alone. I invite people—but I have a hard time deciding which guys I'm going to invite because it's so hard to get them to go home. They will come up, expecting to spend the day and expecting I'll invite them to spend the night because it is so far. It's hard convincing them that I don't want that. How do you say it? "I don't want to sleep with you, but do come visit"? I resent the men whose attitude is, why should I drive one hundred and ten miles just to be your friend? The ultimate act of male chauvinism. I don't know why I resent that, but I do. So stupid. I think later, why should I spend time with them? Sex is a very emotional thing to me, very involving. I don't consider it just a handshake. Why does it have to be like this? Girls run over to the guy's apartment for an hour or two, and they're expected to leave. So I end up standing at the door, yawning, and hinting I have to get up early. People should be able to take up these cues, and most do. But not guys.

A lot of times when I have really strong sexual needs, I either just disregard them—I'll scrub the floor or take a cold shower or

whatever is handiest—or I'll think, eventually I'm going to get
into another affair. Someone is going to come along that I really
like. Sex means a lot to me. I'm not puritanical, but I don't like
getting involved in this swinging stuff. The people I have had sex
with have always meant a lot.

I know I use men; I have a tendency to do that. When I get
lonely or depressed I want them to come, and then want them to
go. It seems very uncaring for them. I would like to marry,
really. I think so. But I'm afraid I'm incapable of the human,
emotional responses necessary to be a wife and mother. One of
the guys I know told me he thought that was why I wanted to be
a doctor. That really got to me, and I've been worrying about it
a lot lately. Oh, I've played the role of wife—always knowing I
can get out of it. And I've played the role of mother with my
brother's kids and enjoyed it, but only because it's for a short
while. Could I go into a do-or-die, let's-try-this-forever type of
thing? There is really a question whether or not I'm capable as a
person to do that. I've been on my own so long, solving my own
problems, fixing my own burned-out lightbulbs, and fending off
bill collectors. Why, I wonder, would I want to change? There's
nobody around to tell me when to buy groceries. If I want them,
I go get them. And this is nice. Very nice.

But there are many pressures. My parents are very old-world,
and their first questions when I come home are, Who are you
dating? How's your love life? That's really their concern. Not
my career.

Mother is very strong, and I respect her very much, although
we're not all that close. She runs a dress shop, which doesn't
make much money, but she loves it. It causes constant conflict
with my father, because he wants her to quit and sell out and go
to California. I admire her for sticking it out; what she's doing
takes a lot of backbone. But I don't know if it's the right thing
for our family. She should be making my father happy. But
would he really be happy if she gave up her shop? I think he

figures she needs her work—if she retired and went to California, she'd probably die much earlier than if she stays home and
keeps working.

Funny, we've never been a close family. It's a family where
when one person is needful, you don't give love, you give money. My parents will say to me when I'm working with some
crisis—exams usually—why don't you go out and get a new
dress? Instead of, why don't you tell us about it? But I certainly
respect my mother; she has really been strong. Really ruled the
roost.

Single girls bring out the mother in everyone, don't you
think? Even my dentist is concerned about me. If I lived the way
the television commercials show single life, I should have a
sports car, very snazzy looking, preferably red. And I should always be immaculately dressed with umpteen bachelors always
running in and out of my home all day long. Of course it hasn't
been that way, but when you are from a small town where
everybody is married at seventeen, it isn't hard to see why they
think I'm strange. Everybody is trying to come up with the perfect
man. It makes me nervous. There are many, many people who
shake their heads and look worried, and I know what they're
thinking: I've either got a real problem or I just haven't met the
right man. And they've all got him. Endless blind dates, and
what jerks.

I'm developing an isolationism since I moved away. It's more
difficult being with people, and I have less in common with my
friends. I come to visit and they will talk about some of these
tremendous new restaurants—I know nothing about them. New
styles—I really know nothing about them. New records. I don't
know much really about that. I'm leading pretty much a one-
track life and I'm happy. I've never been calm before in my life,
and I'm calm now.

So that's where I am—pleased with my work, getting good
grades, and worrying about how everybody wants me to get

married. How would I do it? Take time out to have babies? I'm
so frustrated that they won't realize this is what I want to do. I
would like a companion, though. I'm not sure how to say this
without sounding really dumb, but I would like someone's shoulder to cry on every once in a while. I'm really strong and I can
handle many things and many needs and catastrophes, but every
once in a while it gets to me, and I sense my singleness. I feel it
deeply. And that's very bad, when it happens. But I still think
that what I most want to be is a doctor, and if I have the brains,
I'm going to do it.

Peggy Terry

I was born in MacAllister, Oklahoma, in 1921, within sight of
the penitentiary there. We were sharecroppers. During the Depression years we traveled all around, anywhere where my Daddy could find work—in the oil wells, as a dynamite man, and
when we were in Kentucky, he worked as a coal miner. I went to
the fifth grade, but actually I've got about a fourth-grade education because most of the time I didn't get to go to school. I had to
work in the fields.

My grandmother came from Dublin and she married an
Englishman, which meant she was excommunicated. Religion
doesn't mean much to me. The only thing it has taught me in my
life is all kinds of hatred of all kinds of people. Hate Jews, hate
Catholics, hate blacks, hate Italians, hate, hate, hate. That's all I
can remember.

I've got three children of my own, but actually I've been a
mother since I was twelve, helping to care for my brother who is
the baby of the family. We were so close the gossips in the
neighborhood said he was mine. I loved him very dearly. I never

was young, I never had a childhood. I don't want that to happen to my kids or to anybody's kids. Everybody should have a childhood. You know what I remember best from mine? A lynching. When I was about eleven years old, and I didn't feel anything, which really frightens me now, looking back. I saw this young man hanging there dead, and it wasn't anything to me. I had been brought up that way.

It was during the Montgomery bus boycott that I began to learn some different things, when the black people wouldn't ride at all for a whole year. I saw white men who would wait for a bus to pull up at a corner at the same time a black woman would be walking by, on her way to work. And those men would pick up the woman and throw her on the bus. And with all the dignity in the world, the black woman would just get up and stand there until the bus got to the next corner and then she would get out. They just would not ride that bus.

At first I thought it was absolutely terrible that niggers wanted to ride in the front, and for a long time after the boycott I would stand up if there was no place to sit except by black people.

One day in particular, I was so very tired and I thought, this is crazy, they're sitting down and you're standing. So I sat down on the edge of the seat with one of them and nothing happened to me. Lightning didn't strike me dead, so from then on I would sit by them if I had to. I can't say it seemed a natural thing, but I did more or less accept that that was the way things were going to be.

During the boycott me and some of the neighborhood women decided to go down to the jail and get a look at this black man causing all the trouble, this Reverend King. We were curious—who had ever heard of a black person daring to do anything like this? So about six or eight of us went down to the jail.

They brought Reverend King out, and he had on a white

panama suit and a white hat and shoes. I had never seen a black person dressed like that—in fact, I had never seen a white person dressed like that. Nobody had that money, and I didn't like seeing a black man dressed so nice.

Then about eight or ten white guys came up and jumped on him, and started beating him, right there on the sidewalk. There were a lot of people around and nobody did anything, and I was ashamed. I was so ashamed of the white men. And all the time while I watched, an old saying we have in the South kept running through my head—"Two on one is nigger fun." That meant that only niggers would be so low for two of them to jump on one person.

I had never seen blacks beating up on white people, but many times I had seen more than one white beat up on a black, and I thought, I don't like black people and I don't think they're as good as me, but I wouldn't hurt them.

I began feeling things then. It isn't violence so much—poor people don't have the fear of violence that middle-class people do. Violence doesn't frighten me. I'm not for it, but it doesn't frighten me, I guess because of the atmosphere I was raised in. When we were sharecroppers, I remember the man that owned the land would come out two or three times a week and raise Cain with my grandmother because we weren't producing enough to suit him. We were working from sunup to sundown, sometimes even after dark, and one day my grandmother got fed up. She took the reins off the mule she was plowing with and she beat that old man clear to the road. He got in his buggy and rode off, and never bothered us again.

Women are supposed to be nice and ladylike. You can't go through life being nice and ladylike all the time, at least I can't. As long as they let me be, okay, but I can raise hell, and I have. The things that frighten me are hunger, cold, not enough money to pay the rent, my children's safety. Basic things. I think

Women's Lib is a middle-class sort of thing, not that I'm against them but I only felt the way they do when I was working as a waitress, after coming North. That was after my divorce, when I had nothing and left the South. I was fifteen when I married, and I was really happy when it ended. My husband, he'd been in the Second World War and it just really messed up his mind. He was very brutal and drank heavily and took it out on me. I was just not going to live with a man who acted like that.

I've had so little money. In the South, most of the work we did didn't mean getting money. Southern women, very poor Southern women, held money very seldom, and when I first came to Chicago I couldn't make change for a dollar. A lot of people would find that incredible. I was thirty-four years old.

I got a job in a kind of greasy-spoon restaurant. I was lucky because I had never done anything except farm work and cotton mill work, which didn't require arithmetic. But the first day, handling the cash register, I really messed up. My boss was dumfounded that a grown person couldn't make change, but he was nice about it, and he taught me how.

I became a very good waitress, and I worked myself up to a fancy place—no more greasy spoons—but I never liked it. If I hadn't had to depend on tips, maybe it would have been different, but that just takes away your dignity. People would say sometimes, "You don't have to be so nice, you know I'm going to give you a tip." And I'd almost lose my temper. I wanted to say, "To hell with your tip, I'm nice because I want to be." It makes you feel a little less human to be told, don't bother being nice, I'll pay you anyway. I doubt very much if they would have talked to waiters the way they talked to me. I stayed there only six months, because I resented having to split my tips with the busboys. You could never find them. So I would clean my own tables and set them up, and I would still have to split with somebody I hardly ever saw. I needed the money so badly, I would rather have cleaned my own tables all the time and kept it. But they didn't operate that way.

I went to another restaurant for two years, but I didn't like it, I didn't like having to take a lot of gas. Anything goes wrong, anything isn't cooked right—the people don't go back and say anything to the cook. Oh no, the waitress gets it. There must be something wrong with people who can go around and show so little respect for a human being.

You know what I really learned when I came North? That poor sharecropping uneducated Southern whites are treated the same as blacks. There isn't a single thing that is done to black people that isn't done to what people call "poor white trash." The way the Yankees treated me gave me a great deal of insight into what blacks had been living through for three or four hundred years. Little things just kept going through my mind.

For instance, every time I'd try to get to the Loop, I'd get lost. When I rode the subway, it just blew my mind. I'd go up to white people and ask directions, and most of the time they wouldn't even answer me, and when they did it was in such a down-your-nose attitude.

I remember one time I asked a black man how to get to the subway, and he said, "If you don't mind walking with me, I'll show you how to get there." And I said, "If you don't mind walking with me, I don't mind walking with you." So we walked a couple of blocks together down the street. This would have been absolutely unheard of in Montgomery, and it isn't looked on so good here, either. Northern whites really make me angry. They think all we do is race around lynching black people. I'm not saying things are right in the South, they aren't. But things are just as bad here. In the South they lynch black bodies, but the North, they lynch black minds.

This was such a strange place, and people weren't friendly. I would be walking to the store and I would meet a woman from my neighborhood and I would speak, you know, just "Good morning" or "Good afternoon," or whatever, and they would look at me like I escaped from an asylum. I thought they were just cold, heartless people. When Christmas came and I met these same women on the sidewalk, they were saying "Merry Christmas" to me! I said to one, "Don't you dare wish me a Merry Christmas. All year long you wouldn't even speak to me and so now for a few days you want to be real friendly. To hell with it. Be friendly three hundred and sixty-five days a year or don't bother." She just stared at me. But then the longer I was here, the more I realized that in areas as densely packed as this city, people value their privacy because they have so little of it.

Then my little girl got killed. I was married to my second husband then. She was only six years old, and just starting to school. A doctor backing out of a driveway, he ran over her, and I found people weren't so heartless. People I didn't even know came. They packed the house, and they brought flowers and food and money. And my husband, such a remarkable man, truly strong emotionally, he cried for the first time. He loved my children very much, and it is hard for a man to deeply love children who aren't his own, the children of his wife's former love affairs, marriages, what have you. He helped me so much, was such a comfort, when my child was gone. Now he is gone.

Our backgrounds were so completely different, our cultures. The kind of people he enjoyed being with—he had a very good education and I didn't get out of grade school—I didn't enjoy being with at all. It got to be a real bad situation. Sometimes these things don't matter but again they do, and they just catch up. We were making each other miserable. I still love him. But mainly I respect him. I wanted to write, so much I wanted to write. And anything I wrote seemed so childish to him that in criticizing it he stopped me from building up the confidence to really do anything. In other ways, I tore him down, trying to bring him to my level so we could deal on my level, and it wasn't fair. Bringing people down to your level, whatever it is, is wrong. You should try instead to lift them up to a higher level, not drag them down.

I kind of fell apart after we were divorced, because it wasn't like when I got my first divorce, which I was happy about. It was so lonely. You know, from the time you are a little girl you are nothing unless you've got a man. Women are supposed to have children, bring them up to be law-abiding citizens, keep a nice clean house, and all this, and when it falls apart, and you have to pull yourself together and deal with it, you don't actually know what to do with yourself. I didn't, even though I've always felt like a strong person. I had to fight myself because I wanted so much to just go jump in the lake. Really. That's not just an expression. The whole bottom fell out of my world.

My children have had a better chance in life with me having been married to that man. It never was clear to me how important an education could be, but it was to him. My eldest daughter won a scholarship to Antioch College in Yellow Springs, Ohio, which is one of the fine liberal arts colleges. Coretta King graduated from there. Really a fine place. Now she is working for the American Civil Liberties Union in New York, and I know without the incentives and things I learned from my husband, that would never have been possible. My young son is taking extra courses at the YWCA for electrical engineering, and these things wouldn't have happened. They probably just would have drifted along, and my son would have worked in a gas station and my daughter would probably have married very early like me and had three or four children by the time she was twenty-one. Now she is twenty-three and able to have something of life in this world without being tied down so young with a bunch of kids.

You know how I said little things kept going through my

mind when I saw how Yankees treat poor Southern whites? That was an important time, because I made a decision. I'm the sort of person who, when I feel deeply about something, I believe in acting. So I just went down one day and joined CORE.

It was all my work in CORE and later with JOIN, here in my own neighborhood, that pulled me through that terrible time after the divorce. But it was a tough start. I ended up in jail the first day I belonged to CORE. They were going down to try to meet with the Board of Education and asked me to come along, so I did. We were supposed to sit in front of the steps leading to the offices and try to make some kind of news so people would know we went there. Mayor Daley can get free time on TV and it isn't hard to get his view across, but somebody like me or like a poor black, we have to do something outrageous to get anyone to listen to us. I didn't like getting dragged down sidewalks, getting the skin scraped off my knees. But freedom of speech—if it isn't given to you willingly, then you have to do something to take it. That's what we did. We sat down in a line, and they dragged us all off and put us in the pokey. I had never been in jail before, but I was quite happy.

Another thing happened that taught me a lot. It was at the time when state troopers in Alabama were beating the hell out of women and kids and men with bullwhips and cattle prods. They were having a big outdoor show with outdoor equipment and things at McCormick Place, and they actually sent Alabama troopers to man the Alabama booths. So we went down there with big chains under our coats, just drifting around the place, slowly moving towards their Alabama booth.

I told the troopers I was from Alabama and we had a very nice conversation, me and two cops, just three Southern whites talking. Then we took out the chains and chained ourselves together and to the exhibit. When they saw this, one of the troopers spat on me and called me a dirty bitch. I was working with niggers and we had chained ourselves together. Two minutes earlier, you couldn't have asked for two nicer men or found them anywhere, all that Southern hospitality and jazz.

It wasn't frightening to me, but it taught me a lot. The only time I can say I have actually been afraid—and I didn't let even this bother me too much—was when I started getting letters from the Klan and they started threatening to blow my house up. My kids were little then, and that was frightening.

Later, one of my friends told me about a group that was organizing poor Southern whites in Chicago. At first I didn't want anything to do with it, because knowing me and my background, I didn't quite know whether I wanted that sort of thing—to be among people who were still like I'd been. I was in this righteous period. I'd gotten it together and I didn't hate black people any more, a rather superior kind of thing. But then I came to some neighborhood meetings of JOIN, and for the first time in my life I knew what it meant to be really proud of being a Southern white, and being proud of other Southern whites.

You can't, you just cannot come into contact with the kind of people who reach out to you, and not respond. They helped me a great deal. My neighborhood brought me back to reality after the divorce. There are so many beautiful people here. Most people think there are only a bunch of racist whites, but blacks have moved in and Puerto Ricans and Mexicans and Cubans. Sure there are fights, shootings, cuttings, anything you want to name, but it isn't black against white or white against black or Puerto Ricans. Generally, it's hillbillies fighting each other. In fact, I know of only one incident where it was racist, and that was when two hillbillies killed a Puerto Rican kid.

As soon as I get over this operation, I'm getting back into my work in the neighborhood.

I am fifty years old now and I live alone, just me and the six cats. I'm very lonely at times and I would like to have someone, but it would have to be a man who cares about people and politics, who speaks out—and there just aren't many men my age like that who aren't married. The worst times are at night, when nobody is here. And the only thing to do is just live through it. I know eventually the sun's going to come up and it will be another day. I'm close to my children—my son, he's a poet, a beautiful poet, lives in the same building—and that makes loneliness easier to bear.

I've got to get back into the movement and organize people to fight for what is theirs. I've taught many other hillbilly women in the neighborhood, very quiet and shy women, not to let themselves be bullied. Know your rights, stand up and fight for them. Now I'm not putting down Women's Lib but, like I said, it is middle-class. They know what they need, but they are not working on my level. I don't happen to see life the way they do, but I'm all for them, one hundred percent. I admire Barbara Walters on the *Today* show. I admire her very much. And even the one before her, Pauline Fredericks, who broadcasts from the UN. I admire her deeply because she is a woman and such a forceful person.

Women are making men, all kinds of people, aware that women are tired of being second-class citizens. And that we have been, no doubt about it. But men are so afraid of losing their manhood. It is such a fragile thing, because it is built on hypocrisy and anything built on hypocrisy is fragile, even our democracy. We've just pretended to have real democracy. Wasn't it just 1922 when women were allowed to vote? And blacks have had to fight to vote? That's democracy?

This time since I've been sick has been such a long, depressing period. I want to get well. There are still an awful lot of things I have to say and an awful lot of things I have to do. If people who are lonely would only realize all they have to do is reach out and

someone out there is even lonelier. If you can just bring yourself
to reach out and say, "I'm so terribly lonely," then you will find
someone and you can lean on each other. "Mankind" is a man
word, really—it should be "humankind," that's everybody. My
son coined that word. Women have to be strong and independent. But sometimes they have to lean and get the strength
to get back up. Trying to live with loneliness is like trying to live
without air, and that we can't do.

Bibliography

Books

Aries, Philippe. *Centuries of Childhood*. New York: Vintage Books, 1962.

Beard, Mary R. *Woman as Force in History*. New York: Collier Books, 1962.

Beauvoir, Simone de. *The Second Sex*. New York: Bantam Books, 1953.

Bernard, Jessie. *The Future of Marriage*. New York: World Publishing Company, 1972.

————. *Women and the Public Interest*. Chicago: Aldine-Atherton, 1971.

Bird, Caroline. *Born Female: The High Cost of Keeping Women Down*. New York: McKay, 1968.

Block, Jean Libman. *Back in Circulation*. New York: The Macmillan Company, 1969.

279

Bolitho, William. *Twelve Against the Gods*. New York: The Readers Club, 1941.

Brown, Helen Gurley. *Sex and the New Single Girl*. Greenwich, Conn.: Fawcett Publications, 1972.

Chisholm, Shirley. *Unbossed and Unbought*. Boston: Houghton Mifflin, 1970.

Cooke, Joanne, and Bunch-Weeks, Charlotte. *The New Women*. Indianapolis: Bobbs-Merrill Company, 1970.

Diamonstein, Barbaralee. *Open Secrets*. New York: Viking Press, 1972.

Ellman, Mary. *Thinking About Women*. New York: Harcourt, Brace & World, 1968.

Epstein, Cynthia Fuchs, and Goode, William J., eds. *The Other Half: Roads to Women's Equality*. Englewood Cliffs, N.J.: Prentice-Hall, 1971.

Erikson, Erik H. *Identity: Youth and Crisis*. New York: W. W. Norton & Company, 1968.

Felder, Raoul Lionel. *Divorce: The Way Things Are, Not the Way Things Should Be*. New York: World Publishing Company, 1971.

Fiedler, Leslie A. *Love and Death in the American Novel*. Rev. ed. New York: Dell Publishing Company, 1969.

Firestone, Shulamith. *The Dialectic of Sex*. New York: Bantam Books, 1971.

Friedan, Betty. *The Feminine Mystique*. New York: Dell Publishing Company, 1963.

Frohlich, Newton. *Making the Best of It*. New York: Harper & Row, 1971.

Gornick, Vivian, and Moran, Barbara K., eds. *Woman in Sexist Society*. New York: Basic Books, 1971.

Greer, Germaine. *The Female Eunuch*. New York: McGraw-Hill, 1971.

Grey, Alan L., ed. *Man, Woman, and Marriage*. New York: Atherton Press, 1970.

Hawthorne, Nathaniel. *The Scarlet Letter*. New York: Airmont Books, 1962.

Hellman, Lillian. *An Unfinished Woman*. New York: Bantam Books, 1970.

Hodge, Jane Aiken. *Only a Novel: The Double Life of Jane Austen*. New York: Coward, McCann & Geoghegan, 1972.

Hole, Judith, and Levine, Ellen. *Rebirth of Feminism*. New York: Quadrangle Books, 1971.

Howard, Jane. *Please Touch*. New York: Dell Publishing Company, 1971.

Hunt, Morton M. *The World of the Formerly Married*. New York: McGraw-Hill, 1966.

Ibsen, Henrik. "A Doll's House," in *Three Plays by Ibsen*. New York: Dell Publishing Company, 1959.

James, Henry. *The Bostonians*. New York: Random House, 1956.

Jameson, Storm. *Journey From the North*. New York: Harper & Row, 1970.

Janeway, Elizabeth. *Man's World, Woman's Place: A Study in Mythology*. New York: William Morrow & Company, 1971.

Jones, Eve. *Raising Your Child in a Fatherless Home*. New York: Free Press, 1963.

Komisar, Lucy. *The New Feminism*. New York: Franklin Watts, 1971.

Kraditor, Aileen S., ed. *Up From the Pedestal*. Chicago: Aldine-Atherton, 1971.

Lash, Joseph P. *Eleanor and Franklin*. New York: W. W. Norton & Company, 1971.

Lerner, Gerda. *The Woman in American History*. Reading, Mass: Addison-Wesley Publishing Company, 1971.

Lessing, Doris. *The Golden Notebook*. New York: McGraw-Hill, 1963.

Lewis, Oscar. *La Vida*. New York: Vintage Books, 1965.

Lewis, Sinclair. *Main Street*. New York: Signet Books, 1961.

Lloyd, Trevor. *Suffragettes International: The World-wide Campaign for Women's Rights*. New York: American Heritage Press, 1971.

McCarthy, Abigail. *Private Faces/Public Places*. New York: Doubleday & Company, 1972.

McCarthy, Mary. *Memories of a Catholic Girlhood*. New York: Berkley Medallion Books, 1963.

MacLaine, Shirley. *Don't Fall Off the Mountain*. New York: W. W. Norton & Company, 1970.

Mailer, Norman. *The Prisoner of Sex*. New York: Signet Books, 1971.

Mannes, Marya. *Out of My Time*. New York: Doubleday & Company, 1971.

May, Rollo. *Love and Will*. New York: W. W. Norton & Company, 1969.

Mead, Margaret. *Male and Female*. New York: Morrow, 1949.

Millett, Kate. *Sexual Politics*. New York: Doubleday & Company, 1970.

Montagu, Ashley. *The Natural Superiority of Women*. New York: Collier Books, 1970.

Morgan, Robin, ed. *Sisterhood Is Powerful*. New York: Random House, 1970.

O'Neill, William L. *Everyone Was Brave*. Chicago: Quadrangle Books, 1969.

Perutz, Kathrin. *Marriage Is Hell*. New York: William Morrow & Company, 1972.

Plath, Sylvia. *The Bell Jar*. New York: Harper & Row, 1971.

Pogrebin, Letty Cottin. *How to Make It in a Man's World*. New York: Bantam Books, 1970.

Reeves, Nancy. *Womankind*. Chicago: Aldine-Atherton, 1971.

Safilios-Rothschild, Constantina. *Toward a Sociology of*

Women. Lexington, Mass.: Xerox College Publishing, 1972.

Schneir, Miriam, ed. *Feminism: The Essential Historical Writings.* New York: Random House, 1972.

Scott-Maxwell, Florida. *Women, And Sometimes Men.* New York: Harper & Row, 1971.

Seward, Georgene H., and Williamson, Robert C., eds. *Sex Roles in Changing Society.* New York: Random House, 1970.

Slater, Philip. *The Pursuit of Loneliness.* Boston: Beacon Press, 1970.

Smuts, Robert W. *Women and Work in America.* New York: Schocken Books, 1971.

Sochen, June, ed. *The New Feminism in Twentieth-Century America.* Lexington, Mass.: D. C. Heath & Company, 1971.

Stuhlmann, Gunther, ed. *The Diary of Anaïs Nin,* Vol. 1 (1931-1934). New York: Harcourt, Brace & World, 1966.

Tanner, Leslie B., ed. *Voices From Women's Liberation.* New York: Signet Books, 1970.

Taves, Isabella. *Women Alone.* New York: Funk & Wagnalls, 1968.

Thoreau, Henry David. *Walden and Civil Disobedience.* New York: Harper & Row, 1965.

Tiger, Lionel. *Men in Groups.* New York: Vintage Books, 1970.

U.S. Congress. House Committee on Education and Labor, Special Subcommittee on Education. *Discrimination Against Women.* Hearings, 91st Cong., 2d sess., on Sec. 805 of H.R. 16098. July 1 and 31, 1970. Washington, D.C.

————. House Committee on Education and Labor, Special Subcommittee on Education. *Discrimination Against*

Women. June 17, 19, 26, 29, 30, 1970. Washington, D.C.

Wollstonecraft, Mary. *A Vindication of the Rights of Woman.* New York: W. W. Norton & Company, 1967.

Woolf, Virginia. *A Room of One's Own.* New York: Harcourt, Brace, 1929.

Articles

"The American Woman," *Time* (March 20, 1972).

Beauvoir, Simone de. "Frank Talk on a Forbidden Subject," *The New York Times Magazine* (March 26, 1972).

Bird, Caroline. "Welcome, Class of '72, to the Female Job Ghetto," *New York* (1972).

————. "The Case Against Marriage," *New Woman* (September 1971).

Huber, Joan. "Ambiguities in Identity Transformation: From Sugar and Spice to Professor," *Notre Dame Journal of Education* (Winter 1972).

Hunt, Ridgely. "Enduring Beauty," *Chicago Tribune Magazine* (March 26, 1972).

Kastenbaum, Robert. "Age: Getting There Ahead of Time," *Psychology Today* (December 1971).

Lopata, Helena Znaniecki. "Identity in Marriage and Widowhood," accepted for publication in *Sociological Quarterly*, 1973.

————. "Loneliness: Forms and Components." *Social Problems*, Vol. 17, No. 2 (Fall 1969).

"The Marriage Experiments," *Life* (April 28, 1972).

Riesman, David. "Two Generations," in *The Woman in America.* Boston: Beacon Press, 1965. Original printing: *Daedalus*, 93:2 (Spring 1964).

"Springing the Trap," *The Seed* (August 1971).

Starr, Joyce R., and Carns, Donald E. "Singles in the City," *Society* (February 1972).

Wilkinson, David. "Single Parents in Suburbia: An In-between World No One Expects to Enter," *Evanston Review* (December 9, 1971).